Cross-Cultural Paul

Cross-Cultural Paul

Journeys to Others, Journeys to Ourselves

Charles H. Cosgrove
Herold Weiss
&
K. K. (Khiok-khng) Yeo

To David,
with best wishes
for your ministry,
Charlie

William B. Eerdmans Publishing Company

Grand Rapids, Michigan / Cambridge, U.K.

Wm. B. Eerdmans Publishing Co.
255 Jefferson Ave. S.E., Grand Rapids, Michigan 49503 /
P.O. Box 163, Cambridge CB3 9PU U.K.
www.eerdmans.com

Printed in the United States of America

10 09 08 07 06 05 7 6 5 4 3 2 1

Library of Congress Cataloging-in-Publication Data

Cosgrove, Charles H.
Cross-Cultural Paul: journeys to others, journeys to ourselves /
Charles H. Cosgrove, Herold Weiss, & Khiok-khing (K. K.) Yeo.
p. cm.
Includes bibliographical references and index.
ISBN 0-8028-2843-4 (pbk.: alk. paper)
1. Paul, the Apostle, Saint. 2. Bible. N.T. Epistles of Paul — Criticism, interepretation, etc. 3. Christianity and culture. 4. Cross-cultural studies.
I. Weiss, Herold, 1934- II. Yeo, Khiok-khng. III. Title.

BS2506.3.c67 2005
225.9′2 — dc22

2005040112

Contents

Acknowledgments

We wish to thank the following persons who read drafts of our chapters and gave us indispensable help, including gracious criticisms and encouraging affirmations: Maria Elena Baranov, Aecio Cairus, Hugo Cotro, Enrique Espinosa, Eduardo Ocampo, Isis Quinteros, Mikhail Kulakov, Evgeni Pavlov, Robert Price, Larry Murphy, Brian Blount, Vincent Wimbush, Brad Braxton, Douglas Sharp, Justine and Andy Smith, George Tinker, Jace Weaver, and Leon Matthews. We extend a special thanks to Barbara Wixon, who helped with the notes.

Introduction

The apostle Paul was a cross-cultural missionary, a Hellenistic Jew who sought to be "all things to all people" in order to win them to the gospel (1 Cor. 9:19-23). He may have been at least modestly trilingual, fluent in Greek but also able in a rudimentary way to read and communicate in Hebrew and Aramaic. He became such a champion of the gentiles that some of his Jewish compatriots accused him of disloyalty to his own people. He gave up Jewish dietary laws and Sabbath observance and thought other Jewish followers of Jesus should also accommodate to gentile ways rather than pressure gentiles into "living like Jews" (i.e., into becoming Jewish proselytes as a way of becoming Christians).[1] He carried out missionary journeys throughout Asia Minor and as far as Rome, dying with a mission to Spain on his unfinished agenda.[2]

But Paul was not cross-cultural in a modern sense. The modern concept of "culture" refers to an integrated pattern of beliefs and practices. Cultures, by this definition, are symbolic worlds with their own inner logic. Ancients who reflected on the question of how and why peoples differ recognized that language and "customs" were elements of ethnic identity, often attributed moral personalities to ethnic groups, and sometimes explained differences as a result of environment. But we find nothing in

1. The expression "live like a Jew" (a single verb in Greek that has often been translated "Judaize") appears in Gal. 2:14, where Paul reports how he criticized Peter at Antioch for living like a gentile but pressuring gentiles to live like Jews.

2. On Paul's biography, see Jerome Murphy-O'Connor, *Paul: A Critical Life* (Oxford: Clarendon, 1996). On Paul's sense of his own identity, see James D. G. Dunn, "Who Did Paul Think He Was? A Study of Jewish-Christian Identity," *New Testament Studies* 45 (1999): 174-93.

antiquity like the modern notion of culture as a social construction and integrated system of beliefs and practices.

A bit of Western intellectual history is clarifying here. In the nineteenth century the term "culture" generally meant a form of refinement — in taste, manners, sentiments, judgment, morals. Individuals acquired and lacked culture according to their class. Democratic idealism about culture meant believing that the lower classes (and "backward" peoples) could also embark on personal and corporate journeys toward culture, becoming participants in the great march of civilization. Thus, culture and civilization were widely viewed as unitary concepts — there were not "cultures" and "civilizations" but Culture and Civilization. And Westerners thought of their civilization as the epitome of culture (with various European peoples imaging themselves as the pinnacle of Western civilization and vying for recognition as such by other Europeans).

In the latter part of the nineteenth century, however, Edward Burnett Tylor began using the term "culture" in a novel way, as the subject of a science. Distinctive in Tylor's conception was his idea that a culture is a "complex whole" that defines a human society.[3] In the early twentieth century, Franz Boas developed Tylor's science of culture into modern cultural anthropology, conceiving of each people as possessing its own culture, an integrated pattern of beliefs, practices, values, institutions, etc., arising from particular historical circumstances. For Boas there is not culture but cultures. Each is a world unto itself, like the language that is its own; hence, cultures are to a degree incommensurable.[4] The conceptual framework of modern cultural anthropology provides no basis for assuming that differences between cultures should be interpreted in a hierarchy of superior to inferior. Cultures are just different. This is one powerful intellectual source of cultural relativism in our time. In its hard form it means that all cultures

3. Edward Tylor, *Primitive Culture: Researches into the Development of Mythology, Philosophy, Religion, Art, and Custom* 1: *The Origins of Culture* (London: Murray, 1871), 1. For a dissenting view, arguing that Tylor contributed little to the modern concept of culture but used the concept in the then traditional sense, see George W. Stocking, Jr., "'Cultural Darwinism' and 'Philosophical Idealism' in E. B. Tylor: A Special Plea for Historicism in the History of Anthropology," *Southwestern Journal of Anthropology* 21 (1965): 130-47.

4. See George W. Stocking, Jr., "Franz Boas and the Culture Concept in Historical Perspective," *American Anthropologist* 68 (1966): 867-82; Jerry D. Moore, *Visions of Culture: An Introduction to Anthropological Theories and Theorists* (Walnut Creek: AltaMira, 1997), 42-52.

are equal and cannot be judged by any outside (or universal) standard. Perhaps even communication among them is impossible. A softer form holds that there are bases for communication, comparison, and even evaluation across cultures, even if cross-cultural analysis requires great care to take account of indigenous perspectives and sophisticated modes of translation and interpretation.

By the same token, the concept of cultural relativity calls for cultural self-awareness and its corresponding demand that we make no claims to universality in our efforts to understand the world, that we acknowledge that we always interpret from a limited perspective, from our own cultural vantage point, that we always "read" whatever it may be — books, things, people — from "this place," our place, and not someone else's.[5]

Paul did not think cross-culturally in these terms. An ancient intellectual, not a modern one, he did not claim that his perspective was socially limited (*humanly* limited, yes — 1 Cor. 13:12). He did not think of cultures in the plural, of each culture as an integrated symbolic world with its own inner logic, or of these worlds as social constructions (something human beings make). He did not distinguish nature and society (culture) the way we do. Nature, for Paul, was the created order, including its enduring social formations, right down to hairstyles. Yet in a profound way, for which he does not have clear interpretive categories, Paul shows that he discovered something like the importance of ethnic/cultural difference. When he insists that the gospel does not require gentiles to keep the Law and calls this "not compelling the gentiles to *Judaize*," he speaks something like our language of ethnic/cultural identity. Or at least it appears that way from our (post)modern standpoint — as if he is wrestling in some fashion with the powerful human dynamics of ethnicity, nationalism, and cultural identity. These are our terms, of course. Paul's terms are "the circumcision and the uncircumcision," "Jews and gentiles," "Jew and Greek," "those under the Law," "those without the Law."

"Cross-cultural Paul" is the Paul who crossed cultures, the Jew who lived like a gentile. He is the Paul for whom this embrace of another social identity was not only a missionary strategy but a matter of principle, a way

5. In biblical hermeneutics, the importance of self-aware interpretation from one's own social location is demonstrated in Fernando Segovia and Mary Ann Tolbert, eds., *Reading from This Place* 1: *Social Location and Biblical Interpretation in the United States;* 2: *Social Location and Biblical Interpretation in Global Perspective* (Minneapolis: Fortress, 1995).

of being true to God's equal love for all human beings with impartiality toward their differences as peoples. ". . . since God is one; and he will justify the circumcised on the ground of faith and the uncircumcised through that same faith" (Rom. 3:30, NRSV). Paul's gospel is the warrant for this cross-cultural mission. It is therefore our warrant for reading Paul cross-culturally. The cross-cultural apostle has left us a legacy of writings that have been translated into many languages, Paul encountered and appropriated from different cultural perspectives. Fittingly, the Paul who crossed cultural boundaries has become Paul interpreted from many different cultural perspectives. In our multicultural world, we have much to learn from Paul about living out the gospel in the midst of cultural diversity. We also have much to learn from each other about how to read Paul.

Today the terms cross-cultural, multicultural, and intercultural are often used to distinguish different aspects of culturally sensitive engagement and interpretation. Cross-cultural refers to movement from one culture to another. In biblical interpretation, cross-cultural means the interpretive movement from ancient culture to contemporary cultures, beginning with the challenges of translation. It can also mean the effort to understand the way those from a culture not one's own interpret the Bible from their distinctive standpoint and experience. Multicultural is a descriptive term for a culturally diverse social setting; it is often used as well to express a way of affirming cultural pluralism and valuing diversity. In biblical interpretation, multicultural often refers to the way different cultural perspectives engender different interpretations, which are to be respected and valued. Intercultural refers to mutual interchange, dialogue, and debate between cultures. In biblical interpretation intercultural means sensitively and critically engaging interpretations that come from different cultural perspectives. Thus, intercultural includes cross-cultural movement, the effort to see the world and the Bible from other cultural vantage points. This movement may express multicultural values, the affirmation of diversity in interpretation, but it also entails critical engagement, including judgments about which interpretations are best and what criteria should govern such judgments.

We have chosen to use the term "cross-cultural" throughout this book, since our primary work is making and modeling cross-cultural movements. But we have approached our task with a multicultural spirit. We value cultural diversity in interpretation. Moreover, our collaboration behind the scenes of this book has also included many intercultural exchanges. These exchanges inform our closing chapter, where we engage in some preliminary intercultural reflection in the form of synthesizing observations and questions.

We hope this book provides culturally sensitive interpretations of Paul. More importantly, we hope it encourages our readers toward their own cross-cultural engagements with Paul and other biblical texts, leading them to learn as we have learned how cross-cultural interpretation can be a journey to others and also a journey to ourselves.

The Approach of This Book

We might have written this book as a team of authors from different cultural backgrounds writing on Paul from our own home perspectives. But in that case, none of us would be engaging in cross-cultural interpretation — except passively as listeners to what we each have to say about Paul. There is, of course, great value in this kind of listening. But in a multicultural world it is important to be more than casual in cross-cultural interaction. Understanding a cultural perspective different from one's own through active listening and engagement is a survival skill for many minorities in relation to the dominant culture. It ought to be a cultural virtue of all of us. Each of us ought to work seriously at seeing the world from at least one cultural perspective not our own. Moreover, listening affects us more powerfully when we do it through active engagement with another cultural perspective in an effort to put into our own words what Paul looks like through the lens of that other perspective. How might a book on cross-cultural interpretation of Paul model this kind of seriousness? We decided to write from our home cultural contexts and also from the standpoints of three other cultures. Hence, each of us has provided a chapter on Paul from his own cultural perspective (Anglo-American, Chinese, and Argentine respectively) and also a "cross-over" chapter on Paul from a cultural perspective not his own (African American, Russian, and Native American). At various points in what follows, and in subsequent chapters, we report on the hermeneutics of our enterprise, including moments of failure. We have also sought to make the book cross-cultural in a comparative and synthesizing way by including a final chapter devoted to looking at points of correspondence and difference among the various perspectives. This book is the product not only of individual research but also of ongoing face-to-face dialogue over several years. Each of us has benefited from (and also suffered!) honest criticism from his coauthors.

Each of us discovered that it is not easy to write with self-awareness about Paul and our home cultures without considerable study and critical reflection. We know our home cultures tacitly as that set of skills and practices that make us successful members of our home society. Each of us also participates in a shared cultural ethos, a worldview made of assumptions about moral principles and cultural values, a common sense about what is possible, a common vision (with "family" disagreements) about what a good society looks like and how our own society measures up. But participating in this ethos and knowing it critically are two different things. For each of us, writing from our home cultural perspective was a journey of discovery.

Writing about Paul from and for our own home cultures put us in the role of constructive interpreters, free to address the question of Paul in ways that run the gamut from priestly to prophetic. Each of us felt more freedom to be prescriptive and critical in writing as cultural insiders than when we took the role of reporting on how Paul looks from cultural perspectives not our own. We have been keenly aware from the outset that writing about Paul from someone else's perspective is risky, fraught with possibilities for distortion, and perhaps even ethically dubious. What right does Yeo have to speak for Native Americans about Paul, Cosgrove for African Americans, Weiss for Russians? Each of us well knew that he did not have standing to speak for any cultural group but his own, and even then only as one voice among many. To write about Paul from other perspectives could be done with integrity only if we presented the voices of those other perspectives and not our own voices.

Speaking about Paul from the vantage of cultures not our own is a bit like being foreign correspondents. We are reporters. It is not our place to say what Paul could or should mean to other peoples, only to see how they have understood and appropriated Paul. In this role, we have no right to be either priestly or prophetic, except perhaps vicariously, through the voices of others. But it's not that simple. Every report is not merely descriptive but also interpretive and constructive. We must make sense, discern and present patterns, select and arrange. Hence, we end up in the voices we report. And to a certain extent that is as it should be. To really take another perspective seriously is to engage it empathetically, to seek not simply explanation but understanding, which is always self-involving.

Still, the temptation is always there to dictate and impose, to ignore or manipulate "indigenous" voices in favor of our own preferred portraits of Paul. As keenly aware as we were of this danger, we each succumbed to it nonetheless, to one degree or other, and found ourselves revising and revising in response to feedback from others. No small part of the value of this book is what we learned about the process of cross-cultural interpretation by making mistakes at it.

We have discovered the following interpretive tendencies in our work to describe Paul from the standpoint of cultures not our own. First, we have sought out explicit perspectives on Paul from those cultures — whether in the form of uses of Paul or commentary on Paul. Our primary task has been to identify and assemble these explicit indigenous voices. Second, we have found ourselves imagining ways of interpreting Paul out of indigenous patterns of thought in our crossover cultures. This mode of engagement involves considerable creative work on our part and entails the risk that we will make awkward or forced connections because we have not grasped, intellectually and experientially, the inner logic of a culture not our own. Sometimes this involves using forms of more general Christian theology in that culture as a framework for interpreting Paul. An example is Weiss's reading of Paul through a more general Eastern Orthodox or Russian Orthodox lens. Sometimes this means using other patterns of thought as a framework for interpreting Paul. An example is Cosgrove using the dialectic of nationalism and integrationism in African American understanding as a way to interpret what Paul says about divine impartiality and the election of Israel. In all of this the danger (whether by succumbing to temptation or through well-meaning failure) is that we end up imposing our own prior interpretations of Paul — interpretations we bring to the cross-cultural dialogue — onto a culture not our own by using both those interpretations and our own analysis of that culture as a basis for making relevant connections. Each of us fell into this trap. For example, at one stage of his work, Weiss analyzed the history of Russian and, more specifically Ukrainian, nationalism and then provided a Pauline critique of it — the critique being based on Weiss's own prior conception of a general Pauline perspective on "nationalism." Cosgrove in an early draft drew what turned out to be an artificial construction of African Americans as historically self-identifying with biblical Israel and worked out an "African American" reading of Paul based on this dubious analogical connection.

One could argue that our cross-cultural engagement should be purely "journalistic," a reporting of what others say about Paul, not a presentation of our own readings of Paul from another cultural perspective, much less any suggestions by us about what Paul has to say to cultures not our own. Nevertheless, all reporting is to at least some extent constructive, which means that the choice is not a neat one between "our own interpretations" and those of the others we seek to describe. Not only that, real engagement entails the effort to understand, to genuinely see from another perspective. One of the tests of whether that seeing has been achieved is whether one can reflect back, as an outsider, in ways that indigenous members recognize as valid. This is the mark of authentic "reporting." Another test is whether one can offer a distinctive interpretation, using the resources of the adopted new perspective, that makes sense in indigenous terms as a valid interpretation (not "the" one correct interpretation but one that insiders recognize as plausible and therefore potentially useful). Again, the line between these two types of interpretation — a more reflective, descriptive type and a more constructive type — is fuzzy.

Each of us holds that Paul is open to more than one plausible interpretation and therefore that no one cultural perspective or interpretive tradition on Paul can claim to be *the* correct way of reading Paul. For us, this hermeneutical conviction does not mean that all interpretations are equal — equally convincing or equally good in a moral and theological sense. There is plenty of room for debate and criticism. Nevertheless, there is also room for a plurality of perspectives both within any interpretive tradition and among traditions. If we speak at points as if we have forgotten this principle, it is out of a spirit of advocacy for interpretations we especially prize.[6]

Autobiographical Introductions

The following short personal self-descriptions aim to reveal something of our personal journeys toward cross-cultural awareness and the hermeneutical sensitivities that guide us — what each of us brought to and discovered in the writing of this book.

6. On the whole matter see Charles H. Cosgrove, ed., *The Meanings We Choose: Hermeneutical Ethics, Indeterminacy, and the Conflict of Interpretations* (Edinburgh: Clark/New York: Continuum, 2004).

Herold Weiss

I am a *rioplatense* by birth, a native of the River Plate region shared by Argentina and Uruguay. My ancestors were Germans who went to Russia in search of arable land when Catherine the Great opened the door for them in the eighteenth century. My maternal ancestors farmed in the valley of the Volga. The Weiss family settled in what was then Western Russia and spoke a better German than the Volga Germans. Nobody at home could actually tell me exactly where in Europe the Weisses had farmed. None of them learned Russian, but my paternal grandfather could speak Polish. Years later I learned that they had lived for three generations in Rožišce, not far from Luc'k, in Volhynia. Prejudices against the German farmers were strong both in the Volga region and in Volhynia, particularly against the Lutherans. The Weiss family left Rožišce for Brazil in 1889, but, when they discovered that they could not grow wheat, flax, oats, and rye there, they traveled for three months on horse-drawn wagons to Argentina, where they settled. When in 1998 I visited Luc'k and Rožišce hoping to find some trace of the Germans who lived there for one hundred years, not even a cemetery could be located. At the Orthodox cemetery in Roshische I found only one tombstone with a German surname. After some inquiries I learned that the last ones had left on trains bound for the Gulag in the 1930s.

My parents were born and married in Argentina, but my father's work took him to Montevideo, Uruguay's capital, where the family lived for twelve years. For my first two grades of school I attended the *Instituto Crandon*, a Methodist missionary school. The administrators and some of the teachers had come from the United States. There I was taught not only my ABCs but also the rightness of the Allied cause during World War II, which was being fought at the time. One of my distinct memories from that time, when Uruguay was still neutral, was the arrival of the *Graf Spee*, the precursor of the *Bismarck*, at the port. The tensions produced by her arrival, and the sinking of the ship by her crew just outside the harbor made a deep impression on me. The explosives used for this purpose made the whole city tremble. Uruguay eventually declared war on Germany, and Germans there experienced some difficulties.

Not long afterward, the family returned to Argentina. My mother, who certainly did not approve of the Nazi war but had strong feelings about Germany even though neither she nor her immediate family had lived there, enrolled me at the German school in Rosario, the second largest city in the country. While in Montevideo I had been an enthusiastic fan of the Allies, but now I had to pretend to be a fan of the Germans. That year Germany surrendered and the mood at the school became rather somber. At the German club in the city, one could meet many of the officers of the *Graf Spee* who had found refuge there. Summers were spent on the farms of my uncles in Entre Ríos province, where German was spoken everywhere. It was also the language of the church services I attended at the little white church on my grandparents' land.

Family lore remembered the Russian countryside, the animosity of the Cossacks, the beauty of the land, the hard winters, and the very marked difference between the farmers and the nobility. From my readings as a growing boy I remember Russian fairy tales and their fantastic, imaginary worlds. A stronger influence was the Argentine folklore of the countryside. One of my uncles had a monstrous steam traction engine that moved around and powered a threshing machine. The harvest of wheat, flax, oats, rye, and barley lasted for about a month and a half. My uncle harvested not only his own fields but also the fields of many neighbors. About thirty men were needed for the maximum efficiency of the harvester. The workers stayed with the machine wherever it was stationed and ate and slept in the field beside it. Every evening around the fire in which water was heated for the *mate* (a strong traditional tea typically sipped through a metal "straw"), the men passed the time before bedtime telling one story after another. These stories had to do with evil lights, gaucho duels, horse breaking, racing, etc. My most vivid memories of childhood have to do with the magical evenings I spent listening to the folklore of the *pampas*, the countryside of farms and ranches, as I sat next to the threshing machine in the middle of a wheat field. Even today, the wonderful folkloric music of Uruguay and Argentina the deepest cords in my soul.

Soon after the family's return to Argentina, Perón came to power. Universities were "intervened" or closed. Partisan indoctrination was rampant in the schools. Newspapers that tried to remain independent were first censured and then closed. Everyone learned to check their conduct and speech. People who spoke even the blandest criticism of the regime in public places often found themselves in jail for months while their families remained ignorant of their whereabouts. Student leaders of the opposition just disappeared. *Peronista* pins were worn by people who in their hearts were strongly against *Peronista* rule. Survival was achieved by accommodation, and I grew up thinking that simulation was the most important skill for success.

In that climate I could see no future in Argentina, so in 1954, not quite twenty years old, I came to the United States to study. Since the Argentine peso was very weak and my English was not good enough to get me a job in the U.S., on my way north I stopped in Cuba to work and earn some money. The Cuban peso was on a par with the dollar then. In Cuba I discovered what racial prejudice was. I had been the victim of some religious and ethnic prejudice, but I had not grown racially conscious. In Cuba everyone was instinctively alive to racial distinctions that made life quite difficult for many. I was coming from Buenos Aires, which was proud of being a rather advanced cosmopolitan center. In Argentina my middle-class parents had never owned an automobile, and very few families owned a television set. Certainly we did not. The importation of goods was very limited. In Cuba television antennas could be seen everywhere, even on the poorest homes in the countryside. Cars imported from the U.S. created a continuous traffic jam in the streets of Havana. Sears and Roebuck made it possible for Cubans to buy anything sold in comparable stores in the U.S. Commerce with the States was evident everywhere. The people, however, harbored a vitriolic animosity toward the U.S. for its heavy hand in the economic and political life of the island. In Havana I was unsuccessfully recruited by Cubans to become a guerilla in the jungles of Guatemala, where the CIA had deposed the president.

These experiences left a profound impression on me. They made me come to terms with the gap between the intellectual life I was trying to pursue and the life that was lived in the streets of different cities according to the traditions and histories that hold that life in their grip. It can be very easy to look at life in terms of the analyses done by scholars, but when one is not in touch with the contemporary realities in which one's neighbors find themselves, the validity of one's views is questionable. When I finally entered the United States and began my studies, first in Tennessee and then in North Carolina, I faced yet another situation that was new to me. Unlike Cuba, where segregation became a reality after five o'clock in the afternoon, here segregation was overt and legally enforced at all times. The *Brown v. Board of Education* decision of the Supreme Court had just been issued, but I could not quite understand its significance. I had no doubt, however, that it had disturbed a great many people around me. At the university hospital where I became a ward secretary during weekends to earn my board, I was assigned to a surgical "colored" ward. There I learned about the life of the black people of the South and began to understand how fractured life in this wonderful country actually was. I also began to understand how all cultures have their own strengths and weaknesses.

These preoccupations led me to choose for my dissertation a topic that was quite out of the mainstream at the time. The field of New Testament studies in those days was preoccupied with form criticism and the challenge of demythologizing. My dissertation was on "*Pietas* among Latin Writers of Early Christian Times." I was interested in the religious concreteness of the first pagans who became Christians. What religious and cultural baggage did the pagans who became Christians carry with them? My graduate courses had made me read a great deal directly related to the New Testament. I needed to put all that into a broader cultural matrix.

After I met a young Puerto Rican lady who was to become my wife, my cultural education really began in earnest. I became the pastor of a small Spanish church in Manhattan. Most of the members were from the Dominican Republic and Puerto Rico, but there were also some from Cuba, Nicaragua, and Colombia. It was my good fortune to have members in my congregation with the patience necessary to teach me the great differences among the peoples in the "new" world that was colonized by Spain. Latin America is usually viewed as one homogeneous cultural landscape. Such a simplistic view, however, can only bring about misunderstandings. The differences among the peoples of Latin America are profound, even while the Spanish influence in terms of language and mores is strong. It was only on account of the insights provided by my wife and the patience of my parishioners that this *rioplatense* achieved a modicum of success as a pastor of a *Latino* congregation in Manhattan.

In time I became a professor at Saint Mary's College, Notre Dame. For my first sabbatical I arranged to teach at the Saint Mary's Rome Program. This allowed my family to spend ten months in Rome. One of my secret desires since I had been a student of Kenneth W. Clark had been to visit Mount Athos in Greece. Clark had spent a year microfilming all the New Testament Greek manuscripts in the libraries of the twenty monasteries on that Aegean promontory. For my Master's degree I had done a textual study of one of those manuscripts for the International Greek New Testament Project. One of the highlights of my year in Europe was the days I spent at Athos. Of course, I was eager to visit the libraries, but what I took with me when I left were the liturgies. The deep voices singing the liturgy at four o'clock in the morning still reverberate in my inner ear today.

A few years later I was asked to participate in an archaeological expedition to Capernaum, in Israel. The dig I took part in was conducted at the Greek Orthodox site. There I became friends with two Greek monks who took me to the Orthodox Patriarchate in Jerusalem and initiated me into the riches of Orthodox iconography. One Sunday, Kyrilos and Kyprianos, my two new friends, and Vasilios Tzaferis, the director of the dig, sung for the rest of us the liturgy of Saint Chrysostom at the little church in Capernaum. These experiences left in me an indelible impression about Orthodoxy and the richness of its aesthetic traditions.

Then in 1994 I was invited to present a paper on Paul at a conference in Chişinau, Moldova. As a young nation emerging from the collapse of the Soviet Union, Moldova was (and I think still is) in a rather precarious position. Both of its neighbors, Romania and Ukraine, were not too happy with its existence and had claims on parts of it. Not far away, things were not going well in Yugoslavia, which was experiencing rapid disintegration. In these circumstances, Ion Druze, a prominent intellectual well-known and admired by everyone in Moldova, convinced the new president to convene a conference that would explore how the apostle Paul could contribute to a safe passage for the nation through the troublesome times it was facing. Druze titled the conference "Saint Paul and the Danger of Self-Destruction." I was elated to be invited to attend and present a paper. The trip and the conference were my introduction to Slavic Orthodoxy in its new vitality both in Moldova and in Moscow, where I spent some time on my way to Chişinau. The conference became a significant moment in the life of Moldova. Everyone was talking about how Paul could help in facing the problematic future of the nation. I soon learned, however, that Paul was not a prominent figure in the religious landscape of the Eastern participants. It was Druze's own fascination with Paul that brought Paul from the sidelines to center stage. At the time he was writing a serialized, fictionalized version of Paul's life in a prominent Moscow magazine.

While in Moldova on the eve of the Feast of Orthodoxy, the participants of the conference were taken to a little village to celebrate the evening liturgy. It was an enchanted event in my life. The village people were enthralled by what was happening. When it came time to partake of the body of Christ, the villagers brought out the marvelous breads they had baked at home for the occasion. That moment of mutual participation when all were trying to give their neighbors some of themselves across deep cultural divides was the best demonstration of the power of symbolic actions I ever witnessed.

In seeking to write on Paul from my original home cultural perspective, I soon found myself rereading what I had read as a student in Paraná and Buenos Aires. The challenge was to be faithful to a reality that I knew quite well firsthand but had not experienced on a daily basis for some time. A few trips home during the last forty years have made me aware of many changes in the lives of the *rioplatenses,* but I needed to develop and deepen my memories of my homeland and the impressions I had gained through contacts and news reports over the years. The major problems are that theology and ethics are taught using European texts in translation and that in the dominant Catholic culture there has not been a strong biblical, much less Pauline, influence. When Vatican II directed Catholic attention to the study of Scripture and the *comunidades de base*[7] began to appear, for quite different reasons, they did not make much of an inroad at first in either Uruguay or Argentina. Uruguay has had a longstanding liberal tradition that is rather suspicious of religion in general and the Catholic Church in particular. Argentina has had a strong ultraconservative church that has been on good terms with the government and the army and sought their help in squelching any blossoming of liberation theology and the *comunidades de base.* This has meant that I could not tap interpretations of Paul by the common people. I had, therefore, to develop a dialogue between my native culture and Paul on the basis of my knowledge of both and a cautious scholarly imagination. Of course, I had to select what this dialogue was going to be about. The cultural markers I have chosen are not peculiar to the River Plate region, and some readers may think that they are not the most important. I trust no one will think they are not significant. In the struggle to have Paul interact with my native culture I learned a great deal — most conspicuously how not to go about doing this exercise! The legitimacy of the enterprise depends on the honesty and the openness with which one allows the participants in the dialogue to remain themselves. I will think I have succeeded if my interference does not seem imposing or to be calling attention to itself.

I was greatly helped by friends who read what I was writing, gener-

7. The *comunidades de base* are the "base communities" associated with populist expressions of Latin American liberation theology.

ously offered comments, and seriously questioned some of my observations and assertions. As conversation partners they were invaluable. In general they unanimously endorsed the value of what I was attempting and gave me to understand that I was on the right track. I was particularly encouraged by not being told that I was being too negative in my depiction of the *rioplatenses.* At times I have criticized myself on this account. My aim has been to be as objective as possible when dealing with sensitive issues.

If writing about Paul in dialogue with my native culture proved difficult, dealing with Paul in a culture to which I have rather limited access, particularly to its language, proved almost impossible. Many times I despaired of success. The early drafts are totally absent from what now appears in print. A major obstacle has been the low profile of Paul in Russian Orthodoxy and the fact that he is used in a proof-texting way to advance doctrinal positions. My instincts insisted on interjecting my reading of Paul. These I had to valiantly resist, and when I failed, my coauthors reminded me that as a guest in a foreign land I should be more eager to listen than to talk. Hopefully the readers of these pages will learn to listen so as to be enriched by what others have said. I have known quite a few individuals who have traveled extensively around the world, but who in the process never left home. Writing this essay taught me the importance and the difficulty of abandoning one's accustomed outlook and learning to see things with the eyes of others. The rewards for the effort never fail.

In the mid-1970s a colleague at Notre Dame, John Dunne, opened my eyes to the significance of a theology in which participation was offered as a counterbalance to substitution. He based this insight on Paul who, while saying that Christ had died in our stead, insists that the death of Christ does not mean that Christians are exempted from death but that Christians must die with Christ in order to also be raised with him. Dunne also introduced a new method for doing theology. He described it as "passing over" and "coming back." He explained that theology is constantly seeking to answer new questions that come to the fore on account of experience, and that the best way to gain insight is by passing over into another person's life and then coming back to one's own life. This meant entering sympathetically into the feelings, images, insights, and choices of the other, and then coming back to one's own. Passing over, furthermore, should be extended into another culture. At the time Dunne was trying to gain insights into the question of death and exploring how death was experienced in Buddhism and Islam. The exercise of passing over and coming back, he insisted, would not provide new information but new insights, a new standpoint for seeing information, a new perspective. My conversations with Dunne at the time gave formal authority to what I had been informally doing, on account of my life's trajectory, for some time. In this book I have been challenged to carry out this approach in a rigorous and studious way, to pass over to others and to myself in hermeneutical journeys to the land of my ancestors in Russia and to the land of my birth in the valley of *el rio de la Plata.*

K. K. (Khiok-khng) Yeo

I am an "overseas" Chinese, born and raised in Malaysia, now living in the United States. The Chineseness of my family means that to be human is to be social and ethical beings who establish ourselves so that we can contribute toward the goodness and prosperity of our community. Ethnic identity is an enduring source of meaning for us. Chineseness has also been a means of social and spiritual survival for us.

In the early 1920s, my grandparents moved with their children to Borneo Island in Malaysia in search of a better life and to escape the civil war in southern China (Seotow). This migration from a traditional Chinese identity to a foreign land where we were in the minority had a profound effect on us. In the late 1930s and early 1940s, the Japanese army occupied Malaysia, and my parents witnessed the brutality of racism firsthand as the Japanese pursued an imperialist quest for an east Asian empire. Growing up in Malaysia, I was taught how violence justified by ethnocentric ideologies leads to the horrific events of concentration camps (Nazis against Jews in the Holocaust) and massacres (Japanese against Chinese in Nanjing).

I learned at a young age that ethnic identity can be a blessing and a curse. In Malaysia we valued ethnic diversity and aimed to celebrate diversity, but there were tensions, too. Being Chinese in Malaysia meant that no matter our socioeconomic class, we suffered animosity from other ethnic groups, such as the Malay and other indigenous people (Dayaks, Punans, Melanau, etc.). In Malaysia and Indonesia, anti-Chinese sentiment is common, but these attitudes were difficult for me to understand. Sometimes it seemed that we were attacked for our virtues — for being industrious, family-oriented, attentive to education, morality, and successful in business. I felt this from the time I was in kindergarten. For the rest of my life, my education, my work, my ministry, and my research and writing have been linked with those early experiences, when as a child I struggled to make sense of being Chinese in a multicultural context.

In Malaysia educational opportunities were available to us in Chinese, English, and Malay schools. My parents sent me and all my siblings to a Chinese school sponsored by the Chinese association and subsidized by the government. My parents wanted us to be educated as Chinese, to learn Chinese morality, Chinese ways of thinking, and the Chinese language. As a grade schooler, I thought English was easier to learn than Chinese, but I appreciated the beautiful images, the representation of Chinese characters, especially in Chinese calligraphy. One of my Chinese teachers reminded us that to write Chinese words is to form one's character and to shape one's personality, because writers must be patient and observant and seek to express their will and emotion by practicing thousands of brushstrokes, mastering the control of ink and pressure. Comparing the English, Chinese, and Malay languages I learned in grade school, I knew that being Chinese for me was the most fortunate thing. I still remember how our schoolmasters gave us moral instructions in the morning assembly. Each semester's report card contained our academic score, but also a progress report on our moral aptitude and physical fitness. Great emphasis was placed on how to be a good person and to do the right things. The impression this instruction made on me is illustrated by an incident that occurred one day when I was returning home from the public library and was attacked by a group of Malay boys on the way. I was not hurt physically, but psychologically I was terribly hurt and wished I could retaliate; I hated those Malays. But I reminded myself that to fight with "wild dogs and pigs" is to do evil to oneself. I learned to keep a distance from an "adversary" and to extend a helping hand to those in need. These aphorisms of a traditional Chinese (Confucianist) education were not empty clichés but character-forming paths to virtue.

My parents decided to send me and most of my siblings to an English medium secondary school (middle and high schools). They thought that six years of Chinese/Confucianist education was a sufficient foundation for us. We would continue to learn Chinese and Malay. Second, they thought an English education would guarantee us better employment opportunities and would better serve us if we wished to go overseas for further education. I enjoyed very much the cross-cultural education of my secondary school, where an ethnically mixed student body challenged me to be sensitive to the coexistence of all people. I also noticed that the Confucian moral teachings were absent from my secondary school.

I encountered theology in the secondary school. Christian missionaries established many of the English secondary schools in Malaysia. I went to an Anglican high school and had the option of an elective course on the Bible. I did not take the Bible class, but I did become acquainted with Christianity. I became a Christian after a year of arguing and dialoging with Christian friends.

Becoming a Christian was a high point in my life. It was not so much a moral transformation. I did not give up an immoral life for an ethical one. It was instead a transformation in self-understanding in my quest for meaning. Thus began my pilgrimage to becoming a Chinese Christian — a long journey of learning a new identity of being *both* Chinese *and* a Christian. During the process of my conversion, I sometimes mocked my Christian friends who were "racially" Chinese but did not know the Chinese language or any Chinese classics and Confucianist ethics. I was bothered that the Chinese Bible did not read like Chinese prose. I wrestled with many biblical narratives that struck me as lacking universality, being too narrow in scope, too focused on the Mediterranean world. I wondered how the Bible could be the word of God for everyone when its revelation sounded so limited to particular groups. My favorite parts of the Bible were the wisdom books of the Old Testament. I did not like the historical books, for they did not contain the history of other peoples. To me, the teaching of what I later learned to call the Pentateuch was racist, although I liked the creation account for its beauty and universality. As for the New Testament, I liked Luke and John better than Matthew and Mark, again because I perceived them to be more universal. Paul's letters were my favorite part of the Bible. (Obviously, I had certain Marcionite tendencies as a young Christian!)[8]

Paul helped me become a *Chinese* Christian. Paul's interpretive skill with the Jewish stories engaged me. His passion and edginess grabbed my attention. He was cross-cultural and counter-cultural. I wanted to learn from him and emulate him (a typically Chinese way of approaching a great

8. Marcion, a Christian teacher at Rome in the mid-second century, rejected the Jewish Scriptures and promoted a Christian Scripture made up of an edited Luke and Paul, all in the name of an anti-Jewish universalism and Gnostic anti-materialism.

teacher). During those high school years, I read Paul through Confucianist categories. I was fascinated by his understanding of "sanctification" in Romans 5–7. I dismissed Paul's understanding of eschatology as cultural bias, since apocalyptic did not figure as a credible view of the world in my background and Paul's apocalyptic eschatology seemed to be an artifact of his ancient Jewish and Mediterranean culture. It was at this time that I first thought of doing a comparative reading of Confucius's *Four Books* and Paul's letters.

After high school, I worked for a few years at the Inland Revenue Department. That job never satisfied my thirst for understanding in philosophy and literature. I decided to pursue a theological degree in America and to work on cross-cultural interpretation of the New Testament. I first did undergraduate study at St. Paul Bible College in Waconia, Minnesota (now Crown College), which gave me three years of deep reflection. My wife and I were far away from our family in Malaysia, and three years of homesickness deepened our conviction that we could not be Americanized; we must remain Chinese. During this time, I met a wonderful mentor and friend, Donald Alexander, who had spent seven years teaching as a missionary in Hong Kong and whose doctoral work was on Confucius. He constantly encouraged me to read the Bible from a Chinese perspective. After three years of undergraduate study majoring in Bible and theology, I went to Garrett-Evangelical Theological Seminary. At Garrett, the well-known Paul scholar Robert Jewett became my mentor and eventually guided me through a joint Ph.D. program with Northwestern University. I focused on cross-disciplinary study between New Testament at the seminary and Greco-Roman rhetoric in the Classics and Communication Departments of the university. Jewett's interest in interpreting American culture from a theological perspective served as a model of cultural hermeneutics for me. My doctoral dissertation took up Chinese cross cultural hermeneutics, with a focus on 1 Corinthians 8 and 10 from the standpoint of Chinese ancestor worship.[9]

After my doctoral work, I went to Hong Kong to teach for several years. I spoke Teochiew and Hokien and no Cantonese, so I lectured in Mandarin and learned to engage in conversation with students and col-

9. See K. K. (Khiok-khng) Yeo, *Rhetorical Interaction in 1 Corinthians 8 and 10: A Formal Analysis with Preliminary Suggestions for a Chinese, Cross-cultural Hermeneutics* (Leiden: Brill, 1995).

leagues in Cantonese. I noticed, however, that living in Hong Kong could sometimes be a painful experience for those unable to speak Cantonese. Often I was made to feel unwelcome because I was a Malaysian-speaking Mandarin. Some of my close friends explained this treatment of me as due to an "island emotion," that is, the feeling of those who are slow to open to outsiders because they are protective of their own place in a limited space. I began to understand more fully the complexity of Chinese identity: is it one or many? In seeking to answer this question, I have learned that cross-cultural interpretation is not only a movement outward but also requires a corresponding movement inward, an exploration of one's own cultural identity. For me, learning to be Chinese and Christian in a multicultural world has meant learning the complexity of Chinese identity, not simply assuming that I bear that identity transparently to myself.

In my second English book, *What Has Jerusalem to Do with Beijing?*[10] my goal was to work at bridging the gaps between Scripture ("Jerusalem") and Chinese culture ("Beijing"). I worked with Chinese culture in the concrete specifics of the yin-yang thinking, Confucianist ethics, Taoist spirituality, the June 4 massacre, Vision 20/20, and other cultural events and institutions. I placed biblical theology (ethics, soteriology, eschatology, etc.) in dialogue with these expressions of a diverse Chinese culture. This study reinforced my conviction that other cultural vantage points — ancient and modern — can illumine and offer a critique of one's own culture. And vice versa. I became more self-aware and self-critical as a Chinese, more culturally astute as a student of the Bible, which is a culturally shaped book. I am convinced that cross-cultural interpretation is not just an intellectual exercise or an interesting diversion but a practical necessity for peaceful coexistence among peoples of diverse cultures and religions.

I have chosen in the present volume to study Paul from a Native American perspective because Native American traditions fascinate me. It may be that there are primordial connections between Native Americans and peoples of the eastern hemisphere and thus in a remote way to me. Centuries ago, ancient people of northern Asia likely crossed over a land bridge at the Bering Strait and migrated to what we now call North America. And one may suggest that traditional Chinese culture and Native American culture have certain very general similarities. But these connec-

10. K. K. (Khiok-khng) Yeo, *What Has Jerusalem to Do with Beijing? Biblical Interpretation from a Chinese Perspective* (Harrisburg: Trinity Press International, 1998).

tions are so distant from me and the similarities so vague that I do not imagine for a moment that in seeking Native American perspectives on Paul I am rehearsing another version of my own Chinese tradition. I am a stranger to Native American culture. Most of what I know of Paul and Native Americans I have learned through formal education in American academic contexts and through study using North American research libraries. I have been in conversation with Native American Christians, including pastors and scholars. But I recognize the limitations of a Chinese person reading Native American history and culture in a North American academic setting. I am not so naive as to claim that my description is objective or that my presentation is how Native Americans should read Paul.

As an outsider, I adopt a sympathetic posture in reading the Native American tradition. As one who does not live in the complexity and nuances of Native American cultures, I aim to understand, not to offer my own judgments. For this reason, my treatment of Native American culture(s) focuses on ideals and values. Here one must distinguish between cultural ideals and actual behaviors. For example, when I speak of the values of peace and harmony in certain Native American cultures, I do not assume that participants in these cultures never engage in violence, only that they embrace nonviolence and harmony as ideals. In the same way, the Confucian ideal of *ren* or benevolence does not mean that Confucianists are never violent.

My study of Native American cultures depends mostly on published material, but I have gathered some information through interviews. In using these sources, I have tried to be very cautious. I know that cultures have many shadings and complexities that do not fit neatly into a simple interpretive system. I have discovered that in some published academic material there is a leftist slant typical of much academic thought in the humanities in the U.S. These perspectives from the Left are very important. Native American academics have taken up the critical tools of ideological critique to expose and interpret Euro-American imperialism toward Natives and to resist White domination. In the academic literature the opinion of many is that assimilation to White culture is bad and that dialogue between Natives and Euro-Americans has proven hopelessly unfruitful. For some Native American intellectuals, Native worldviews are fundamentally superior to Euro-American worldviews and can only be diminished through dialogue or accommodation. I have listened carefully to this radical perspective, but I have been more attracted to views that are more integrative and, in my view, more balanced. I have also sought out non-academic voices. Native Americans are a very diverse population in America. They are by no means monolithic in how they think about their own traditions, about Christianity, or about the Western world. There have been significant movements in Native American history to forge creative syntheses of Native culture and Euro-American culture. There have been important Native American Christian movements.

I have tried to be a descriptive reporter in presenting Paul through Native American eyes, but in understanding and reporting I also make hermeneutical choices, focusing on what I find meaningful and making connections in a way that makes sense to me. For example, I think I pay a lot of attention to cosmology, anthropology, and ethics in the Native American chapter because these themes resonate with me as a Chinese. Another factor is at work here as well. Generally speaking, Paul has not been an attractive figure for Native Americans exposed to Christianity or a major voice in Native American Christian theology. Therefore, I probably end up doing more of my own synthesizing and making more suggestions of my own about a Native American perspective on Paul than I would have liked. I hope that, where I have done so, I am following Native American cues and patterns of thought. But inevitably, my reading of Paul through a Native American lens is a constructive work influenced not only by Native American sources but also by the Chinese and Euro-American assumptions and categories of thought that have shaped me culturally and educationally.

Charles Cosgrove

I grew up in a middle-class family in a very small suburb of Chicago. Although in academic settings I am often distinguished ethnically as "Anglo-American" (and am willing to accept the general cultural symbolism of that label), I am technically German-Irish American.[11] And in my father's Irish Catholic ancestral past, "Anglo" is not a self-descriptor but conjures up a condescending neighbor, an occupying presence, and sometimes an enemy.

11. According to the 1990 census, the two largest immigrant groups in the U.S. are Germans and Irish, suggesting that I am ethnically super-typical as an American and probably should have gone into politics! By the 2000 census, however, those of Irish origin had been surpassed by both Hispanics and African Americans.

Nevertheless, these European ethnicities — German, Irish — play almost no role in my personal sense of identity. I think of myself as simply American in the way of most Americans whose ethnicity is not "contested." I am named after my father, who was named for his father, who was named for his teenage uncle, fallen in combat July 1, 1863 on the first day of the Battle of Gettysburg — a Union soldier and an Irish immigrant.

This connection with the Civil War has special meaning for me. We have no idea what our ancestral soldier's Civil War politics were (and I know that immigrants in nineteenth-century America quickly assimilated white prejudice toward blacks to some degree or other), but I like to think of him as a symbol of my family's beginnings in America (my mother's side arrived later), an Irishman fighting against the South's claim to independence and against preservation of the Southern way of life, with slavery at its foundation. And I think of my great-great-uncle when I recall Frederick Douglass's comment, in his tour of Ireland, that the Irish peasants he saw had the same look as many American slaves — a sullen, lifeless, unintelligent look, proof to the white mind of black inferiority and to the English mind of Irish inferiority but a sign in truth of the ravages of oppression and the survival tactics it evokes in the oppressed.[12]

For free American blacks like Douglass, Great Britain offered an escape from American racism; for many nineteenth-century Irish, America offered an escape from English prejudice. Nevertheless, I know that it is important not to draw the parallels too closely between what the Irish and the Africans suffered at the hands of the English. There are some huge differences. Comparing the Irish journey to America with the importation of Africans to America, James Baldwin comments, "The Irish Middle Passage was as foul as my own. . . . But the Irish became white once they got here and began rising in the world, whereas I became black and began sinking."[13] My parents taught me to distinguish similarly between such differences of prejudice — to distinguish the prejudice experienced in their own ancestral history from the more deadly prejudice directed toward African Americans. I imbibed their anger and criticism against all forms of discrimination against anyone, anywhere, but especially against "Negroes" (a

12. I can no longer locate the source of this reference in Douglass's papers.

13. James Baldwin, *The Price of the Ticket* (New York: St. Martin's, 1985), xv. I owe this reference to Brad Ronnell Braxton, *No Longer Slaves: Galatians and African American Experience* (Collegeville: Liturgical, 2002), 18.

respectful 1960s name for African Americans). Martin Luther King was a national hero for my family. I don't remember what we thought about Malcolm X and Black Power. I think we tended to conceive the solution to racial problems in terms of "black assimilation" and "white acceptance." These bits of my history are significant for what follows.

Perhaps the best way for me to describe my journey to the joint effort that is this book is to begin with my first academic sabbatical, which I spent in Buenos Aires at ISEDET working on a biblical theology project entitled "justification and social justice." ISEDET — Instituto Superior Evangélico de Estudios Teológicos — is a united Protestant seminary and a seat of Latin American liberation theology. I went to study with José Míguez Bonino, improve my Spanish, absorb the political-theological atmosphere of the seminary, and use the ISEDET library as a resource for the liberationist angles of my topic. Buenos Aires and ISEDET also had a poignant association for me as the place where Ernst Käsemann's[14] daughter Elisabeth carried out work as a human rights activist and in 1977 became one of Argentina's 30,000 *desaparecidos* during the days of the brutal military regime that lasted from 1976 to 1983.[15] She represents in my mind the kind of social justice commitment that her father's kind of Pauline theology warrants, a way of reading the apocalyptic Paul in the service of social justice.

I never completed the book that was supposed to emerge from my sabbatical project because I was stymied by unresolved hermeneutical questions. One was "indeterminacy," the increasingly unavoidable awareness that no matter how rigorously I (or anyone) might work out an interpretation of Paul for my topic, other plausible interpretations might be — had been, were being — just as vigorously and resourcefully defended. Eventually — and almost a decade later — I came to terms with this in a book entitled *Elusive Israel,* a study in biblical hermeneutics, really, that used Paul's treatment of Israel in Romans 9–11 as an example.[16] In addition to dealing with the question of indeterminacy, that book also took up the question of nationalism. My thinking about nationalism also owes a great deal to my Argentine experience, as I will explain in a moment.

14. Ernst Käsemann, one of Rudolf Bultmann's most influential students, was a giant of New Testament studies in the post–WW II era.

15. It was eventually established that Elisabeth was executed in secret, along with others, by orders of an Argentine general.

16. Charles Cosgrove, *Elusive Israel: The Puzzle of Election in Romans* (Louisville: Westminster/John Knox, 1997).

During my time in Buenos Aires, Michael Novak's *Will It Liberate?* was published in Spanish translation.[17] I was invited to join a group of ISEDET graduate students to discuss this book, which I read in Spanish to make sure I would be primed with useful vocabulary for the discussion. These were the Reagan years, a time when antipathy to the U.S. was particularly strong among left-leaning people in Latin America. To the ISEDET students, Novak, a fellow of the American Enterprise Institute and a harsh critic of the socialist assumptions of most Latin American liberation theology, was an intellectual version of Reagan, someone they despised.

Sometimes we learn what should be the simplest and most obvious lessons not at home but in a new place, where strange surroundings give us a heightened awareness of the world and our place in it. In Buenos Aires I sat in the circle of discussants and listened to very bright and politically attuned Argentine theology students talk about the United States. It was immediately apparent to me that they knew almost nothing about the United States. Then it occurred to me that I did not know a great deal more than they, at least not enough to do the kind of contextual theology that liberation theology calls for and that I affirmed as a student of the liberationist approach.

Of course, I had a lot of passive cultural awareness about my own country, a kind of tacit cultural knowledge, but not a reflective knowledge well informed by history and careful study. Obviously, if theology is to be contextual or "correlational" (Tillich), those who do theology ought to be as devoted to studying their own time and place as they are to studying the subjects of their particular theological discipline. And I had never really done this — at least not beyond taking certain required courses in high school and college, watching the news, and doing some desultory and unorganized reading here and there. So, one could say that I went to Argentina to learn firsthand about the Third World and discovered that I needed to learn about my own home world in an active and intellectually rigorous way. Both of my chapters in this volume reflect something of the seriousness with which I have taken American history and cultural analysis since my Argentine sabbatical.

Back home I considered how to make good on my resolve to become more culturally self-aware. But "American culture" is a huge subject, espe-

17. Michael Novak, *Will It Liberate? Questions about Liberation Theology (Será liberadora? Interrogantes acerca de la teología de la liberación)* (New York: Paulist, 1986).

cially when regarded historically. Where to begin? It seemed to me that I should start with an American experience and history not my own and that the lasting and powerful ways in which matters of "race" — racism, racism's resisters, and racism's active and passive agents and allies, personal and institutional — have figured in America argued for beginning with the African American experience. I had read some James Cone, so I turned to his newly published book, *Martin & Malcolm & America.*[18]

As I worked through Cone's analysis of the dialectic between black particularism and black universalism throughout African American history, I was continually reminded of the preoccupation (especially at that time) of so many Pauline scholars with how to make sense of Paul's simultaneous affirmation of some kind of Jewish particularism in Romans 11, for example, and his otherwise emphatic universalism (no distinction between Jews and gentiles). I became convinced that African Americans had thought about the relation between particularism ("nationalism") and universalism ("integration") in ways that could illumine the interpretation of Paul, providing categories and insights that might place Paul's statements about Jews and gentiles in a new light. So I immersed myself in the literature of black nationalism. My book *Elusive Israel* was influenced in important ways by this study, and in quoting from black abolitionist William Watkins at the beginning of my chapter on nationalism in Paul, I meant to symbolize my debt to the African American tradition.

I remain convinced that the interpretation of Israel in Paul has been too dominated by "white" Establishment thinking about nationalism, which tends to see nationalism as inherently bad, no matter what form it takes. But some Christians make an exception for Jews, according them the theological right in the name of Paul to be elect Israel, a people whom God values in a unique way and upon whom God bestows a vocation in history (whether in a political statist sense or in a non-political religious sense). This view of the Jewish people is some kind of nationalism, and I have learned, thanks to categories from Cone and other African Americans, a logic by which to affirm a form of Jewish nationalism (the Jewish people as Israel, God's elect people in history) without excluding other legitimate non-Jewish forms of nationalism. I think there are merits in "soft" black nationalism (defined later in this book in my chapter on Paul in African

18. James H. Cone, *Martin & Malcolm & America: A Dream or a Nightmare* (Maryknoll: Orbis, 1991).

American perspective) and I criticize my own country not for being "nationalistic" — an inherent characteristic of being a distinct people in a world of many peoples — but for being too often nationalistic in a "hard" sense, an arrogant and imperialistic nationalism. Black Christian nationalism in its soft form offers a prophetic alternative to the dominant hard form of American nationalism — an alternative that I do not expect to see become a dominant ethos and policy in the U.S. but that nonetheless provides a framework for Christian political theology and prophetic critique. There are also important traditions in Jewish thought that provide a similar alternative for political theology.[19]

My excursion into the subject of black nationalism led me back into nineteenth-century America. I read thousands of pages of primary African American sources and became absorbed not only in the history of black nationalism but also in the various expressions of black religion, black abolitionism, debates about equality, and a host of other subjects, including African American antislavery constitutionalism (an obscure topic linked historically to the equally obscure subject of Anglo-American antislavery constitutionalism). These studies led me, naturally enough, into broader reading in American history and culture that I need not describe in itemized detail here. I will only mention that an awakened interest in the American legal tradition, especially its hermeneutical aspects, led me eventually to spend some time in law school, another important supplement to my "American education."

When it came time to prepare my chapters for this book, I decided on "Paul in African American perspective" as my cross-cultural contribution for reasons stemming from the autobiography I have just shared. On one hand, this seemed like a manageable cross-cultural move for which I was well-suited, an effort to see Paul from the perspective of nearby neighbors who share with me, in a more general way, the same larger American culture and whose religious, political, cultural, and intellectual history I have spent a lot of time studying. But in other respects, the task seemed daunting. My sense of not having "standing" to write about Paul through African American eyes was and remains very keen. I am not a neutral outsider to the black tradition, a visitor from afar who can look, describe, and

19. In *Elusive Israel* I draw attention to the important contributions of Daniel Boyarin and Jonathan Boyarin to contemporary thinking about nationalism/ethnicity, etc. The Boyarins approach these questions from a Jewish perspective.

comment with impunity. I am a white neighbor, culturally linked to the brutal history that continues to burden and wound the lines of communication and understanding between blacks and whites in America. The only argument in favor of my saying anything about what Paul looks like through an African American lens is that my aim is reflective listening — listening long and hard and then putting into words what I have heard and think I understand. All white Americans owe some kind of sustained, serious listening to African Americans, and listening can become communication, with the hope of dialogue, only if we speak after we have listened. The first kind of speaking should be to say what we have heard, so we can be corrected and guided to better listening.

My approach to Paul in African American perspective has been affiliative rather than prophetic. It is not my place to be a prophet to African Americans or the black church. Moreover, in view of the history of appeal to Paul to buttress the institution of slavery (and the memory of that history), there is a continuing need for a certain degree of reconciliation between Paul and many African Americans. Of course, the danger of affiliating Paul to the African American tradition is that one can easily fall into the role of mere apologist for Paul rather than taking a meaningful look at Paul from the African American perspective. I hope I have avoided this pitfall.

I do have standing to speak as an American about dominant American culture in Pauline perspective, and I feel confident that what I describe gets authentically at traits and tendencies in the diverse American character that all Americans share or encounter in some way or other. Nevertheless, here, too, I have limitations and blind spots. My focus, American "individualism," is a subject that everyone agrees is central to American self-understanding and character, but there are many subcultures in America and they are not all individualistic in the same ways or to the same degrees. I interpret the cultural codes of American individualism in part out of my own experience as a Midwestern, baby-boomer, middle-class, white male with a Ph.D., etc. My take on individualism does not draw on any personal attunement to how, say, migrant Mexican-American cherry pickers understand and experience the American ethos I describe — or how suburban southern California members of Generation X do, or Pennsylvania steel workers (are there any left?), or urban teenage moms who fall below the poverty line, and so on. Building on the work of Koen Goudriaan, Brad Braxton observes that ethnic groups sharing the same culture may interpret and experience that common culture differently because their different ethnicities provide interpretive filters that organize and interpret the common culture differently.[20] I suspect the same goes as well for social class as a filter, gender as a filter, and so forth. Moreover, the compounding of multiple filters in a given group (African American rural women) and in a given person (an unmarried northern, urban, blue-collar, Italian male named Frank who plays guitar in his free time) shades experience of the common culture in distinctive, idiosyncratic ways. The rise in recent years of local ethnographies couched in narrative style — socio-anthropological efforts to describe a subcultural patch of experience in the flux of time without imposing neat categories or interpreting through broad generalizations — reflects increased awareness of the differences of perception and experience of a common culture that exist within that culture. A "subculture" is not simply something additional to the broader shared culture; it is also an interpretation of the common culture and is therefore a distinct experience of that culture.

None of the above persuades me that there is no place for generalization. It is simply very important to keep checking generalizations against the specifics of diverse experiences and not to press categories of the "typical" too far. Learning how one is typical is itself an important part of maturation in self-understanding, since we are usually least aware of the ways in which we are typical. What we all take for granted or all practice as a matter of cultural habituation — whoever "we" are — is usually invisible to us until it is pointed out (usually by an outsider). Then it appears "natural" to us once we contemplate it, another sign of how difficult it is to see what is typical as a social construction, a particular cultural formation that people in other cultures do not find "natural" and may not even think is appealing.

I learned from conversations with my coauthors about my chapter on Paul and American individualism that I am *typically American* in thinking that individual rights are very important, something we cannot afford to do without, even if rights doctrines can be carried to individualistic and legalistic extremes. The section of my chapter that deals with rights went through many revisions and my final stance both defends in some respects and criticizes in other respects classic American notions of human rights. But the entire intellectual effort revealed to me (and demonstrates, I hope,

20. Brad Ronnell Braxton, *The Tyranny of Resolution: 1 Corinthians 7:17-24* (Society of Biblical Literature Dissertation Series 181; Atlanta: Scholars, 2000), 79.

to my readers) how tricky culturally sensitive hermeneutics can be. Connections between the Bible and our world that seem patently obvious to us as "clear implications" of the text often dissolve under close logical and historical examination. On the other hand, I take it as inherent to the concept of the Bible as the church's *Scripture* that Christians are supposed to make connections between the Bible and their lives and, therefore, that *constructive analogical reasoning,* as the only way to make connections, is an appropriate hermeneutical approach. Still, the line between reasonable construction and arbitrary invention is sometimes a fine one — and is always a matter of judgment.

Some may find my chapter on Paul and American individualism too hard on America, others too soft. I have conflicted feelings about my home culture and national identity. The so-called "culture wars" in the United States today have those on the Right accusing those on the Left of being unpatriotic and anti-American and those on the Left accusing those on the Right of being blindly patriotic and jingoistically pro-American. I think of myself as politically on the left-leaning side of the *middle.* The military conflicts involving the U.S. during my lifetime have never stirred patriotic emotions in me — not even the few I supported. I am ambivalent about celebrating the Fourth of July because I think the American Revolution was morally unjustified and because I regard the original U.S. Constitution as racist. I do not think the U.S. is the "greatest country" on earth. On the other hand, there are many things I treasure about being an American. I value (and am proud of) America's commitment to individual freedom. I like how ethnically diverse/multicultural America is and is increasingly becoming. I believe in democratic capitalism (with due criticism for America's way of practicing it). And I love America as a *place* — the cities and small towns of America, its landscapes, its wildernesses.

I could go on with balancing lists of things to criticize and things to admire about America and outfit each point with qualifying comments. But my American identity probably has less to do with positions and attitudes and more to do with the sheer facticity of origin and experience in all its virtually unanalyzable detail, of growing up American the way one grows up in a family and loves it and belongs to it quite apart from having opinions about it. I learned this powerfully during two years of study in Germany when I was a graduate student. German university students (especially those in the humanities) were (I would guess still are) rather anti-American in the early 1980s. Reagan's presidency was deeply disliked and

U.S. plans to establish American Pershing II missiles in Germany were strongly opposed by the German students I knew. But they also did not like all kinds of other things about America. During the first months of my German experience, none of this anti-Americanism bothered me. I sympathized with much of the political critique and brushed off the cultural attacks (touching on everything from American food to the American personality type). In time, however, all of this anti-Americanism began to grate on me and even to hurt. It also awakened strong feelings of patriotism in me that had nothing to do with any particular views I held about American politics or culture. I also learned an *a fortiori* lesson from this experience. If being the object of just a little bit of prejudice, comparatively speaking, in a setting where I was in no danger of being disadvantaged politically or socially, in a country I would soon leave to go back home, and in a place where I had no enemies and was never personally hated — if that experience of mild prejudice could produce real discomfort and resentment in me (and awaken some of my strongest patriotic feelings!), what must strong prejudice and actual discrimination feel like in a setting where one has real enemies, is hated by some, in a place from which one has no practical means of escape and in a land that one also rightly claims as home!

Here is what I have learned about the personal dimensions of cross-cultural understanding and Christian community. We reach out to others in empathy by finding something in our own experience that seems to connect with theirs. We become community when we go on to the hard work of testing these empathetic intuitions, accepting correction, and also opening ourselves to *receive* empathy, understanding, and a new perspective on ourselves from those we have sought to embrace.

Our Limited Horizons

We are keenly aware of the grounds on which one can criticize this project. Here is one criticism: *The authors have a right to speak from their own cultural perspectives but have no business writing about Paul from the vantage of cultures in which they are not members.* We have already addressed this question, but our defense may not be convincing to some. In the end, we take a risk of speaking where we do not have standing. We hope we have done so as careful and respectful listeners who believe that active study of other perspectives is vital to cross-cultural dialogue and understanding. Here is another potential criticism: *The authors are all male and perhaps assume that gender does not affect cultural interpretation.* We do not assume that, but we also confess that we have not done justice to the question of gender in our cultural interpretations. Another criticism might be as follows: *The authors are academics, which means that however cross-cultural they try to be it is a bookish kind of cross-culturalism.* We do not deny this. We offer a set of intellectual journeys that are largely dependent on libraries, not on "field" research or "immersion" in other cultures. This is certainly a weakness in some ways. On the other hand, library research supplemented by personal dialogue is a way to understanding that we highly value. One can cross great distances of time and space in a library; one can listen to many competing voices; one can find tools of critical analysis there. Some may observe: *The chapters cover different subjects, which makes them difficult to compare.* This is certainly true. It may be a drawback. On the other hand, we did not want to set up in advance a set of themes or questions and end up treating the different cultural perspectives as mere respondents to our questions. People in different cultural settings do not simply give different answers to the same questions, they ask different questions. They ask their own questions. We hope this book displays the cultural diversity of ways we can question Paul and find answers in Paul.

CHAPTER 1

Paul's Journey to the River Plate

Herold Weiss

In his study of Paul in *El hombre de hoy ante Jesús de Nazaret,*[1] the Uruguayan Juan Luis Segundo gives an acute and illuminating study of Paul's letter to the Romans. He develops an argument for the centrality of piety in the divine-human relation and the centrality of justice in the relations among humans. Using a hermeneutic of suspicion that advances from a rather simple first reading to a more mature second reading, Segundo argues that the gospel of Paul represents a continuation of the message of Jesus in the Synoptics. His presentation of the *hombre de hoy,* contemporary humanity, however, never quite touches ground in the living social reality and culture of his native Uruguay and the wider River Plate region. His discussion remains at the level of an abstract anthropology, very much in the tradition of European theology. In these pages I would like to bridge the gap between anthropology and the human reality in the socio-cultural concreteness of the River Plate basin.

The River Plate *(el rio de la Plata)* is one of the shortest and the widest rivers in the world. It is formed by the confluence of two great rivers that originate in Brazil: the Paraná and the Uruguay. Thus the River Plate region is in the first instance the fluvial basin of the Paraná and the Uruguay rivers. These two rivers form the Argentine mesopotamia, which in some ways is culturally closer to Uruguay. The full name of this republic is The Eastern bank of the Uruguay (river).[2] When its waters get confused

1. Juan Luis Segundo, *El hombre de hoy ante Jesús de Nazaret,* II *Historia y actualidad,* 1 *Synópticos y Pablo* (Madrid: Ediciones Cristiandad, 1982), 316-22. Segundo is arguably the most academic of the Latin American theologians of liberation.

2. La Banda Oriental del Uruguay.

with those of the Atlantic Ocean, the river is 125 miles wide. By then it influences the climate of the Argentine pampas. On this account it also gives its name to a vast region that includes the whole of Uruguay and the central and eastern part of Argentina. On both sides of the border dividing these two nations the people identify themselves as *rioplatenses.* The most important *rioplatense* figure is the gaucho (comparable in some ways to the North American "cowboy"), the inhabitant of the open land with distinct clothing and diet. In his wardrobe most characteristic is the *facón,* the knife he carries behind his back under the belt. His diet distinguishes itself by the frequent drinking of *mate,* a tea made from the leaves of a rather large tree indigenous to the northern mesopotamia and drunk by sucking a small amount of hot water that has been poured on a gourd containing the chopped, dried leaves and a small tube with a filter.[3]

Fate and Destiny

The first cultural marker of the River Plate region I will consider is the sadness of the gaucho and its causes. A good starting point is the folk songs of the region. Besides the *vidalas* (to life) and the *cielitos* (little heaven) are found the *tristes* (sad). These are the typical dances of the pampas. In his analysis of the social psychology of Latin America, Carlos O. Bunge ventures the opinion that the *tristeza criolla* is due to the fact that "as much in the Indian as in the Spaniard the moorish joy of life has been suffocated by the Inquisition."[4] Of course, the tango, the creation of the urban *arrabales* (lower class suburban barrios), is the classic expression of the misfortunes that confront the living. In every tango story someone ends up dead, disgraced, or alienated. In the faces of tango dancers there cannot be a hint of joy. Rather, the poses and the faces express the need to face one's destiny with determination and seriousness. Love is a matter of mastery and surrender.

The greatest expressions of gaucho poetry, *Martín Fierro* (1872) and *La vuelta de Martín Fierro* (the return of Martin Fierro) (1879) by José Her-

3. For a very revealing study of the strengths and the weaknesses of the gaucho, see Andres M. Carretero, *El gaucho argentino. Pasado y presente* (Buenos Aires: Editorial Sudamericana, 2002).

4. Carlos Octavio Bunge, *Nuestra América. Ensayo de psicología social* (sixth ed., Buenos Aires: La Cultura Argentina, 1918), 181. Unless acknowledged, all translations from Spanish works and the Greek New Testament are my own.

nández, contain many proverbial lines. These works have been described as sententious on account of their memorable apophthegms. One stanza reads

> Let's go, Fate, let's go together
> since we were born together:
> and since we live together
> in an indivisible bond,
> I will open with my knife
> our way up to the front.[5]

Here one's fate is depicted as a Siamese twin with whom one must travel through life. It would appear that since Martín Fierro will open the road ahead by his skill with a knife, his fate is just a fellow traveler. Such, however, is not at all the case. The road he travels with his fate is the road of *ausencia.* His life is distinguishable by what is absent in it. As the poem points out, he misses father and mother (ll. 1333, 1339), children and wife (l. 1349), a home of his own (ll. 1316, 1355-56), friends and patrons (l. 1351), and the understanding of others (ll. 1361-66). In the eyes of others, he is a *vago* (a bum, l. 1315), *maldito* (accursed, l. 1322), *mamao* (drunk, l. 1343), and *ladrón* (a thief, l. 1360). Worst of all, there is no use trying to change things. That is his lot. If he tries to point out the injustice of his circum stances, his cause never receives a hearing:

> In his mouth there are no arguments
> even though he has reasons to spare;
> wooden bells are
> the reasons of the poor.[6]

5. J. Hernández, *Martín Fierro,* ll. 1385-90:

> Vamos, suerte, vamos juntos
> dende que juntos nacimos:
> y ya que juntos vivimos
> sin podernos dividir,
> yo abriré con mi cuchillo
> el camino pa seguir.

6. *Martín Fierro,* ll. 1375-78:

> En su boca no hay razones
> aunque la razón le sobre;
> que son campanas de palo
> las razones de los pobres.

Así lo quiso el destino (Destiny wanted it this way), or *Yo nací pa pobre* (I was born to be poor) are explanations monotonously repeated by Latin American lips.

That Destiny determines the affairs of humans is freely expressed in the novels of the region. Ernesto Sábato in *Sobre héroes y tumbas,* describes Alejandra as one who does not believe in God or hell, but does believe in "Destiny." She says,

> Destiny chooses its instruments; immediately incarnates itself and then the screwing begins. . . . Destiny, though incarnated in Benito, did not see things exactly like him, had small disagreements. This happens quite frequently, obviously, because Destiny cannot go around choosing discretely the people who will serve as its instrument. That is why Destiny is a confusing thing and it equivocates: It knows well what it wants, actually, but the people who carry it out, not as well.[7]

In his acclaimed presentation of the inner life of the best-known Argentine dictator, *The Perón Novel,* Tomás Eloy Martínez constructs a conversation between Perón and Descalzo, an army buddy of his, at the time when Yrigoyen had become president in the 1920s. When Perón was a cadet at the army college, the Argentine army was being trained under the supervision of Prussian officers. Reflecting on the new government taking power, Perón comments that a great shift is taking place in Argentina and that from now on the army will be taking a more prominent role in national politics. Descalzo asks: "Do you want the power, Perón?" To which Perón replies, "It's not a matter of wanting or not wanting. It's a matter of fate."[8] This motif permeates the whole novel. As Perón reviews his life at the end of his career, it cannot be said that he forged ahead and achieved what he had achieved on account of his superior talents, the power of his will, or his political skills. He has just run the course his destiny had traced

7. "El Destino elige sus instrumentos, en seguida se encarna y luego viene la joda. . . . El Destino que aunque se había encarnado en Benito no opinaba exactamente como él, tenía sus pequeñas diferencias. Cosa que sucede muy a menudo, porque claro, el Destino no puede andar eligiendo en forma tan apretada a la gente que le va a servir de instrumento. Por eso el Destino es algo confuso y un poco equívoco: él sabe bien lo que quiere, en realidad, pero la gente que lo ejecuta, no tanto." Ernesto Sabáto, *Obras de Ficción* (Buenos Aires: Editorial Losada, 1966), 237.

8. Tomás Eloy Martínez, *The Perón Novel,* trans. Asa Zatz (New York: Pantheon, 1988), 175.

for him. In the same vein, in his presentation of Facundo Quiroga, a second-rate *caudillo* of the 1830s, Domingo Faustino Sarmiento wrote that he is describing him because he is a mirror of the nation "due to unstoppable forces not related to his will."[9]

Another famous poem in the gaucho repertoire is *Fausto* (1866) by Estanislao del Campo. It tells the story of a gaucho who has gone to Buenos Aires and ends up at the Colón theater, the most prestigious opera house in Latin America, attending a staging of *Faust,* the famous opera by Gounod based on Goethe's tragedy. Having returned to the countryside, he tells a friend what he had seen on the stage. The gaucho version of *Faust* does not identify any of the characters by name. In it, "the doctor" gets the devil to become his accomplice in gaining favor with "the blond." This allows "the doctor" to leave "the blond" pregnant. The story ends with "the blond" in jail for having killed the baby born on account of the successful seduction accomplished by "the doctor." In this telling "Don Juan" pays the devil nothing for his help and suffers no consequences. According to del Campo, events are governed by Fate, which in the case of women is "more cruel."[10] A lyric poetic interlude between the first and the second act of the theatrical performance is used by del Campo to establish the importance of this theme. Ostensibly the passage is an ode to the sea. Its place in the structure of the poem is clear, however, in the lines:

> On the rocks it is divine
> to see the waves break apart
> just like at the end collide
> men with their destiny.[11]

The fatalism that informs the culture of Latin America is more pervasive among those who find themselves at the bottom of the socioeconomic pyramid. The intellectuals of the upper middle class, on the other

9. D. F. Sarmiento, *Facundo. Civilización y barbarie* (Buenos Aires: Sur, 1962), 24.

10. "Las hembras, en mi opinión, Train un destino más fiero." Estanislao del Campo, *Fausto* (Buenos Aires: Centro Editor de America Latina, 1955).

11. En las toscas es divino
Mirar las olas quebrarse
Como al fin viene a estrellarse
El hombre con su destino.

hand, have been imbued with an idealistic determinism based on romantic and positivistic views of history. In this view the cycle that guides the rise and fall of civilizations has determined that Latin America is next in line to take its place as the center of human achievement and glory under the sun. Simón Bolívar, a leader of the wars of independence from Spain in the northern half of South America, had a vision of the whole continent as one united expression of the superiority of Hispanic culture. In Mexico this utopian vision of Latin America was given expression by Minister of Culture José Vasconcelos in his book *La raza cósmica* (1925).[12]

This expectation of imminent cultural and political fulfillment was also expressed by Domingo F. Sarmiento in the 1840s. In *Facundo* he examines the condition of Argentina at the time and offers his vision for the future. According to him, Buenos Aires "is called to be one day the most developed city in both Americas."[13] The way he expressed this prophecy is most telling. Even though the source of this "call" to grandeur is not identified, it is clear that it is none other than Fate. Latin America has also felt that it has a manifest destiny. The destiny of Catholic Latin America, however, is not to expand its land holdings and become a military, industrial, and mercantile power to be reckoned with around the world. Latin America's destiny is to triumph in the realm of the spirit, to triumph on account of its high ideals. This was given ultimate expression by José Enrique Rodó in his *Ariel*, published in 1900. Rodó uses the protagonists, Ariel and Caliban, from Shakespeare's *The Tempest* to contrast and compare the cultures and the futures of North and South America. While Caliban stands for the materialistic culture of the North, Ariel represents the idealism of a youthful South America. Rodó refers to his creation as

> the sweet and serene image of my Ariel — the benevolent genie in whom Shakespeare skillfully blended . . . such high symbolism. . . . Ariel is the superior reason and feeling. Ariel is this sublime instinct

12. José Vasconcelos, *La Raza Cósmica: A Bilingual Edition*, trans. and annotated by Didier T. Jaen (Baltimore: John Hopkins University Press, 1997). Unlike Rodó, who contrasts the materialism of the North with the spiritualism of the South, Vasconcelos contrasts the racial exclusivism of the North with the racial embrace of the South. The ultimate triumph of the superior Latin culture is based on the superiority of its racial inclusivism. This argument has become quite relevant to Latino pride in *mestizaje* (being of mixed race).

13. Sarmiento, *Facundo*, 35-36.

> for perfectibility, by whose virtue the human clay is magnified and transformed into the center of things to which light is attached.[14]

Rodó himself is one of the highest exponents of that Hegelian liberalism that expected the triumph of the spirit. Thus he became the apostle of a spiritual education that carried into the future a "pious veneration of the past." This creative spirit, however, had to be free from clerical dogmatisms if it was to be "the noble power that in the present communicates . . . the sense for the ideal."[15] It was because the youth of Latin America were developing "the sense for the ideal," were, in other words, becoming imitators of Ariel, that Latin America was to become the beacon for the rest of the world. Whether evident in the resignation, sadness, or hopelessness of the masses or in the confidence with which the elites assign superior spiritual values to the Latin soul, a pervasive determinism informs the culture of the River Plate. Of course, the intellectual elites who place their hope in history look down upon the more traditional, ahistorical masses.[16]

The idealism of the beginning of the twentieth century was somewhat justified. Uruguay, for example, enjoyed for many years one of the highest standards of living in the world, certainly among the top ten nations. In the 1920s it reinvented itself with one of the most progressive constitutions and a host of social laws that placed its cultural experiment on the map. The course of the second half of the twentieth century, however, has radically diminished those historical hopes. A different political climate with hardly any reasons for hope has been neutralizing the fears of cultural homelessness, so that a large proportion of the population has migrated or is contemplating leaving. When, at the beginning of 2002, the Argentine economy imploded and the country had five presidents in a period of two weeks, there was some real anger among the masses. It was evident that the politicians had been taking care of themselves and not of the people. Still, to an amazing degree, the people have resigned themselves to the situation as one more tragedy that a cruel fate had determined for them.

14. José Enrique Rodó, *Obras Completas. Editadas, con introducción, prólogos y notas por Emir Rodriguez Monegal* (Madrid: Aguilar, 1957), 242a.

15. Rodó, *Obras Completas,* 241b.

16. On the tensions between historical elites and traditional masses, historical and ahistorical cosmological postures, see Mircea Eliade, *The Myth of Eternal Return: Cosmos and History* (New York: Harper, 1947).

Paul's Concern for Justice

Paul would understand the determinism of Latin American culture. One of the main characteristics of apocalypticism is its determinism. The outcome of the struggle between the forces of evil and the power of God is never in doubt. In fact, everything taking place in history is already determined. Paul gives ample expression to this determinism. According to him, futility and corruption came about only because God himself subjected creation to them. It is to be noticed, however, that God subjected creation "upon hope," already envisioning "the glorious freedom of the children of God" (Rom. 8:20-21).

In the same way, the failure of Israel to believe in Christ as the manifestation of God's righteousness had come about because God hardened their hearts. The gentiles' affirmative response to the power of the gospel that is being preached among them is due to God's desire to make Israel jealous. However, since God had "known" Israel, it is impossible for them ever "to stumble so as to fall" (Rom. 11:11-12). As Paul sees it, "the gifts and the call of God are irrevocable" (Rom. 11:29). Thus, the Jews' rejection of the gospel, the gentiles' acceptance of it, the eventual jealousy of the Jews that will cause them to accept the gospel, and the ultimate salvation of Jews and gentiles have all been "prepared beforehand" (Rom. 9:22-24).

Paul opens the discussion of these issues with a rhetorical question: "Who can resist his will?" (Rom. 9:19). This question, posed by an imaginary interlocutor who does not understand Paul or does not agree with him, is paired to another, "Why does [God] blame?" The conversation partner considers it a contradiction to say that everything is determined by God but human beings are accountable, capable of being blamed. Paul's take on the rhetorical questions is not a philosophical *tour de force* on the relationship of God's sovereignty to human freedom. Tacitly, he admits that the answer to the first question is "nobody," and to the second "because he is God." His answer is an echo of the rhetorical questions the God of the whirlwind throws at Job (Job 38–40), or the lesson learned by Jeremiah on his visit to the potter's workshop (Jer. 18:1-10). "Oh man, who are you wishing to audit God? The clay does not say to the potter, 'Why are you shaping me this way?'" (Rom. 9:20). Humans may fail to understand God's ways, but they are not to question his sovereignty. Thus, Paul says three times in Rom. 1:18-32 that God "hands over" human sinners to all kinds of wickedness. This impression of a strict divine determinism is modified, however, by the fact that the fate of evildoers is what they have already chosen for themselves.

While recognizing the legitimacy of the intellectual tension between the two questions, Paul maintains that the obvious answers must be sustained. For him this is an aspect of "the mystery that has remained sealed from time eternal," the mystery at the core of his gospel and at the core of the *kerygma* of Jesus Christ. This mystery "has now been revealed . . . , becoming known to all the nations in order to elicit obedience of faith according to the decree of the eternal God" (Rom. 16:25-26). The mystery has to do with the divine ways. How a crucifixion can bring about redemption and why humans may be held accountable within a world fully under God's decrees are not for human minds to understand. This is the wisdom of God that seems like idiocy to humans (1 Cor. 1:21), the hidden mystery of God's wisdom (1 Cor. 2:7). Confronting God's ways, Paul can do no more than throw up his arms and exclaim: "How unexplainable are his decisions; how incomprehensible his ways!" (Rom. 11:33).

The events that mark the lives of Christians are predetermined in order to bring to fruition the divine design. As Paul sees it, those whom God foreknew, he also predestined, called, and justified. Now it is certain that God will also glorify them (Rom. 8:29-30). For him glorification is the ultimate goal. As he says, "These light, temporary afflictions are preparing us for the weighty, eternal glory which surpasses any comparison" (2 Cor. 4:17). As he insists, "The one who has prepared us for this is none other than God" (2 Cor. 5:5).

Paul's determinism, however, contrasts sharply with Latin American determinism in that his is highly optimistic because of his understanding of the gospel as the revelation of God's justice (Rom. 1:17). The Latin American masses reflect their determinism in their sadness and their resignation. The optimism of the Latin elites, on the other hand, is based on a reading of fate that borders on triumphalism. The optimism of Paul, on the other hand, is based on his faith that God has acted creatively in the cross and the resurrection of Christ, a faith backed up by Paul's experience of the power of the Spirit in the lives of those who believe. Within the new creation, Christians are being transformed from glory to glory, even to the likeness of their glorious Lord (2 Cor. 3:18).

For Paul, the tension involved in keeping God's overwhelming power and will together with human responsibility for one's deeds is essential to the prevention of historical triumphalism. An example of such triumphalism is the assumption that the church has "arrived" and is bringing history to ever nearer approximations of the kingdom of God, thanks to God's providential power, which has given Christians a superior moral character and wisdom to assert their domination of history under divine providence. But for Paul, divine control over the world is at the moment not complete. Nor is it evolving in a gradual, historical fashion. Human activity in the world does not just follow divine designs. The powers of the air, thrones, dominions, and angels are real and active in the world, even though there is only one God (1 Cor. 8:5-6). The certainty of God's eschatological triumph, however, may not be regarded as historical predestination. Historically, God's ways remain hidden. Knowledge of God's intention to save does not take away the mystery of God's ways. Salvation is not certain in the knowledge of the mystery now revealed. Hope is not knowledge, and God has established salvation on hope (Rom. 8:24). Individual responsibility for one's deeds is grounded on the tension between knowledge and hope.

It would seem, then, that Paul offers a very strong message of hope for the sad masses who feel overwhelmed by a fate that has dealt them a bad hand. He would agree with their pessimism if viewed apart from God's hidden transformation of the world. Hope is possible only on the foundation of faith, and faith is grounded on the reality of the new creation accomplished at the resurrection of Christ. The optimism of the *rioplatense* elites, on the other hand, is like that of the elites in Paul's time. They conceived the social structure as static and hierarchical and had, therefore, very conservative political views. This was the case even when, as the Roman emperor Marcus Aurelius testifies, their views of the personal life were quite enlightened by Stoic ideals. To the elites imbued with the idealism of a romantic view of history, who consider their success in the world secure, Paul would say that God's triumph is not worldly success but the revelation of God's righteousness. Therefore, history is controlled not by forces working within it but by the power of the risen Christ, who must be believed and obeyed in order to bring about God's ultimate goal.

Caudillos and *Vivos* Are above the Law

My second focus will be on the cult of personality that militates against the rule of law. Its roots may be traced to the deep divide that has characterized Latin American society since its very inception. In colonial times the division was primarily between the agents of the *Consejo de Indias* residing in Seville, who administered things from the great urban centers in Mexico City, Bogota, Lima, and Buenos Aires, and the common people who made life for the administrators and their acolytes easy. In general the division was between the urban centers and the large barren lands in the interior of the continent. In the primitive factories that processed the natural riches and in the mines that extracted the gold and silver that eventually funded the industrial revolution in Europe, life was ruled by the *capataz* (foreman). Those who labored under his command knew that he had power of life and death over them. The revolution of 1810 put an end to the viceroyalty of the River Plate but sadly did not bring about the liberation of the masses who had been exploited by the Spanish overlords. The people in the countryside soon realized that the creole urban elite, many of whom had been educated in Spain, was replacing the old masters without making any major difference to their lot.

Faced with a new oppressor in place of the old one, the gauchos of the countryside rose up against those who wished to concentrate all power in Buenos Aires. The leaders of the different provinces who wished for a more equitable distribution of power among all the inhabitants of the land came to be known as *caudillos.*[17] The classic portrait of the *caudillo* was painted by Sarmiento in his *Facundo,* a broadside written in exile against the strongman Juan Manuel de Rosas couched as a study of a provincial chieftain, Facundo Quiroga. For Sarmiento the existence of *caudillos* threatens the nation and is preventing it from achieving its glorious destiny. In broad outline, the options are either to follow the path of civilization that prospers in an urban environment, where civic institutions and education make for an enlightened culture, or to be led by *caudillos,* ignorant gauchos who personify barbarism. Sarmiento's description of the different gaucho types has become classic, but his desire to tar the *caudillos* as gauchos fails to convince. Basing his analysis on geographic and ethnic explanations of historical development, Sarmiento pictures the *caudillo* as a leader shaped by the barbarism of the sparsely inhabited desert who on ac-

17. Charles Chapman writes, "Broadly defined, the caudillos were military men, almost literally on horseback, who were at the same time political bosses and absolute rulers, either of a country or a district, notwithstanding the alleged existence of republics and democracies, and despite the contrary provisions of constitutions and laws." See Charles E. Chapman, *Republican Hispanic America: A History* (New York: Macmillan, 1938), 106.

count of exceptional skills imposes his will on the uneducated. The *caudillo* is the man on horseback who leads his men in war and rules over them on account of his personal authority. He is a reincarnation of the *capataz. Caudillismo,* then, is a political system instituted neither by ideas or laws, but by individuals and their personal authority. As Bunge writes, "The spirit of this system meshes very imperfectly with the letter of republican constitutions."[18] Sarmiento, likewise, laments "the preponderance of brute force, the preponderance of the strongest, the authority without limits and without responsibilities in those who govern, the administration of justice without process and without debate."[19]

For Sarmiento the *caudillos* are an anachronism, a leftover from more primitive societies without great urban centers as the carriers of culture. They represent the provincial interests of backward peoples. In line with this view, it has been claimed that in Argentina the presidency of Bartolomé Mitre (1860-68) represents the end of *caudillismo* and the birth of a national identity. This is true if *caudillismo* means the prioritizing of regional interests over the centripetal force of the national megalopolis. But this is not quite the case. As Chapman perspicaciously points out, "Over all the countries of Hispanic America there is still the shadow of the man on horseback."[20] Carlos Menem, president of Argentina until 1999, was a typical *caudillo* who ruled on account of personal authority over the masses.[21] He appeared before his people with a horse's technological equivalents, race cars and jet airplanes. When the Italian manufacturer Ferrari presented him with a shining red racer, a reporter reminded him that official presents belong to the state. To this he answered that no one was to tell him what he could or could not do with what had been given to him. Then he explained: "People follow me because I am a transgressing

18. Bunge, *Nuestra América,* 226.

19. Sarmiento, *Facundo,* 38.

20. Chapman, *Republican Hispanic America,* 110. The language still retains the idea that a horse is indispensable for the life that is worth living. The story is told of an Argentinean exiled in Chile who was met by a friend and asked how he was doing. To express his discontent and frustration, he answered: "En Chile y de a pie" ("In Chile, and on foot"). A popular folk song made famous by Eduardo Cafrune is entitled "Sin caballo y en Montiel" ("Without a horse and in Montiel"). Montiel is a town in the province of Entre Rios. In this case the sentiment is quite different. Montiel is home, but how can one feel at home without a horse?

21. Tomás Eloy Martínez, *El sueño argentino* (Buenos Aires: Planeta, 1999), repeatedly refers to the authoritarianism of the governments.

president." Not long after he drove the car from Buenos Aires to Mar del Plata at over 130 miles an hour.[22] In a highly hierarchical culture it is accepted that Fate has given to this or that individual the "genius" with which to rule on the basis of his superiority. As such he is above the law.

Bunge describes another aspect of the political system of *caudillos* somewhat ironically. The demagogues who succeed to power are obscurantists who, even while pretending to be the patrons of culture, do not understand and actually hate the arts, sciences, and letters. Thus, "because they are incommoded and blinded by the light sent out by civilization, our politicos stigmatize universities."[23] They want young people to study only to serve as secretaries and assessors. But the young should not expect the fatherland to be grateful in return.[24] On this account, Latin America has lost most of its intellectuals to different kinds of exiles. As a young student in Buenos Aires in the early 1950s, I well remember the graffiti found in many an empty wall all over town: "Build the Fatherland. Kill a Student."[25] Perón's demagogic appeal to the masses was based on his opposition to both the British owners of the railroads and to the creole oligarchy who had benefited from commerce with Britain for over a century. He was also against the universities, who questioned his methods and his goals.[26] Universities were "intervened." In some, a *peronista* mediocrity was appointed rector. Others were closed for years.

To instruct the people in the virtues of abiding by the law is not a primary objective in the educational systems of Latin America. Politicians prefer the young to be ignorant of what the constitution says. Admiration for the personal authority of the *caudillo* translates itself into admiration for the ability to evade the law in every way possible, to assert one's power over the law. This is true as much in reference to traffic laws as to tax laws, labor laws, and the rest. The culture lacks a civic sense of responsibility and accountability. The constitution is not the sacred text that provides the Scriptures for a civic religion. Employment by the government is not a

22. Alma Guillermoprieto, *The Heart That Bleeds: Latin America Now* (New York: Vintage, 1994), 142. Newspapers at the time also reported that when asked about his risky behavior, Menem answered: "Nobody dies one hour before his time."

23. Bunge, *Nuestra América,* 231.

24. Bunge, *Nuestra América,* 232.

25. "Haga patria, mate un estudiante."

26. A well-remembered slogan runs, "Alpargatas sí, libros no" ("peon footwear yes, books no").

form of quasi-religious "service." Rather a government job is a way of getting a salary without having to work. Police officers and sheriffs can be the law in themselves. To survive within this jungle one must create a wide web of protective relationships.

The culture, then, is not the culture of hard work under law-abiding conditions, but of *el vivo. El vivo* is literally "the alive one" but it means the person who knows how to take advantage of situations. Most of all, he knows how to talk his way out, and how to talk his way in. *El vivo* is able to get ahead by doing what is necessary in order to achieve what he wants. His power is in his wits.[27] In his novel *El Mal Metafísico* (1916), Manuel Gálvez, a member of the *Arielista* generation, portrays the sufferings of the romantic idealist who refuses to compromise while all his friends have been able to prosper by adopting the ways of *el vivo.* Idealism is a metaphysical illness that affects those who live bound to an aesthetic and ethical image of perfection and therefore find themselves socially disjointed.[28]

In the culture of *el vivo,* loyalty to one's friends is very important, and having a circle of friends is essential. One gets things done by being referred by a friend to the friend of a friend. This is also true when doing business with the lowest of government agencies. Approaching a government agent without mentioning the name of someone known to one's interlocutor means that one's petition at this agency will languish in a tray for months. Knowing people and having friends is the only way to accomplish things. What Bunge says concerning *caudillismo* is also true of daily life in society: "The caudillos are not instituted by ideas but by persons and proper names."[29]

The Spanish sense of *hidalguía* has to do with a lifestyle. Central to it is the ability to dispense favors to others and thereby establish one's superiority. It is also important to have others do the menial tasks necessary to the maintenance of one's lifestyle. In a culture of honor and shame, it would be extremely shameful to be seen engaged in a task that might cause one to perspire or to soil one's clothing. Hence, society presents well-established roles to be played according to the class to which one belongs.

27. For the best analysis of *el vivo,* see Julio Mafud, *Psicología de la viveza criolla* (Buenos Aires: Américalee, 1965), 105-31.

28. Manuel Gálvez, *El Mal Metafísico* (Collección Austral 433; Buenos Aires: Espasa-Calpe Argentina, 1943).

29. Bunge, *Nuestra América,* 230. Bunge prefers to call *caudillismo "cacicazgo."* The word comes from the noun *cacique,* the tribal chief.

The Uruguayan Carlos Reyles traces the origins of the antipathy to manual labor to the adventurers who crossed the sea to conquer the continent. He writes as follows:

> The conquistadors, the viceroys, the noblemen of proud lineage accustomed to build their fortune on the broad land with the tip of the sword or the lance the way the Cid did, the most daring adventurers and invaders of the globe, for whom there are no impassable obstacles or infernal enterprises that deprive them of their valor, they categorically refused, judging it no doubt degrading, to get involved in the modern adventure of work. They do not wish to debase their noble hands in labors that they always consider those of village folk.[30]

Unlike Rodó who, as mentioned above, abhorred the utilitarianism of the culture of the North, some *rioplatenses* have expressed admiration for the "work ethic" of the United States. They have lamented the low esteem accorded to work in Latin America. Bunge, for example, like Sarmiento, sees the solution to the problem of Latin America in the influx of immigrants who would bring with them the culture of work. According to him the three problems in the continent are *la arrogancia* (haughtiness),[31] *la pereza* (laziness), and *la tristeza* (sadness). They have to be displaced by modesty, work, and joy.[32]

It must be noted, however, that with the globalization of the economy new forces have brought about significant changes among the young and better educated, who are also informed by the feminist revolution and the cultural propaganda of Hollywood. Among them one may see men who help in household chores. Still, the classic notion of the *intelectual puro,* the wise man who lives above the cares of the world, exerts a powerful influence. *Estar ocioso* is the best way to be. That is, doing nothing in particular, having free time with no cares. To be, like the Stoics of antiquity, totally impervious to all pressures is what one should aim at. This ideal is so powerful that even if one is working hard it is important to appear to be above it all.

30. Carlos Reyles, "Don Quijote: La locura del famoso hidalgo y nuestra locura," in *Incitaciones* (Santiago de Chile: Editorial Ercilla, 1936), 63.

31. Sarmiento already noticed "the arrogance of these Argentine gauchos who have seen no one better than themselves" (*Facundo,* 46).

32. Bunge, *Nuestra América,* 216-218.

The culture of *el vivo* also informs the relationships between the sexes. The prowess of the Latin male has traditionally expressed itself in two ways. One is that of the Don Juan whose pleasure is derived not as much from sex as from the deceptions necessary to seduce his ladies and from bragging about his conquests among his friends.[33] He cares nothing about the women he seduces or the children he may father. As noted above, the *Fausto* of Estanislao del Campo exposes and criticizes this behavior, lamenting the harsh fate of women. Male prowess is also exhibited by the institution of concubinage, which allows a man to keep several *queridas* ("loved ones") in their homes while being married to one legal wife. The children of his *queridas* may have his family name and recognize him as the father who visits the house regularly. The Islamic roots of this institution are clearly evident, even if in Latin America it has developed its own *modus operandi.* It represents the sexual behavior of the conquistadors. Thus in Latin America a distinction is made between the children of the legal marriage, the children of non-legal stable arrangements, and "natural children" born out of casual encounters. In some countries, at the death of the father only the children of the legal marriage inherit. Concubinage's social legacy has been rather tragic.

Concubinage is an institution outside the law. Maybe it best exemplifies the culture of *el vivo,* whose economic position, power, and reputation allow him to live above the law. The open existence of institutions such as this encourages illegitimacy in all aspects of life. It also fosters the living of a double life, the acceptance of social lies, and the need to tell one's friends what is going on behind the curtains, to expose the verbal and the social charades. One of the tests of friendship is whether one is entrusted with all the gossip. The sharing of social secrets keeps the *camarilla* (those who share the closet) glued together. The tensions thus created are well illumined by Isabel Allende in *The House of the Spirits.* Much of the political, economic, and social tensions in Latin America may be traced to the anger of illegitimate children. A long list of revolutionaries could be composed of such sons and daughters. The most visible ones lately have been Eva Perón and Fidel Castro.

33. One of the best analyses of Don Juan is by Carlos Reyles, "Don Juan. Materia literaria y esencia donjuanesca," in *Incitaciones,* 79-108. Reyles, however, fails to exhibit the flaws in the type. He gives too much credit for the existence of the type to the admiration on the part of women for the qualities of Don Juan. This is another case of blaming the victims.

Again, it must be said that, as in the case of the attitude toward work, the globalization of culture is bringing an end to the institution of concubinage. Allende makes the point in her novel by telling the story of four generations of the Trueba family. The last (the youngest) generation finds itself a bit out of joint with the lifestyle of its elders. Attitudes toward work and sex are changing, primarily because of the new position that university-educated women are gaining in the workplace. They no longer need a man to take care of them as a *querida* (lover). Hollywood has also taught young males that it is cool to help washing dishes. Work is beginning to be viewed as a status symbol. Women are finding their place in all aspects of the new economy and have reaped some of the benefits of the feminist revolution. Socially they have become liberated to come and go by themselves as they please. Living with a *novio* (boyfriend) is no longer a socially devastating stigma. Within the constraints of less developed, weaker economies they are becoming somewhat self-sufficient. In these aspects *rioplatense* culture has been undergoing quite significant shifts as it becomes North-Americanized.

It would be irresponsible to end this description of a prominent cultural type without referring back to the importance of friendships, and bringing out *la nobleza gaucha.* The ties of friendship are at the root of the society. In many ways friendships are more binding than family ties, and friendships are for life. There is no privacy with friends and no secrets. It is not necessary to ring the bell in order to enter the house of a friend at any time of day. One can always depend that, aware of one's need, a friend will act with compassion.[34] People who visit the region never cease to be amazed at how they are taken in and befriended by the *rioplatenses.* In fact, it should be said that this is very much the hallmark of Latin America. The people are always eager to make new friends and to open their hearts and homes in demonstrations of hospitality. This openness to strangers reveals itself also in the compassion that informs their dealings with others. The initial response to another is intuitively generous, compassionate, friendly, eager to lend a hand. To be such is to be *gaucho.* This is to be a native son or daughter. Characteristically the *rioplatense* is a Good Samaritan.

Spanish translates straight from French the expression *nobleza obliga.* In the River Plate region this has taken a distinctive turn to be known as *nobleza gaucha. Noblesse oblige* had to do with the European titles of nobil-

34. See Mafud, *Psicología,* 96-99. Mafud entitles this section, "El culto de la amistad" (the worship of friendship).

ity, which placed certain responsibilities on the shoulders of those with "blue blood." It was a leftover from the rules of chivalry, only that for the nobility there were no written rules. Their obligations were dependent on their own self-respect and virtue. Thus, even though the poor and the lower classes could not make claims on the nobility, aristocrats understood themselves as obligated to be compassionate and helpful to those in need. When the *criollos* took the government of the Viceroyalty of the River Plate into their own hands in 1810, one of their first official declarations abolished all titles of nobility. Nobility had to be reconceived without reference to economic or political power. The culture immediately re-created it in the characteristic way of being a *gaucho*, the generous, hospitable, helpful, compassionate dweller of the pampas who has suffered much on account of his unpretentiousness. His resourcefulness and self-reliance, however, give him a quiet confidence and pride in who he is. *La nobleza gaucha* imposes its claims on those who carry within not blue blood but the dignity that comes from knowing themselves the depository of the family's honor in the present generation and are totally contented being who they are.

Paul and Life in Community

Paul's apocalyptic universe is undoubtedly hierarchically constituted. The problem of the universe is precisely that the powers of the air are at the moment not subject to God. It is the task of the risen Christ to subject these powers to himself and then to present himself before God "so that God may be in everything all things" (1 Cor. 15:28). Paul's explicit advice to all Christians is, "Let everyone submit themselves to superior authorities. . . . The one who stands against authority stands against what God instituted" (Rom. 13:1-2). In another context, Paul draws a flow chart with authority coming down from God to Christ to the husband and to the wife (1 Cor. 11:3).[35] Within this universe human beings do not have ultimate freedom. As creatures in a fallen creation, humans live under the power of

35. 1 Cor. 11:2-16 is considered by many scholars to be a non-Pauline interpolation. It is extremely difficult to interpret on account of its internal contradictions as well as its tensions with 7:3-4 and 14:34-36 (of course, the second of these is an even more likely interpolation!). Our purpose at the moment is only to point out that Paul lived in a hierarchical universe. See William O. Walker, *Interpolations in the Letters of Paul* (Sheffield: Sheffield Academic, 2001).

sin. On account of the resurrection of Christ, however, human beings now may live under a new Lord. It seems that for Paul, freedom exists in relationships and is dependent on power. This means that any mention of freedom must include a prepositional clause. Human freedom must be defined as freedom *from* sin, death, and the powers of the air, freedom *in* Christ, freedom *for* obedience and righteousness, freedom *for* God (Rom. 6:17-22). A person either enjoys these freedoms or is a slave of the Law, the powers, sin and death. In Paul's universe freedom is not a human right. Freedom as such does not stand by itself. Relationships define freedom.

It is incumbent on men and women, therefore, to be particularly careful about the circle of relationships in which they live. For Paul the crucial question is "Whose slave are you?" The choice is not between freedom and slavery but between slavery to sin, to the passions, to the Law, to death and slavery to Christ and the power of the Spirit, wherein alone there is true freedom (2 Cor. 3:17). It is in this context that Paul draws the contrast between Christ and the Law. Those who are slaves of the Law are not servants of Christ. Thus either one is living in the realm of the flesh, where the Law rules and God's wrath is revealed, or one lives in the realm of the Spirit, where faith rules and God's righteousness is revealed. Paul does not envision the best possible human community as one under the rule of Law. Does this mean that Paul would endorse the *caudillo* and his junior, *el vivo,* the people who act above the law, as the models for the ideal community? Not at all.

To live above the law, or to ignore the law, is lawlessness. Autonomous freedom is not an option. For Paul the good society is under the power of the Spirit. The paradox is that it is only as slaves of the Spirit that humans are free (2 Cor. 3:17). To change the image, it is in weakness that they are powerful (2 Cor. 12:9). The absoluteness of the power of God, or of the Spirit, relativizes the Law. For Paul the Law has definite and useful negative functions, which it performs most effectively. Its basic function is to transform sin from an abstraction into a concrete instance and to condemn the evildoer (Gal. 3:19; Rom. 4:15; 5:13; 7:7-9). By itself, however, the Law does not have the power to create a just society. True human community needs for its constitution the power of the Spirit, which essentially is the power of love. The ultimate Pauline injunction, therefore, is not quite "Submit to superior authorities." It is, rather, "pursue love," which he recommends after his panegyric extolling love above faith, hope, and every other spiritual gift (1 Cor. 14:1).

In contrast to the Law, love cannot exist outside living beings; therefore, the control exercised by love is a process in the mind. This is how Paul radicalizes obedience and shows himself a true intellectual. He places full confidence in the capacity of the mind renewed by the Spirit to know the will of God (Rom. 12:2). Thus, while obedience to the will of God is of the essence, the Law is not the ultimate expression of that will.

Readers of Paul's letter to the Romans agree that the "therefore" at the beginning of ch. 12 marks a shift from a rather theological discussion to its practical consequences:

> I appeal to you therefore, brothers and sisters, by the mercies of God, in your reasonable worship to present your bodies as a living sacrifice, holy and acceptable to God. Do not allow this age to mold you according to its designs. Rather, be metamorphosed with a new mind from above so that you may evaluate what is the will of God, that is, what is good and acceptable and perfect.

These are remarkable words. Paul gives two twists to traditional temple worship. The first is one that the prophets of Israel had already insisted on. To fail to do the will of God in one's daily affairs at home and in the marketplace annuls whatever one does at the temple. The second proposes that what is to be sacrificed is not a heifer but one's "living body." When these two conditions are met, one is involved in "reasonable worship" of God.

Why is this kind of living, this living sacrifice, worship in accordance with reason? Because, as Paul explains, the essential element is a mind that is renewed from above and is therefore able to function properly, discerning what is good. In other words, the human mind properly empowered by the Holy Spirit is the sole arbiter of the will of God. Here we are not introduced to an authoritarian, hierarchical world but to a world in which the reasoning powers of every person are considered as good as those of anyone else, and therefore everyone is held personally accountable.

Paul is not privileging the intellect, or knowledge as such. He very carefully qualifies the effective moral agent as the mind renewed from above. He is not setting up an intellectual elite, but a community in which those guided by the Spirit have equal say. Authority belongs to the human mind enlightened by the Spirit of the risen Christ which, then, seeks the good of the neighbor. Throughout his correspondence Paul makes numerous appeals to the reasoning powers of his readers. He insists that they must evaluate what he or anyone else tells them. Even when he appeals to their emotions, reminding them that he was a mother in travail for them or a nurse who nurtured them, or that as a father he had been kind to them,[36] he also puts before them arguments or propositions for their consideration. He values both the power and the ways of reason.

Reason may be viewed both as that which gives the mind the structure within which any thought is possible and as the steps taken by the mind according to certain agreed-upon rules. Following these rules one may argue for the superiority of one proposition over another. Conclusions arrived at without following these rules are judged unreasonable or illogical. A person who lacks the built-in structures of reason is said to have lost his or her mind or to be retarded. Arguments that do not stand the test of logic are said to be weak.

Paul trusts the ability of his audience to use their minds and reason properly. He writes, "I speak as to reasonable people. Judge for yourselves what I say" (1 Cor. 10:15). After having had a serious disagreement with the Corinthians he writes to them, "Examine yourselves, to see whether you are in the faith. Evaluate yourselves, or do you not know that Jesus Christ is in you?" (2 Cor. 13:5). Christians with Christ in them do not need to be evaluated by others. Their own judgment is valid. Paul loses his patience with the Galatians who ignore the evidence of their own experience, against which there can be no argument, and, rather harshly, calls them "morons" (Gal. 3:1). To the Corinthians, who consider themselves mature people of the Spirit and therefore affirm that "all things are lawful" (1 Cor. 6:12), Paul says, "Brothers and sisters, don't become children in your thinking, even if in evil you make yourselves babes. In thinking be mature" (1 Cor. 14:20). Describing the wrath of God at work in the pagans who have been delivered by God to their sinful ways, he locates their problem in their mind, or in the heart, which, according to Hebraic terminology, is where desires and plans are harbored. According to Paul the power and the glory of God in evidence within creation are capable of being perceived by the mind (Rom. 1:20), but the senseless heart of those who change the truth for a lie has been darkened and their reasonings are futile (Rom. 1:21). God has given them up to a mind that lacks the ability to make judgments (Rom. 1:28). Paul assigns great significance to the power of the mind.

36. See Abraham J. Malherbe, "'Gentle as a Nurse': The Cynic Background to 1 Thessalonians 2," *Novum Testamentum* 12 (1970): 203-17; and in *Paul and the Popular Philosophers* (Minneapolis: Fortress, 1989), 35-48.

To explain his understanding of God's salvation Paul usually depends on passages from the Old Testament.[37] A few times he also appeals to a saying of the Lord (1 Cor. 9:14), to an early Christian confession of faith (1 Cor. 15:3-5), or to an early Christian baptismal formula (Gal. 3:27-28). These clearly function as authorities to which reason may appeal. Even if today allegory is not considered the means for a strong argument, Paul, like his Jewish contemporary Philo of Alexandria, used it as a valid way of arguing (Gal. 4:21-31). As a good Jew trained under a Pharisaic master, Paul also knew how to do *midrash,* arguing by elaborating imaginatively on a biblical passage (2 Cor. 3:4-18). On some occasions Paul uses the more rabbinic way of limiting the meaning of a particular word by bringing together two uses of the word in the Old Testament in order to define one by means of the other. For example, in Rom. 9:33 he sets Isa. 28:16 next to Isa. 8:14-15 in order to define the "stone" on which Zion is built. In other cases Paul quotes the Old Testament but insists on a detail of scriptural language. In 1 Cor. 15:27 he quotes Ps. 8:6, but finds it necessary to make clear that when it says "all things" God is excluded. Quoting Gen. 12:7 in Gal. 3:16, he makes his case on the fact that the noun "seed" is singular rather than plural.

Paul also builds arguments that depend strictly on the logic of the case, rather than on appeals to authority. In Gal. 3:15 he makes an argument based on what humans would commonly agree upon; it appeals to common sense. No one expects another person to add clauses to a contract after it has been signed; therefore, we should not think God did so. In Rom. 5:10, 15, 17 Paul builds a more complicated argument *a minori ad maiorem* (from the lesser to the greater). It rests on the reader's willingness to grant "this" (a commonly recognized smaller fact) to be the case. If "this" is the case, *how much more* is "that" (which logically stands higher than "this") the case. If the sin of Adam is credited with having caused the entrance of sin and death in the world, how much more are the death and resurrection of Christ to be credited for the entrance of righteousness and life in the world. If Adam did accomplish "this," how much more did God accomplish "that"! While the argument affirms the effectiveness of Christ's work, contradicted by the present work of sin and death in the world, it presupposes that Christ's mission is the work of God, which is of a higher

37. Paul's foundational texts seem to be Gen. 12:1-3; 15:5; Deut. 10:16-17; Jer. 18:6; Hos. 1:10; 2:23; Hab. 2:4, and many Psalms.

order and more effective than the work of a man. In these arguments Paul shows himself trusting the ability of his audience to follow logic.

Another way in which Paul exhibits his high estimation of the power of the mind is his reluctance to become the judge of what others are doing. As stated above, for Paul the crucial question is, Whose servant are you? But being a servant does not involve the suspension of one's reasoning powers. To the contrary, good servants are distinguished by their good use of the mind. As far as Paul is concerned, his identity is that of a servant (slave) of Christ. No one is Paul's servant. No Christian can be a servant of anyone else. Therefore, no Christian should give orders to another Christian. Thus to Philemon Paul, following rhetorical usage, writes, "Having in Christ much audacity to order you, rather in love I plead with you" (Phlm. 8-9). No Christian should judge what another is doing. Only the Master has the authority to judge the work of his servant (Rom. 14:4). This way of understanding the conditions of life places a great deal of responsibility on the servant. In other words, it trusts the ability of the servant's mind to determine the will of the Master.

Paul repeatedly writes about "having your mind set" on something. He contrasts "having the mind set on the flesh" with "having the mind set on the Spirit" (Rom. 8:6-7). When acting, individuals must be "fully persuaded in their own mind" (Rom. 14:5). To act against one's better judgment, to live with a split mind, is what Paul considers sin. Actions must reflect full conviction. His understanding is that "he who has doubts is condemned . . . because he does not act with confidence [out of faith]" (Rom. 14:23). For Paul, faith is living as a servant in full obedience to the judgment arrived at by a Spirit-renewed mind. Submission to authority, however, should not be blind, and Christians have only one Lord. Service of their Lord calls for the intelligent exercise of the full powers of the Spirit-renewed mind in order to determine what is good. Paul was well acquainted with those who claimed authority on account of their skills or personal spiritual endowments. Comparing himself to them, he considers himself "not in the least inferior to those super-apostles" (2 Cor. 11:5). Still, he insists that he does not seriously wish to make such comparisons, even if he engages in "a little foolishness" by doing so (2 Cor. 11:1). Power, for him, is effective when he finds himself crucified with Christ, weak. Boasting is legitimate only when one is boasting "of the Lord" (2 Cor. 10:17). Superior gifts or wits do not give one authority over others or power over the Law. Paul dismisses the super-apostles, who are trying to undermine his mission, because as far as he is concerned they work in the realm of the flesh and he is trying to forward the work of the Spirit.

In the Latin American imagination, the appeal of *caudillos* rests on the predisposition to admire superior individuals. The relationship of the *caudillo* with his followers is symbiotic. They depend on each other. The *caudillo's* demagogic message is reinforced by the people's need for authority figures within a hierarchical symbolic universe. These needs are not primarily rational but emotional. By contrast, Paul's message is not an appeal to the emotions. His is a rational approach. His authority as an apostle, of which he is quite conscious, does not rest on his personal power. To establish his authority he appeals to the experience of his converts. They can determine whether the Spirit changed their mind (Gal. 3:3). His appeal is to reason. The good society is one in which the power of the Spirit, which is the power of love, is what everyone submits to. As a result, in this society there will be room for differences in praxis, because when the Spirit is Lord there is freedom (2 Cor. 3:17).

In the exercise of freedom as servants of Christ (Gal. 5:1), Christians cannot ignore their neighbors. The central conviction of Christians is that "Christ has died for all," and therefore "love controls" them. It would seem that for Paul the consequence of Christ's death is not that therefore those who believe in him need not die. Rather, his logic draws the conclusion that "therefore all have died" (2 Cor. 5:14). He insists that Christians live "crucified with Christ." The one who lives is the one who died for all. Therefore, he professes, "I live no longer, but Christ lives in me" (Gal. 2:20). In this condition, Christians "have the mind of Christ" (1 Cor. 2:16). For them, therefore, it is impossible to place themselves first. Their actions, like Christ's, demonstrate that in their mind the other is more valuable than themselves (1 Cor. 10:24).

This theme is a constant refrain in Paul's letters. Since all Christians live in Christ, they are of one mind. In the mind of Christ the other is first. It is certainly not the case that in all things all Christians think the same and agree on what in every case should be done. Clearly Paul allows for quite different behaviors in terms of foods and the observance of days (Rom. 14:3-6).[38] What Paul insists on is that according to the mind of

38. See Herold Weiss, "Paul and the Judging of Days," *Zeitschrift für die neutestamentliche Wissenschaft* 86 (1995): 137-53; *A Day of Gladness: The Sabbath among Jews and Christians in Antiquity* (Columbia: University of South Carolina Press, 2003), 121-31.

Christ, where love controls, the neighbor is number one. A society in which everyone agrees that placing the other first is the primary cultural value has never been created. Still, the envisioning of such a society is for Paul the criterion by which a culture is to be judged. It would seem that Paul insisted upon this as the foundation of the Christian community because he had determined that the revelation of God in Christ had to do with the power of love, which is the power of the gospel, which is the power of the Spirit. Thus, for Paul, what counts about Jesus' life is his obedience unto death "for our sins" (1 Cor. 15:3). It reveals God's love (Rom. 5:8, 19) and righteousness (Rom. 1:17; 3:21).

Above it was claimed that Paul's ultimate demand is not "submit to superior authorities" but "pursue love." There can be no doubt that Paul would consider Christ as the superior authority, the Master whose servant he was. We may legitimately ask, therefore, what is the relationship of submission to Christ and the pursuit of love, in other words, submission to love. It may be said that in Paul's view the climax of the human drama is reached when "all things," including Christ, are subject to God, "so that God may be in everything all things" (1 Cor. 15:28). Paul's eschatological vision also includes love abiding at a higher level than faith and hope (1 Cor. 13:13). This exceedingly high love is what God demonstrated when "Christ died for us" (Rom 5:8), and is the love that "has been poured into our hearts by the Holy Spirit" (Rom. 5:5) so that now "the love of Christ controls us" (2 Cor. 5:14). But Paul does not distinguish between the love God demonstrated at Christ's cross and the love of Christ that controls us. Even if in his description of the eschatological triumph of God Christ turns over the kingdom to God, so that all things are finally subject to God, this does not quite indicate a submission of Christ to God's love. Christ's submission is also a demonstration of God's love. It may not be said, therefore, that submission to Christ takes second place to submission to love. It is impossible to distinguish the synergy of Christ and love in Paul's thought. It is the obedient (to God) mind of Christ that pursues love.

Immediately after Paul advises his readers that they should live guided by a mind renewed from above, rather than by the constraints of their cultural *milieu,* he tells them, "Let no one among you think of him/herself more highly than he/she ought to think. Rather think of yourself reasonably" (Rom. 12:3). This general exhortation is followed by more specific recommendations: "Excelling among yourselves in brotherly love; outdoing each other in giving the other honor; not being lazy in your work; being alive in the Spirit; being slaves in the Lord" (Rom. 12:10-11). These guidelines for living in society are built upon the principles of the supremacy of love and the power of the Spirit to transform the mind so that honoring the other is a way of life.

While trusting the power of the mind that is capable of being determined by the Spirit and love, Paul does not endorse a life above the Law, the establishing of a network of human influences that allow escape from responsibilities, or the institutionalizing of unlawful conduct. It is easy to imagine what Paul would say to the *vivos* of the River Plate "who have seen no one better than themselves," as Sarmiento said.[39] The *vivo* lives by his wits, by his rhetorical skill. Paul would classify the wisdom of *el vivo* as "wisdom of the world." To it he opposes the "wisdom of God." Christians are no longer under the Law, but also not above the Law. Living crucified with Christ, they no longer live in the world where the Law rules. They live not "according to the flesh," but "according to the Spirit." In this environment their lives produce the fruit of the Spirit, against which "there is no law" (Gal. 5:23). As Paul sees it, the controls imposed by love and the Spirit are more formidable than those of the Law or the conscience. There is no way to rationalize them.

Paul would find very congenial the innate compassion and the hospitality of the gaucho. The strong friendships undergirding *rioplatense* society would be very attractive. It is somewhat curious to note that in the extant writings of Paul friendship is not a prominent theme. The binding of those who hold things in common, *koinōnia,* on the other hand, is his favorite way of referring to the Christian community. This word is usually rendered as "fellowship," but its characteristic force points to the glue that makes for commonality. The fellowship of those in Christ holds them together and gives them their identity, making them share both the sufferings and the glory of their risen Lord. There is no question that Paul would look favorably on that which works toward uniting in a wholesome way those who otherwise would be separated. That is what love is about. For him, the mind of Christ also works as the glue that holds together a body whose members are organically connected. The mind of Christ gives structure and unity to a society that, even though composed of distinct members who function in different ways, shares an identity in Christ. By contrast the mind of the *caudillo,* or *el vivo,* which seeks his own good in an

39. Sarmiento, *Facundo,* 46.

autonomous way, makes impossible the consolidation of a community. It rather works toward the formation of cliques, which Paul explicitly decries (1 Cor. 1:12). In his mind the whole body of Christ, guided by the mind of Christ, is the form in which Christians actualize in the world the work of the Risen Christ. In this way Christ is not absent from the world, even if he is not personally present. His body, those who have died and live in Christ, perform his message in the world even now. Fellowship must be broadly based, involving the whole body. Paul would also find quite congenial *la nobleza gaucha,* which is based not on blood but on the spontaneity and the openness of the self toward the other. But he would anchor it in Christ as the true source of identity.

Life and Death

Finally, I would like to examine a third cultural marker in the landscape of the River Plate. It may not be totally peculiar to the region, as none of the features considered above are, but a valid grasp of the culture of Latin America cannot ignore that there is in it a different understanding of death, of the relationship of the living and the dead. In Latin America death is an event to be lived intensely, to be celebrated. As has often been pointed out, the fathers and the heroes of these countries are not remembered on their birthdays, but on the days they died. In Buenos Aires, La Recoleta is the most important monument, a cemetery admired for its concentration of magnificent architectural and sculptural works of art.

In his novel portraying the dilemmas faced when crossing a frontier, *El gringo viejo,* Carlos Fuentes creates a most ironic situation by having an old veteran from the Civil War, who has become a journalist in the employ of Randolph Hearst, go to Mexico to die. "The old man imagined Mexico as a gigantic corpse with bones of silver, eyes of gold, flesh of stone, and balls hard as copper."[40] Once across the frontier,

> the desert told him that death is nothing more than the exhaustion of the laws of nature: life is the rule of the game, not its exception, and even the seemingly dead desert hid a minute world of life that originated, prolonged, imitated the laws of human existence. He could not

40. Carlos Fuentes, *The Old Gringo* (New York: Harper Collins, 1985), 14.

> free himself — even if he wanted to — from the vital imperative of the barrenness to which he had come of his own free will.[41]

The irony is that in the land of death the old man speaks as a true *gringo* when he says to himself: "I am in control of my destiny."[42] Later in the story, the old gringo hears a conversation between an officer and General Arroyo, the Mexican revolutionary, in which the latter asks: Which is more important, the way we live or the way we die? For Mexicans the answer is obvious. The narrator then tells us that the old gringo began to ponder this honor code. The ongoing conversation makes the point that life and death are never separated. Bravery before death must be matched by bravery before life, "since they were the same thing; the old man had come to Mexico to learn that, and he'd learned it, hadn't he?"[43] It would seem that Fuentes would like the whole world to learn this lesson: life and death are inextricably conjoined. This perspective is given poetic expression in the lines of the Uruguayan poet Juana de Ibarbourou:

> In the lazily burning match of death
> life moves about, throbbing fruit and being.
> Everything turns warm and suffering
> in the card game of luck.[44]

For our purposes, a more relevant example is provided by Tomás Eloy Martínez. In *The Perón Novel* it is not always clear when the information provided by the historical documents that he studied exhaustively ends and the dramatic imagination takes over. The result is not only a remarkable portrait of Perón but also an insightful study of the Argentine psyche. Its first paragraph ends with the words, "His horoscope had predicted for him an unknown misfortune. What could it be if the only misfortune he had not already experienced was the desired one of

41. Fuentes, *The Old Gringo,* 16.
42. Fuentes, *The Old Gringo,* 17.
43. Fuentes, *The Old Gringo,* 85-88.
44. Juana de Ibarbourou, "Espera" in *Tiempo* (Barcelona: Plaza y Janes, 1963), 164:

> En el fósforo vago de la muerte
> Anda la vida, fruta y ser latiente.
> Todo se vuelve cálido y sufriente
> En el juego de dados de la suerte.

death?"[45] The novel ends with a montage of Perón's return to Argentina on June 20, 1973, and his apotheosis at death, which in turn is described as the exit of the placenta from the uterus. This montage is the artistic expression of the pervading identification of death with life, making death have a very peculiar ambiguity. In a memorable passage, while preparing in Madrid for his return trip, Perón reminisces with Cámpora, the Argentine President who had gone to Madrid to accompany him on the return, about an aide of his who was a genius, "the world's greatest statistician." Perón recalls, "Figuerola once called it to my attention that Argentineans are death-oriented. He used the word: 'thanatophiles.' . . . We are cadaver cultists."[46] The word refers to love of death. In his masterful novel, *Santa Evita,* Martínez elaborates on this obsession with the dead and the passions it arouses among the living. Gossip has it that the corpse of Perón now lacks both hands, likely due to the eagerness of a devout worshiper.

The roots of this fascination with the bodies of the ancestors go back to Roman classical times. Early Christians went to the cemeteries for the celebration of their *agapē* meals in the company of the ancestors in the faith, the saints, particularly the martyrs. To bring the faithful back to the churches for the celebration of the mass the eucharistic table was made to double as a tomb with the corpse of a saint, sometimes in full display. In Latin America most loved ones become saints at their death. This motif, death as "the desired misfortune" that reveals the person's destiny, is at the center of the Latin American soul. Thus, through life one is to imagine one's death, live one's death, prepare for one's death. The words of Socrates, "True philosophers are always occupied in the practice of dying" (Plato, *Phaedo* 67E),[47] are taken seriously. Martínez's presentation of Perón's return as a wake in which the General is both the icon who is venerated in a makeshift altar and the cadaver in the coffin is most telling.

Spain exported to Latin America the austere Catholicism memorialized by Philip II at the Escorial, a building that is more of a mausoleum than a royal palace in which life is to be enjoyed. At the center of its devotions was a crucifix with a profusely bleeding Christ. The most respected

45. Martínez, *The Perón Novel,* 3.

46. Martínez, *The Perón Novel,* 316.

47. *The Dialogues of Plato,* trans. B. Jowett, 2 vols. (New York: Random House, 1937), 1:451.

form of devotion were *escarmientos,* punishments of the flesh. The true Catholic is a *penitente,* a *flagelante.* This vision of life as a perennial bleeding death does not consider death a stranger. Rather, it views life and death as irremediably intertwined. What Octavio Paz wrote in reference to Mexico is very true of Latin America as a whole:

> The word death is not pronounced in New York, in Paris, in London, because it burns the lips. The Mexican, in contrast, is familiar with death, jokes about it, caresses it, sleeps with it, celebrates it, it is one of his favorite toys and his most steadfast love. True, there is perhaps as much fear in his attitude as in that of others, but at least death is not hidden away: he looks at it face to face with impatience, disdain, or irony.[48]

Poets have been particularly concerned with death. The immense power of the dead over the living is wonderfully expressed by Gabriela Mistral, the great Chilean poet.

> The bones of the dead
> know how to spray a subtle ice
> over the mouths of those they loved.
> They can no longer kiss!
> The bones of the dead
> shovel their whiteness profusely
> over the intense flame of life.
> They kill its ardor!
> The bones of the dead
> triumph over the flesh of the living.
> Even disarticulated they form strong bonds
> which keep us submissive and captive![49]

48. Octavio Paz, *The Labyrinth of Solitude: Life and Thought in Mexico* (New York: Evergreen, 1961), 49.

49. Los huesos de los muertos
hielo sutil saben espolvorear
sobre las bocas de los que quisieron.
Y éstas no pueden nunca más besar!

Los huesos de los muertos
en paletadas echan su blancor

All actions undertaken by the living must be weighed against the wishes of the dead.

Juana de Ibarbourou, who in her youth rebelled against death but later in life found it ever present, wrote:

> Humans alone
> alive or dead,
> God's eternity,
> in the deserted sky.[50]

In other words, the eternity of God is found in the eternity of humans. José Asunción Silva in his "Día de los difuntos" observes that on the Day of the Dead the bells toll in order to tell the living about the dead, but then he laments that the living forget them too soon. One of the most grievous of sins is to forget the dead. Amado Nervo laments "How lonely are left the dead!" It never crosses anyone's mind that they are really dead.[51]

Editorial Sudamericana in Buenos Aires has been the publisher of most of the work of the Colombian Nobel Prize winner Gabriel García Márquez. In the blurb intended to promote sales for *Crónica de una muerte anunciada,* the publisher writes:

> sobre la llama intensa de la vida.
> Le matan todo ardor!
>
> Los huesos de los muertos
> pueden más que la carne de los vivos.
> Aún desgajados hacen eslabones
> fuertes, donde nos tienen sumisos y cautivos!

Gabriela Mistral, *Desolación,* Colección Austral 1002 (Madrid: Espasa-Calpe, 1951), 115.

50. Juana de Ibarbourou, *Tiempo,* 165:

> Sólo es el hombre,
> Vivo y muerto,
> La eternidad de Dios,
> En el cielo desierto.

51. Jorge Luis Borges, the Argentine antihero who lived troubled about the self, alternately denying its existence while affirming it, openly hoped for total extinction. In a lecture on immortality, he said, "I don't want to continue being Jorge Luis Borges; I want to be someone else. I hope that my death will be total; I hope to die in body and soul." *Selected Non-Fictions,* ed. Eliot Weinberger, trans. Esther Allen, Suzanne Jill Levine, and Eliot Weinberger (London: Penguin, 2000). See also "The Immortal," in the same collection. One may wonder how much is due to his desire to shock his complacent compatriots.

> The reporter dives deep repeatedly into the past, asking himself about this death and the silence surrounding it. If he is to discover anything, it is that the world is not a reality to be named, but a mystery that may never be deciphered. Possibly he will glimpse at the final cipher of the inexplicable in the fiercely familiar presence, simultaneously far away and immediate, of the myth that underlies every life and every death.[52]

The myth that gives meaning to every life and every death is the myth of Fate as the fixer of how and when we live and how and when we die. As the investigating judge is reported to have written on the margin of his summary, "Fate renders us invisible."[53] Life and death are livable because they are fixed quantities, but human attempts to decipher them are doomed. This myth equalizes both quantities to the same level in the divine eternity. But when life and death are equated, life is devalued. *Crónica de una muerte anunciada* is one of the best mirrors of the Latin American view of life. The Vicario twins, who have carried out the crime in order to reclaim the honor of their sister (quite against their own will, but driven by a palpable social force and too many coincidences), exhaustedly confess, "How difficult it is to kill a man!" At the end, the fully eviscerated Santiago Nazar, who is determined to reach his home, is asked by a neighbor from across the river, "What has happened to you, son?" To her he announces, "They have killed me."[54] Life and death are surreal.

Paul and the Tragedy of Death

Paul fully understood the intertwining of life with death. In his time everyone knew the Stoic maxim "Practice dying." To live is an exercise in living and dying. Thus Paul envisions himself fully alive only when he is crucified. This language resonates in the labyrinths of the Latin American psyche. He proclaims in a thundering voice from the rooftop "I die every day" (1 Cor. 15:31). He travels over the Mediterranean world "always carrying around in the body the death of Jesus," as he explains, "because we the living have been delivered to death because of Jesus" (2 Cor. 4:10-11). When he

52. Gabriel García Márquez, *Crónica de una muerte anunciada* (Buenos Aires: Editorial Sudamericana, 1981), back cover.

53. García Márquez, *Crónica,* 180.

54. García Márquez, *Crónica,* 192.

lingers in a place to preach, his preaching portrays the crucifixion so vividly that his audience thinks Christ is being crucified right then and there before their very eyes (Gal. 3:1). This kind of permanent attachment to a dead loved one is quite familiar to a Latin American. It was, of course, well established also in the world in which Paul lived. A generation or two later Christian martyrs seem to have been quite eager to embrace death, as made amply clear by the letters of Ignatius of Antioch or the *Martyrdom of Perpetua*.[55]

For Paul, the greatest manifestation of the love of God is the death of Jesus on the cross (Rom. 5:8). The crucified evokes the most wonderful visions of God having to do with faithfulness, justice, and love. Paul's obsession with the crucified (1 Cor. 1:23-24; Gal. 3:1), however, never crosses the line that would make him into an object of worship. For Paul the difference between God and Christ is quite clear. Adoration can be given only to God; otherwise worship is idolatrous. His continuous identification with the crucified is not *thanatophilia*. His desire to live crucified with Christ is predicated on the understanding that the death and the life of the risen Christ are inextricably intertwined. He takes with him always the death of Christ in order to also share in the life of Christ. The two are inseparable. His interest in them, however, is not a sadistic or a masochistic fetish.[56] As he says, "we the living have been delivered to death by Jesus so that also the life of Jesus may become visible in our mortal flesh" (2 Cor 4:11). But even if the mortal flesh may serve, if crucified with Christ, to manifest the life of Christ, Paul still "eagerly longs . . . for the mortal to be swallowed up by life" (2 Cor. 5:4). For him, as a true apocalypticist, there is no doubt that the current intermingling of life and death is a struggle that will end with the ultimate defeat of death, the last enemy (1 Cor. 15:25-26). For the final triumph shout he quotes the words "Death is swallowed up in victory" (1 Cor. 15:54). His ultimate concern is not really with the dead Christ but with the risen Lord. He would not agree with an emphasis on the bleeding, suffering Christ that forgets about the resurrection.

Paul's fascination with the death of Christ must be understood in context. Death is the end of the road that begins in sin and is ruled by the

55. See E. R. Dodds, *Pagan and Christian in an Age of Anxiety* (New York: Norton, 1965), 135 ("there is evidence for thinking that in these centuries a good many persons were consciously or unconsciously in love with death").

56. This way of reading Paul is adopted by Richard Rubinstein, *My Brother Paul* (New York: Harper and Row, 1972), 54-77.

Law. It is "the wages of sin" (Rom. 6:23). His argument with fellow Christians who have a strong attachment to the Law as the ruler of life is that in fact the Law is only capable of condemning to death. Therefore, if humans are to live they must be guided and empowered by something other than the Law. In the realm of flesh, which is the normal, natural life of all human beings, sin has taken over because the flesh is weak. As a result every one dies. Within this environment the presence of the Law brings about not salvation but death. As Paul sees it, "the sting of death is sin, and the power of sin is the Law" (1 Cor. 15:56). The alternate road that leads to life begins with the resurrection of Christ and is guided and empowered by the Spirit that raised Christ from the dead. This is the road of righteousness, lived by the Spirit and in the Spirit rather than in the flesh. Life on this road is characterized by freedom from the Law, sin, the powers of the air, and death.

Telling the Corinthians about the great affliction he has recently experienced in Asia, Paul confesses that at one point he despaired for his life, thinking death was imminent. Reflecting on this experience, he writes: "We had in ourselves a death sentence, in order to rely not on ourselves but on the God who raises the dead, who has liberated us and liberates us, and who we hope will liberate us from greatest death" (2 Cor. 1:9-10). The death from which Paul feels liberated by the God who raises the dead is not his biological death. We lack the details of the tribulation to which Paul refers. Whether his despair was caused by a physical illness or the persecution of others is not detailed. What is clear is that here Paul contrasts liberation from physical death with liberation from eschatological death, the "greatest death." At the beginning of the fourth century, Athanasius described the death that Jesus died on the cross, which he died in our stead, as "the death."[57] Christians very early distinguished between biological and eschatological death, just as they made the same distinction about life. On that account they had nothing but disdain for biological life and death. Death as the result of sin under the Law is not to be confused with biological death. Life in the flesh, which seems to be triumphing over biological death, is not to be compared with life in Christ, which is not under the condemnation of the Law and triumphs over eternal death.

Admittedly, the death of Christ on the cross was also the death of the body of Jesus. This means that in the cross of Jesus Christ biological and

57. Athanasius, *The Incarnation of the Word of God* (New York: Macmillan, 1946), 6.22.

eschatological death were conjoined. All the eyewitnesses to the crucifixion, however, saw only the death of Jesus in the flesh. Post-Easter faith alone can see the death of Christ "for our sins in accordance with the Scriptures" (1 Cor. 15:3). Paul's intermingling of life and death, it would seem, is not between life in the flesh and the "greatest death," but between this life and biological death. In 2 Corinthians he is quite eager to be able to resolve the impasse between the Corinthians and himself. He wishes to be able to continue his ministry, which he considers more glorious than even that of Moses (2 Cor 3:7-8). He feels under pressure by the love of God to carry on (2 Cor 5:14). Still, it is quite clear that he considers biological life and death as *adiaphora*, indifferent. Languishing in prison, thinking that his incarceration may end with an execution, he writes, "My firm desire and hope is that in nothing I shall end up looking bad, rather that as always in the past also now I shall by my conduct with boldness exalt Christ, either living or dying. Because for me to live is Christ and to die gain" (Phil. 1:20-21). Now that he is looking at death in the flesh from close range as a possibility he does not consider it, as some poets have, to be the mother of philosophy and theology, the great equalizer, the dignifier of coarse lives. He relativizes biological life and death on account of the value he places on the life in Christ that has triumphed over "greatest death." To the one crucified with Christ, who is crucified to the world and for whom the world is also crucified (Gal. 6:14), to live is to be in Christ. Not to live in the flesh is gain.

To the Corinthians, who did not distinguish between biological and eschatological life, Paul quotes the slogan guiding those who live according to the flesh: "Let us eat and drink; tomorrow we die" (1 Cor. 15:32). According to this view, life and death are morally indifferent. Life is short, and one must take as much advantage of it as possible. There are no consequences to be taken into account in a moral equation. For Paul, on the other hand, the value of the new creation in Christ's life is such that life in him is of unsurpassed value. Every human endeavor now is to be evaluated in its light. While biological life and death have become for him *adiaphora*, the reality of eschatological life grants humans a sovereign new vocation in Jesus Christ (Phil. 3:14). His concern is not with death, even as he faces it squarely, but with life. Neither death nor the dead are to determine our conduct but the love of the God who gives life eternal. Biological death is not the revealer of our Fate. Our destiny is in the life of the risen Christ.

CHAPTER 2

Paul and American Individualism

Charles H. Cosgrove

In *Paul the Apostle to America*, a very thoughtful book on Paul's significance for American culture,[1] Robert Jewett provides a brief history of the study of Paul in the United States. Jewett judges that interpretation of Paul in America has remained largely European in orientation.[2] Most American work on Paul strikes Jewett as "Eurocentric," by which he means a tendency to project a universal Paul who needs no cultural adaptation. The construction of this universal Paul typically takes its cues from the European (and especially the German) tradition of Pauline interpretation, which is a culturally specific collection of interpretations purporting to transcend culture. Interpretations of Paul shaped by European experience are often taken over into the American context with little modification.

Jewett also notes a number of exceptions to Eurocentric interpretations of Paul. Among them are Josiah Royce's analysis of individualism from the perspective of a distinctively American interpretation of Romans 7, Reinhold Niebuhr's use of Paul in constructing a theology of individual and social moral conduct, Graydon Snyder's interpretation of 1 Corinthians from an American Anabaptist orientation,[3] William Thompson's look at Paul from the American faith-development tradition,[4] Amos Jones's ef-

1. Robert Jewett, *Paul the Apostle to America: Cultural Trends and Pauline Scholarship* (Louisville: Westminster/John Knox, 1994).

2. Jewett, *Paul the Apostle to America*, 13-31.

3. Graydon F. Snyder, *1 Corinthians: A Faith Community Commentary* (Macon: Mercer University Press, 1987).

4. William G. Thompson, *Paul and His Message for Life's Journey* (New York: Paulist, 1986).

fort to show Paul's relevance for the African American experience,[5] Jewett's own application of Romans 12–14 to the question of pluralism and the conflict between liberals and conservatives in America,[6] and Marva Dawn's exploration of community in Paul with special attention to contemporary forms of American community experience.[7]

Notwithstanding the more distinctively American contributions just mentioned, Jewett concludes that, all in all, very little has been done "to relate [Paul's] theology to the distinctive issues of the American ethos."[8] He offers *Paul the Apostle to America* as a pioneering effort to plant Paul more firmly on American soil.

In what follows, I propose to follow in Jewett's footsteps, not by repeating what he has done but by exploring a theme that he treats only incidentally, namely, American individualism. The distinctly American forms of many cultural traits that the United States otherwise shares with other Western nations is owed largely to American individualism. Hence, it makes sense to approach Paul with questions arising out of the individualistic American ethos, exploring both the resonances of Paul with the American ethos and Paul's challenges to America. To anticipate, I find certain Pauline resonances with the American tradition of human rights and important Pauline challenges to American ideals of economic self-reliance, personal freedom for self-realization, and "the pursuit of happiness."

Individualism

It is a commonplace that Americans are emphatically committed to individualism. This assertion runs through the history of commentary on the American ethos, from Alexis de Tocqueville's remarkably durable observations about America in his 1840 book to Bellah and company's engaging 1985 sociological study of individualism and commitment in American life.[9]

5. Amos N. Jones, Jr., *Paul's Message of Freedom: What Does It Mean to the Black Church?* (Valley Forge: Judson, 1984).

6. Robert Jewett, *Christian Tolerance: Paul's Message to the Modern Church* (Philadelphia: Westminster, 1982).

7. Marva Dawn, *The Hilarity of Community: Romans 12 and How to Be the Church* (Grand Rapids: Eerdmans, 1992).

8. Jewett, *Paul the Apostle to America,* 31.

9. Alexis de Tocqueville, *Democracy in America,* 2 vols., the Henry Reeve text as re-

Individualism is not easy to define. The history of the term[10] begins in France, where *individualisme* was coined as a negative epithet in counterrevolutionary critique of the Enlightenment in the aftermath of the French revolution. The word later found a place in the German Romantic tradition of the nineteenth century, which celebrated individual uniqueness, originality, and self-development, along with individual freedom in morals and judgment. Steven Lukes notes that "individualism" comes into its own in America, where it signifies a new order "of equal individual rights, limited government, laissez-faire, natural justice, and equality of opportunity, and individual freedom, self-development, and dignity."[11] I would add to this list the concept of the superiority of the individual over the group, the virtue of self-reliance, and the value of social disengagement into private life. All these elements of individualism are interrelated and can be organized conceptually in any number of ways to define the nature, way, and purpose of a life well-lived in American terms. I have chosen to treat *self-reliance, human rights,* and *freedom* as focal centers for the discussions to follow, concluding with a reflection on *the purpose of a human life.*

Self-Reliance

Self-reliance is a broad American concept. Over the last hundred years, its economic meaning has become closely associated with a psychological meaning, notably in positive thinking, mind power, and like movements.[12] It is also linked to a certain style or vision of maleness, the highly individuated, autonomous man, idealized as a frontiersman — rugged, gloriously

---

vised by Francis Bowen, further corrected and edited by Phillips Bradley (New York: Knopf, 1966); Robert N. Bellah, et al., *Habits of the Heart: Individualism and Commitment in American Life* (New York: Harper and Row, 1985).

10. I rely here on Steven Lukes, "Types of Individualism," in *Dictionary of the History of Ideas: Studies of Selected Pivotal Ideas,* ed. Philip P. Wiener, vol. 2 (New York: Scribner, 1973), 594-604.

11. Lukes, "Types of Individualism," 596.

12. For a historical survey, see Richard Weiss, *The American Myth of Success: From Horatio Alger to Norman Vincent Peale* (New York: Basic, 1969). The movements Weiss describes have not diminished but, if anything, have intensified over the thirty-five years since he wrote his book.

alone on the prairie and in the crowd. Garry Wills observes the ways in which John Wayne has come to epitomize this "American Adam":

> The archetypal American is a displaced person — arrived from a rejected past, breaking into a glorious future, on the move, fearless himself, feared by others, a killer cleansing the world of things that "need killing," loving but not bound down by love, rootless but carrying the Center in himself. . . .[13]

Of course, there are also humbler and more humane versions of the autonomous male, like the common man who lives out the sort of lowly heroism Ernest Becker describes in *The Denial of Death,* an "earthy heroism wrought by gnarled working hands guiding family through hunger and disease."[14]

"Self-reliance" — as defined by the self-help and mind power movements, by Horatio Alger stories of "self-made men," by Hollywood images of western cowboy and space cowboy, and by many other American traditions of individual power in autonomy — is a multifaceted myth.[15] I have chosen to focus on the myth of *economic* self-reliance because of its importance and because it is the root metaphor of other kinds of self-reliance. However, one drawback of this narrowing of focus is that to a significant extent our different myths of self-reliance provide clues to each other. For example, a comprehensive treatment of economic independence would require close attention to how our violent tales of self-reliant heroes suggest a hidden connection between violence and economic self-reliance. I can make only brief reference to this connection in the discussion to follow.

Americans are as economically interdependent as any other peoples and in many ways more interdependent than people in some societies (including pre-industrial American society). But Americans tend to suppress the truth of their inescapable interdependencies in the self-reliance stories they tell about themselves.[16] Henry David Thoreau's retreat to Walden

13. Garry Wills, *John Wayne's America: The Politics of Celebrity* (New York: Simon and Schuster, 1997), 302.

14. Ernest Becker, *The Denial of Death* (New York: Free, 1973), 5.

15. I use the term "myth" in the sense of a guiding conception that gives people a sense of their identity and place in the world but at the same time distorts reality.

16. For a recent brief discussion see Bellah, et al., *Habits of the Heart,* 55-58.

Pond is one such story, an enduring symbol that epitomizes the self-deception in much American glorification of self-reliance. Thoreau's famous Walden experiment in self-reliance[17] required the borrowed land of a wealthy property holder (Emerson) — property protected by government, one might add. Thoreau was so close to society at Walden that he could hear nearby farmers chopping wood, watch the daily steam engine chug past the southern border of the pond, make a thirty-minute walk along the railroad track to town almost every day (for socializing or to visit a shop), entertain frequent visitors (including his mother and sisters, who brought him pies and doughnuts), and eat dinner with friends in town.[18] It is true that he lived frugally; he did not live independently. After about two years he grew tired of life at Walden and moved into the Emerson household. Thoreau was economically dependent his whole life on the kindness of friends and family.

The American enchantment with self-reliance is epitomized in the stories we tell of frontier Americans, self-made businessmen (rags-to-riches tales), and other American icons. The popular nineteenth-century Horatio Alger books (still reprinted) offer many examples. Our self-reliance stories are morality tales in which an individual begins with little or modest means, pursues a self-chosen goal through discipline and hard work, and ultimately prospers. Stories of this kind suggest that the virtues of self-reliance are sufficient for success in America. Most of us know, however, that circumstances beyond the control of our heroes helped make their success possible. Indeed, part of the pleasure of self-reliance tales is the dramatic interplay between the hero's effort and the uncertainty of the outcome. Nevertheless, the core message of the American self-reliance myth is that when one works hard and virtuously, even against all odds, powers outside our control — a kind of providence of the American

17. Thoreau's retreat to Walden Pond had a number of purposes, only one of which was to demonstrate the possibility and the benefits of self-reliance. Nevertheless, the association of Walden with self-reliance is what sticks in the American memory. This meaning of Walden is symbolized by Thoreau's moving into his cabin on Independence Day; it is also suggested by the opening lines of *Walden* ("I lived alone . . . in a house which I had built myself . . . and earned my living by the labor of my hands only") and by Thoreau's advocacy of independence as one of the traits of an authentic life. See Henry David Thoreau, *Walden: An Annotated Edition,* ed. Walter Harding (New York: Houghton Mifflin, 1995), 1, 12.

18. Thoreau's time at Walden is described in the standard biography by Walter Harding, *The Days of Henry David Thoreau: A Biography* (New York: Dove, 1962), 179-98.

system or of the God who blesses America — will see to it that our efforts meet with success in the end.

The American myth that the U.S. is a land of "*equal* opportunity" demands the success of self-reliance and encourages us to interpret our society and our own lives in distorting ways. Although Americans today do not imagine that radical self-reliance in the old frontier fashion is practical,[19] we still try to envision ourselves as highly self-reliant and hold up economic independence as an ideal. We are helped in this by the more impersonal and interchangeable forms that our economic relations take, which give Americans a sense of independence unknown in ancient Mediterranean cultures. People in Paul's day experienced dependence as clients in the patronage system, slaves, freedmen working for former masters, and tenant farmers, to name a few prominent examples. These types of dependence on others were direct, personal, and largely static, by contrast with the impersonal, often indirect, and interchangeable forms of dependence in modern post-industrial economies.

Another distortion appears in how we join the myths of self-reliance and equal opportunity to forge a chain of cause and effect between effort and success. We can tolerate evidence that the chain sometimes breaks, but we are strongly predisposed to believe that the chain usually holds. This partly explains why Americans are so ambivalent about (and many are very hostile to) "welfare" and why we avoid applying the term "welfare state" to our society as a whole, preferring to restrict the term "welfare" to programs aimed at a relatively small underclass.[20] Nevertheless, if by welfare one means financial assistance of some kind or other through state appropriation and redistribution of private wealth, then there is a much larger American welfare state that benefits not only poor Americans but the middle class.[21]

19. Our ideas of frontier self-reliance are largely mythical as well. People on the frontier banded together and depended on each other for survival. Very few went it alone.

20. In addition to the ideology of individualism, racism is also a factor in dominant American perceptions of welfare. On both elements, see Martin Gilens, *Why Americans Hate Welfare: Race, Media, and the Politics of Antipoverty Policy* (Chicago: University of Chicago Press, 1999).

21. In popular American conception, "welfare" refers to programs like AFDC (now Temporary Assistance to Needy Families) and *not* to Social Security or Medicare, although economists have traditionally included the latter within "welfare state." In addition to Social Security, Medicare, and Medicaid, there are many other redistribution programs or mecha-

The American creed of self-reliance refuses to use the term "welfare" for all this middle-class assistance because to do so would imply that almost all Americans today rely on the mechanisms of regular, state-sponsored redistributions of other peoples' money in order to succeed in America and that sometimes we receive this kind of help when we are, by the standards of the American ethos, undeserving (not exhibiting the virtues of honesty, hard work, etc.). Admitting this about ourselves goes against the grain. Although we depend on each other and accept coerced (tax-based) help from each other, we refuse to call it welfare because depending on welfare of any kind is deemed un-American.

Paul lived in a hierarchically structured communitarian society, where interdependence was not only acknowledged but stressed as a social good. The idea that a social group is like a body with interdependent parts was a favorite commonplace. Although Paul valued hard work and certain forms of independence, neither he nor his contemporaries knew anything like the economic creed of American self-reliance. In what follows, I examine six topics in Paul's letters that throw light on the question of self-reliance and how we might take a Pauline approach to it: (1) Paul's "sufficiency" (Phil. 4:10-13), (2) earning one's own living, (3) the church as body, (4) the collection for the saints, (5) the exemplary dependence of the Son on the Father, and (6) the gracious love of God in Christ.

One might take Paul's discussion of his "sufficiency" (Phil. 4:10-13) as implicit praise for some kind of self-reliance. Paul draws on the language of popular philosophy in Phil. 4:11 when he says that he has learned to be *autarkēs,* a word that carries a Stoic association of "self-sufficiency." In Philippians 4, however, this sufficiency turns out to mean the moral-spiritual capacity, with God's help, to accept all circumstances with equa-

---

nisms which benefit not only the poor but also the middle class. On the welfare state as a collection of federal and state programs that benefit the vast majority of Americans (and not just the non-working poor), see Christopher Howard, *The Hidden Welfare State: Tax Expenditure and Social Policy in the United States* (Princeton: Princeton University Press, 1997), and Gilens, *Why Americans Hate Welfare.* Moreover, before the development of this welfare state, Americans depended on each other for social help through countless voluntary associations (fraternal societies, insurance cooperatives, etc.). See David T. Beito, *From Mutual Aid to the Welfare State: Fraternal Societies and Social Services, 1890-1967* (Durham: University of North Carolina Press, 2000). Whether the older welfare society was better than the modern welfare state is a question that need not be debated here. My point is simply that in both pre– and post–New Deal America, practically no one was economically *self-reliant* in a robust sense of the term.

nimity. This is quite the opposite of a theory of worldly success through the virtues of self-reliance.

The topic of earning one's living appears in 1 Thess. 4:9-12 and 2 Thess. 3:6-12. Paul tells the Thessalonians "to work with your own hands as we directed you, so that you may behave properly toward outsiders and be dependent on no one" (1 Thess. 4:11-12). His concern is that the reputation of the church in the world not be tainted by the charge that Christians are "idlers" (cf. 5:14) who depend on alms. The focus here is not individual self-reliance but the economic independence of the community, maintained by the able-bodied doing their share.

In 2 Thessalonians the focus seems to be more on relations within the church. Paul insists that those who refuse to work should be denied a share in the common goods and urges the idle to "earn their own living" (3:12). The circumstances are not entirely clear. The most plausible interpretation is that expectation of an imminent return of Christ led some to quit working and to rely for daily sustenance on the common meals of the church. Paul's instruction reflects a concern for ordinary fairness, but self-reliance is not in view. Presumably the church is to continue to have common meals and to provide for the poor and the sick. The able-bodied are to do their part.

Paul also rehearses to the Thessalonians and the Corinthians his own apostolic practice in regard to work and accepting monetary support. Paul received money from some churches (notably the Philippians) but not others (the Corinthians and Thessalonians). Dale Martin makes a persuasive argument that status considerations govern Paul's approach to financing his mission.[22] As Martin sees it, accepting monetary gifts without reciprocating could imply that Paul is a client of the church that supports him, a perception that could undermine his apostolic authority. Hence, when thanking the Philippians for their gifts to him, Paul describes those gifts as a "fragrant offering . . . *to God*" (Phil. 4:18). In this way he avoids the appearance of being put in their debt, which might make him look like their client. A different social situation existed at Thessalonica, where the church was predominantly lower class. Paul reminds the Thessalonians that he and his companions "worked night and day" so that "we might not burden any of

22. Dale B. Martin, *The Corinthian Body* (New Haven: Yale University Press, 1995), 79-86; *Slavery as Salvation: The Metaphor of Slavery in Pauline Christianity* (New Haven: Yale University Press, 1990), 117-35.

you" (2 Thess. 3:8), implying, Martin argues, that he lowered himself socially in order to show solidarity with the Thessalonians. Paul sees such acts of downward social movement as imitation of Christ. By contrast, at Corinth a church dominated by upper-class sensibilities finds Paul's resort to manual labor shameful. Moreover, Martin suggests, the Corinthians' efforts to get Paul to accept gifts were probably intended to gain some control over him, to adopt him as a kind of "household philosopher."[23]

Martin's sociological analysis alerts us to how different Paul's language of independence sounds in his social world than in ours, where it is easily misinterpreted as advocacy of rugged economic individualism. Paul uses limited strategies of economic self-reliance in certain settings to protect his apostolic status and to model the downward social mobility of Christ. But he also accepts gifts to support his mission. The mission involves coworkers and supporters of many kinds; it is a financially interdependent network.

Paul's ecclesiology provides another justification for financial interdependence among Christians. Paul uses the metaphor of the church as "body" to stress that each member of the community needs the others (1 Corinthians 12 and Rom. 12:3-8). His focus is on the essential contribution of each spiritual ministry to the body as a whole. Among the spiritual gifts are forms of financial giving (Rom. 12:8), which implies that, by the Spirit's design, the individual members of the body are not economically self-reliant.

A grand undertaking in financial gift-giving is the collection (or "offering") for the saints in Jerusalem. Paul mentions this collection obliquely in Gal. 2:10, discusses it at length in 2 Corinthians 8–9, and touches on it again briefly in Romans 15. Paul spent perhaps as many as ten years soliciting monetary gifts from the gentile churches to assist poor Christians in Jerusalem. This assistance is charged with symbolism. It represents the indebtedness of the gentile churches to the Jews for the spiritual blessings the gentiles have received through Christ. Its acceptance by the leadership in Jerusalem symbolizes their affirmation of Paul's mission to the gentiles (Paul's "priestly offering" of the gentiles to God). In Paul's understanding, God has so arranged history that both wings of the church are made dependent on each other: "for if the gentiles have come to share in [Israel's] spiritual blessings, they ought also to be of service to them in material

23. Martin, *The Corinthian Body,* 84.

things" (Rom. 15:27). Although Paul speaks of the gentiles "owing" this help to the Jerusalem Christians, Romans as a whole shows that all interhuman debts are relativized by the incalculable debt of humanity to God. Hence, at a deeper theological level, we become indebted to one another only because God gives us to each other.

Paul's christology also speaks to the American ideal of self-reliance. In an arresting statement, Paul tells the Corinthians that Christ "was crucified in weakness, but lives by the power of God" (2 Cor. 13:4). In short, Jesus was not self-reliant but depended on God. Paul's story of Jesus in the Christ-hymn of Philippians implies that Jesus *chose* the path that made him weak and reliant on God: "he did not regard equality with God as something to be exploited but emptied himself, taking the form of a slave" (Phil. 2:6-7). The metaphor of choosing slavery signifies embrace of a lowly social status, that is, the acceptance of dependence and the vulnerability that goes with it. As a slave, Jesus is obedient to God and remains so even when threatened with death (Phil. 2:8). I interpret Christ's obedience as an expression of faith, and I take Paul's use of the Greek expression *pistis Christou* (and its variants) to mean "the faith of Christ," that is, Jesus' own faith or faithfulness.[24]

Jesus' way of faith is exemplary. We are to trust God as revealed in Christ and to embrace his kind of faith as our own. As Rom. 3:26 says, "God justifies the one who shares the faith of Jesus" (my translation).

Jesus' faithful obedience led him to live for others. Paul expresses this idea in several places where he tells parts of the story of Christ: "Christ did not please himself" (Rom. 15:3); "though he was rich, yet for your sakes he became poor," that "you might become rich" (2 Cor. 8:9); Christ "gave himself" for us (Gal. 2:20); Christ became "a servant of the circumcised" (Rom. 15:8). Phil. 2:5-11 may involve the idea that Christ became a servant of God for humanity. In at least three of the passages just mentioned, Paul holds up Christ as an example for us to follow (Rom. 15:1-7; 2 Cor. 8:8-10; Phil. 2:1-11). Sharing Jesus' faith includes sharing his other-centered way.

In Rom. 5:8 Paul interprets Christ's self-giving as an expression of God's unconditional love: "But God proves his love for us in that while we were still sinners, Christ died for us." Since Paul uses the generous love of

24. These Greek expressions have often been translated as "faith in Christ," meaning our faith in him, but they can just as naturally be taken as references to Jesus' own faith. See Rom. 3:22, 26; Gal. 2:16, 20.

God in Christ as an example for Christians to imitate, it follows that the moral structure of this love applies to our love for others. Love is not to be based on merit. As a generous or unconditional act, love creates indebtedness, thus producing forms of dependence. This is what the traditional Christian concept of *agapē* means. The love of Christ is not a basis for exchanges of help by those who are otherwise self-sufficient. It is not the libertarian friendship of independent equals, based on intrinsic worth or earned respect. Those who love generously may recognize and honor intrinsic worth or merit, as a matter of justice, but they live nevertheless by a higher rule of obligation to love others generously because God has loved them generously. This higher rule is the "law of Christ" (Gal. 6:2), and to live by this law means seeing oneself as both needing generous love and obliged to show generous love to others.

Love outlasts the present evil age, remaining the highest value even in the morally perfect world of the new creation (1 Cor. 13:8-13). This gives us a clue to the nature of love in Paul's understanding. If love is inherently gracious, then the centrality of love for the new creation means that the grace of love is not only a way of dealing with sin but is intrinsically good, a value in itself. This makes sense only if Paul thinks of grace as the basic order of unity in Christ, an order of interdependence in which we know ourselves indebted to others and wholly dependent on God who has graced us with each other. Freedom from sin does not obviate love's grace; it enables us to live fully in the grace of love, as both givers and receivers.

By contrast, the pursuit of self-reliance implies a life of working oneself out of grace. This involves two fictions, applicable to economic self-reliance as to any other kind of self-reliance. One fiction is that it is possible to be self-sustaining. The other fiction is that self-reliance, even if it were feasible, is a good thing, that it makes us our best selves. In Paul's understanding, our best, most mature selves know their dependence on God and others, seek the interdependence of gracious love, and embrace generosity and gratitude as their way of living in the world.

Many American Christians probably do not see a contradiction between the virtue of self-reliance and Christian teaching about generosity and concern for the poor. They reason this way. Self-reliance is a good thing, but sometimes hardworking people are reduced to poverty by illness, accident, a layoff, or some other misfortune. The church, other charitable organizations, and perhaps the government should provide assistance to people in these emergency situations and help them get back on their feet. Christian "charity" should aim at helping people toward financial independence.

There is some limited wisdom in this reasoning, but it is deeply flawed in its tacit assumptions about economic conditions in America. These assumptions are: (1) that in America individuals earn their wealth in a way that makes them morally deserving of it, (2) that everyone has roughly an equal economic opportunity, and (3) that only in relatively rare emergencies does any American really need to depend on strangers (charitable organizations, the government) for assistance. As for the first assumption, economic earning does not equate to moral desert. A corporate manager who ends up a millionaire in retirement thanks to salary, benefits, and investments is not *morally* deserving of being wealthier than a teacher with modest salary, limited benefits, and scarcely any discretionary money for investment. As for the second assumption, vast differences of opportunity prevail in America. A child in an upper-income family starts out in life economically far ahead of the millions of children living under the poverty line in America. As for the third assumption, most Americans are routinely dependent on others, including the government, for their economic security (see above).

When "self-reliance" is not just a synonym for initiative and hard work but a creed that involves some or all of the assumptions just described, it amounts to a form of moral self-deception. In his indictment of humanity in Romans 1, Paul speaks of this kind of deception as "suppressing the truth in unrighteousness" (v. 18), which I take to mean self-deception through and *for the sake of* unrighteousness (including injustice). We engage in this suppression of the truth because we want to satisfy our own passions (v. 24), even at the expense of others (1:29-31). As creatures with consciences, however, we need moral cover for the unrighteous lives we live. Idolatry provides us with that moral cover (vv. 23, 25). We exchange the truth for a lie, making injustice look like justice, approving of what, at a deeper level, we know is wrong (v. 32). The truth we suppress (v. 18) is truth in the largest sense: the truth about ourselves, the truth about God (v. 25), the truth about the social world we have constructed. We exchange the truth about the God of justice for a god who justifies rationalizations that serve our own selfish interests. The American creed of self-reliance is one such rationalization. When sanctioned by Christian theology, it is an idolatry.

The creed of self-reliance is an ideology by which we Americans justify economic inequalities that most of us would find morally unacceptable if we looked at them honestly. We know that such an honest look would put moral obligations on us that we do not want, so we perpetuate myths about our socioeconomic system. Among the victims of these myths are many who are poor, including children who go to school hungry, lack adequate medical care, and live in isolation from the experiences and privileges that give most Americans self-confidence and hope. This is the hidden violence behind the myth of self-reliance.

Human Rights

In the American political tradition, the primary meaning of individualism is personal rights. One font of this rights tradition is the utilitarian philosophy of the eighteenth-century Englishman John Stuart Mill, which asserted the equal rights of all over the privileges of the few. In Mill's brand of utilitarianism, each individual counts for one and social class counts for nothing. This humane value of egalitarianism is what made utilitarianism revolutionary. It justified political redistributions of "utility" according to the thesis that every individual has an equal right to happiness. However, utilitarianism conceives of this equal right as finite and calculable. Hence, the happiness of the majority can outweigh the happiness of the few according to the utilitarian principle of utility maximization: the greatest happiness to the greatest number. By a strict utilitarian calculus, one could morally justify harvesting the organs of a single unfortunate person to save the lives of five other people on the grounds that the happiness of the five outweighs the happiness of the one. Almost no utilitarian wants this, so most forms of utilitarianism entail some constraints on utilitarian logic.

The most important set of constraints comes from the Enlightenment human rights tradition of Immanuel Kant and John Locke, which lodges rights in the single person against the group. The language of the American Declaration of Independence stands in this tradition when it asserts that "all men are created equal and endowed by their Creator with certain inalienable rights."

In the American rights tradition, the individual is thought of as having a certain superiority over the group. Nevertheless, when we think of the group as an aggregate of individuals, the value of the majority seems greater than that of the minority. Almost every area of American life reveals compromises between our commitment to individual sovereignty and our utilitarian concern for the good of the many. Generally, Americans are utilitarian when it comes to shared risk for the sake of the whole and individual-rights-oriented when it comes to direct violation of personal rights. For example, we do not permit the harvesting of organs from living human beings without their individual consent, but we do put those very same organs at risk, without their owners' individual consent, in the construction of highway interchanges based on utilitarian cost-benefit analysis (which always includes likely cost from injury and death versus expense of increased safety).

Paul lived in a culture with no tradition of equal freedom based on human rights. Rights in Paul's culture were privileges attached to "station" and inseparable from duty. Equality, where it was affirmed, was almost always conceived as *proportional*, which meant *equity* in accordance with social status. Hence, a slave had certain rights and duties pertaining to his or her status (varying with the type of servitude). Likewise, masters had certain rights (far more rights than slaves) and also duties. Rights and duties were thought of as attaching to social status, not to the person apart from the status.

Did Paul believe in human rights, rights attaching equally to all human beings regardless of social status? In Paul's language the term for authority *(exousia)* carries the sense of a "right" in certain contexts, where it always has to do with rights attached to social status or role. For example, the potter has a right over the clay (Rom. 9:21); the apostle has a right to support (1 Corinthians 9 and 2 Thess. 3:9); those in Christ have the right to eat idol meat (under certain circumstances; 1 Cor. 8:9). The question of human rights in Paul is not, however, simply a matter of terminology. We can also approach the question by asking whether human rights are logically implied by any of Paul's basic convictions, beginning with his conviction that the church is called to proclaim the gospel and that every human being is summoned to obey God's call in the gospel.

The Right to Heed the Gospel

Paul's conviction that the gospel is a universal call aimed at universal human (and cosmic) subjection to God (Phil. 2:10-11; 1 Cor. 15:20-28) implies a universal duty of every person to obey God as revealed in Christ. That duty stands above every human claim and therefore amounts to a right above every human claim. We can express this more precisely as follows: every human being, regardless of social status or any other distinction, has a spiritual right — in relation to other human beings, including political institutions — to hear and obey the gospel. For Jews and Jewish Christians, the duty to obey God and not human beings, including the state and state-sponsored religion, is axiomatic. For Paul, this duty appears in the gospel, which claims the allegiance of Israel to the God of the fathers revealed in Christ and seeks the "obedience from the gentiles," which is the aim of Paul's mission (Rom. 15:18).

This already hints at the three conditions that must be satisfied for the duty to heed the gospel to count as a human right. First, the duty must have a moral standing that is independent of law or social convention. Second, it must apply universally to all human beings. Third, the duty must apply not only to humanity as a whole or humanity in community but to the individual. I think all three of these conditions are fulfilled in the thinking of many ancient Jews, including Paul. For Paul, the duty to obey God is ultimately independent of human law, convention, or institution. It derives from God alone. No human being or institution has a right to interfere with this duty. This implies a corresponding human right to obey God and not to be interfered with in the exercise of this duty. The duty itself entails a right. Moreover, according to Rom. 1:18-32, the whole world has the duty to obey God. All human beings owe God faith, honor, thanks, and moral obedience. As noted above, the gospel aims at universal subjection to God (Phil. 2:10-11; 1 Cor. 15:20-28). It follows that every human being has a corresponding right before other human beings or institutions to live in obedience to God. The gospel reasserts this universal claim of God on all humanity and shows that obedience to God is to a significant extent an individual duty and right. The preaching of the gospel calls the individual hearer to embrace Christ's lordship above any other human claims.

An apocalyptic faith like Paul's that evangelizes individuals, calling them from "this evil age" into a new world (Gal. 1:4), must assume that the evil age (including its institutions) has no legitimate religious claim on them. The convert has a duty to God and therefore a moral or spiritual right — what might be called a "conversion right" — from God to exercise faith freely in word and practice without constraint from the world. Hence, the idea of a political right of conversion is logically implicit in Paul as a human right *from* God and *before* the powers that be. I hasten to emphasize, however, that Paul never worked this out as a theory and that the political powers of his day (the Romans) did not recognize this sort of right. The Romans granted religious rights only on prudential grounds as privileges.

A further question is whether the conversion right is sufficient as a basis for other rights. In the American political tradition, freedom of religion has been seen as entailing other rights, notably the right to free speech and the right to free association. We may note here that the Baptist doctrine of "soul liberty" is closely akin to a conversion right and has been seen as a foundation for political rights. Affinities are also found in Karl Barth's argument that the preaching of justification by faith is the church's right before others, including the state.[25]

One can indeed argue from a basic conversion right to other rights, specifically rights that establish the conditions under which life in Christ can be fully practiced. It is inherent to the basic Pauline conception of God's rights over the world that the church — and the individual believer — has authority (a right) from God to live in Christ without hindrance from the world. But it is equally inherent to Paul's theology that the world tramples this authority, causing Christians to suffer in the world (as Christ suffered). Moreover, developing a human rights conception based on the church's duty to obey God produces something like "Christian rights," not universal human rights in the ordinary sense of that term. Finally, we should keep in mind that Paul and his fledgling congregations were in no position even to contemplate "lobbying" the state or any other institution for their Christian rights. Certainly in the first century of the Common Era, Christians had no common ground with the state on which to found such a claim. When they came in conflict with the state or other human institutions, they looked instead to the near end of the world as the vindication of their rights to live in accordance with the revelation in Christ.

A General Right to Freedom of Religion?

The argument from a conversion right to other rights concerns the rights of those in Christ before the state, but it does not address the question of

25. Karl Barth, "Church and State" and "Christian Community and Civil Community," in *Community, State, and Church,* ed. Will Herberg (Garden City: Doubleday, 1960).

any *general* human right to freedom of religion. This question has been addressed in two ways in America. One is the prudential argument that if any religious group wants to enjoy religious freedom, then it would be wise for that group to recognize the same freedom for others. The second approach rests on the theological judgment that faith that is coerced (by other human beings or human institutions) is not authentic faith; hence, any state establishment of religion, including a state establishment of my religion, undermines genuine faith. This second approach may have a warrant in Paul's understanding of faith as entailing inner personal conviction (Rom. 4:8-21; 14:20-23). However, an ancient person who held that his or her religion was the one true religion might have reasoned that a state establishment of that religion protects people from false religious practice and does not hinder them from embracing the true faith from inner conviction. This is what led to Christendom in the West. If we can muster a Pauline argument against the Christendom concept, it will not be based on the authentic human self as "free inquirer." The strongest Pauline argument against Christendom is Paul's apocalyptic view of the world and the "powers." It is inconceivable in this view that the powers of the world might establish the one true faith. Hence, the political freedom of the church requires a state that is restrained from any establishment of religion.

Therefore, contemporary Christians might argue that freedom of religion in the modern liberal democratic state has a *theological* warrant in the supra-social (divine) grounding of the right to live in Christ *and* in Paul's apocalyptic conception of the powers opposed to Christ. The state ought to make space for the church, but not in such a way as to create a state church of the one true faith backed by governmental authority. This means that the state can make room for the church only by guaranteeing political freedom of religion.

If this argument for a general human right to religious liberty sounds plausible, it must surmount a difficulty. Certainly Christians may prefer to live in a state that behaves liberally toward religion, but that preference is not a *theological* ground for a general political right to religious freedom. A theological grounding must show that granting religious freedom to all (not just Christians) is something the state *ought* to do, that this kind of liberality is what God calls the state to do. But this assumes a state that is responsive to God, which shifts us away from the apocalyptic premise that the powers resident in the state are opposed to God. One can certainly argue that Paul has a complex view of the powers (and of government as inhabited by the powers), a view that allows the state to be both in opposition to God (1 Cor. 2:8) and also in the service of God (Romans 13). Nevertheless, as we shift away from the apocalyptic premise of a state opposed to God, we have begun logically down the path toward Christendom, not toward freedom of religion as a general human right. That is, in a Pauline framework, for the state to be responsive to God, it must show *loyalty to Christ.*

By contrast, the liberal brand of American civil religion has a place for a state that is responsive to God by being neutral toward religion. The idea of a human right to religious freedom makes sense in this perspective because American civil religion supplies two important requirements: the idea of benign neutrality on the part of the state and a model of religion in which people are conceived of as free rational inquirers after truth.

But there is no place in Paul's worldview for benign neutrality or free rational inquiry as the path to truth. Paul thinks in terms of two spheres of lordship, one in which sin (or the passions, other powers opposed to God) dominates and one in which Christ is Lord. This is basic to apocalyptic thinking. It allows no neutral space in between. There is interaction between the two worlds — a conflict with existential consequences for believers in their moral lives (Rom. 6:12-19; Gal. 5:16-17). There are also possibilities for choosing sides. But there is no third option outside these spheres of power, no neutral ground, certainly no third condition in which the mind is functioning properly in rational deliberation about competing religious claims.

In summary, one can derive a political right of Christian obedience from Paul, and one can oppose government establishment of religion on the basis of Pauline apocalyptic suspicion of the state. But neither of these nor their combination leads logically to a general human right to religious freedom.

Paul's Creation Theology as a Basis for Human Rights

Another approach to the idea of human rights in Paul is through his creation theology. Human rights means the equal rights of all human beings in relation to each other. Equal rights follow from equal status. The human rights tradition arose in the West as a challenge to what was perceived as unjust distinctions in social status. It asserted that *superior* forms of equal status exist above the authority of the state and the conventions of any society. God, they said, is the author of equal human rights. Common expressions for this from the American revolutionary period are "all men are born free and equal" and "all men are created equal." These assertions refer not to social fact but to a divinely bestowed status that state and society ought to honor.

Equality of creaturely status before God is implied by Paul's teaching that God shows no partiality (Gal. 2:6; Rom. 2:11; cf. Rom. 3:29-30), his assertion that God has undone the distinctions between (or hierarchies of) Jew and gentile, slave and free, male and female (Gal. 3:28), and his insistence that God has made every member of the body of Christ equally necessary and valuable (1 Corinthians 12). These are fundamental Pauline convictions, residing at the core of his gospel. They also show that, for Paul, the new creation fulfills the intent of the original creation expressed in the theology of divine impartiality toward all people.

Paul's law-free mission to the gentiles is rooted in his perception that the oneness of God means divine impartiality toward Jew and gentile.[26] In drawing this conclusion, Paul relies on a rich tradition of Jewish teaching about divine impartiality, which applied this theme primarily to socioeconomic distinctions. Paul's rebuke to the Corinthians for "despising the church" by "humiliating those who have nothing" (1 Cor. 11:22) shows that the socioeconomic meaning of divine impartiality shapes his conception of the new creation in Christ. Paul's teaching about the Lord's Supper runs counter to typical Greco-Roman practice of making dinner parties an occasion for acting out status gradations through seating arrangements and food allocation.[27] The gospel pronouncement in Gal. 3:28 (perhaps a baptismal formula) shows that for Paul divine impartiality ultimately spells the end of gender and master/slave hierarchies. His discourse about the gifts of the Spirit distributed throughout the body of Christ (1 Corinthians 12) further develops the meaning of God's impartiality in Christ for inner church culture, this time in response to a status hierarchy based on "greater" and "lesser" manifestations of spiritual power. The traditional language of divine impartiality does not appear in 1 Corinthians 12, but the

26. See Jouette M. Bassler, *Divine Impartiality: Paul and a Theological Axiom* (Society of Biblical Literature Dissertation Series 59; Chico: Scholars, 1982).

27. See Gerd Theissen, *The Social Setting of Pauline Christianity* (Philadelphia: Fortress, 1982), 153-58.

idea of divine impartiality is surely implicit. Paul uses a well-worn topic, human community (society) as "body," a unity of different parts working together harmoniously. In the Greco-Roman world, this body-politic metaphor was used conservatively, typically in admonishments to lower parts of the social body to keep their place and not cause trouble. Paul calls this entire ideology into question. Dale Martin's sociological analysis of the Corinthian letters is again illuminating. In what he calls a "compensatory move," Paul argues, by analogy to the human body, that the lower is deserving of high status and the higher of low status.[28] Nevertheless, Paul implicitly accepts the traditional gradations as well when he confers high status on the lowly: "those members of our [literal] bodies that we think less honorable we clothe with greater honor" (12:23).[29] Paul does not say that what we regard as less honorable is really more honorable and vice-versa. He describes a double attitude in conventional understanding of the body, a paradox in which the least honorable is also the most honorable. The effect of this in application to the church as body is a kind of leveling in which each member has both high and low status. Here divine impartiality works dialectically in God's arrangement of the body through apportionment of gifts.

The thesis that Paul's understanding of God's divine impartiality provides a basis for a theological human rights theory is strengthened by the fact that Hellenistic Jews in his time readily drew this conclusion from similar teachings about God. In a meditation on Lev. 25:23, Philo speaks of human rights as duties that human beings owe to one another because all are equally God's creatures; for this same reason, human rights are not claims on God. "In relation to each other," Philo says, "all created beings rank as men of equal honour and descent and highest birth; all enjoy equal honour and equal rights, but to God they are aliens and sojourners" (*De Cherubim* 120-21).[30] In a similar vein, Josephus quotes the Jewish writer Aristeas as saying that freedom is a right for all people as creatures of God (Josephus, *Antiquities* 12.23). And Philo also comments in another place that "rights" exist "by nature" (God's design), while laws are by convention (*Quaestiones in Genesim* 4.184).

28. Martin, *The Corinthian Body,* 96.

29. Martin, *The Corinthian Body,* 95.

30. *Philo,* vol. 2, trans. F. H. Colson and G. H. Whitaker (Cambridge: Harvard University Press, 1979), 79.

For Paul, too, the cosmos belongs to the one God, who shows no partiality. All human beings are indebted to God as God's creatures and as sinners, hence there can be no human rights claim on God. But we can draw the inference from Paul that the status of all human beings as creatures of the one God makes them equal to one another. This is especially evident in the way he argues against a distinction between Jew and gentile from God's impartiality and from the confession of the one God (Rom. 2:1–3:31; 10:12). Paul's appeal to the confession "God is one" is especially important because it shows that for Paul the christological and ecclesial notion of equal status (equality in Christ) has a basis in *creation*. God is the creator of the world and therefore God of all, both Jews and gentiles. The equality in Christ we find in the formula of Gal. 3:28 has its foundation in the creation theology of Rom. 3:27-31 and *therefore applies to all humanity.* Hence, when we see Paul using the term "new creation" to describe a world in which the distinction between "circumcision and uncircumcision" no longer counts (Gal. 6:15), we may conclude that the new creation fulfills an intent of the impartial God toward the original creation.

Freedom

Freedom is a defining concept for Paul and for Americans, but the term has a very different application in Paul than in contemporary American thinking. For Paul, freedom means liberation *from* moral enslavement to the passions, sin, the present evil age. It is a deliverance by God's power in Christ and makes us free *for* a new moral and spiritual existence, *for* a life lived in the interest of others, *for* the coming new creation. In the American conception, freedom is the right not to be interfered with in the pursuit of one's own interests. It is freedom *from* incursions of the state upon our speech, our movement, our religious practice, our economic pursuits, and our political power as citizens. It is freedom *from* the norms, roles, and values that society imposes on us. It is freedom *from* the expectations and agendas that family and friends have for us. We recognize that certain limitations of all these freedoms are necessary, but we begin, so to speak, with the strong presumption of our individual right to a robust and all-encompassing freedom and see limitations on that freedom as encroachments — some necessary, some acceptable, some odious. And what is freedom for? Popular language suggests that freedom in the American conception is *for* the pursuit of personal happiness, *for* a life of self-realization, *for* success and prosperity in this world.

Rights and Duties

The contrast between Paul's notion of freedom and ours has much to do with the question of rights and duties. The question of freedom reveals a unity of rights and duties in Paul and a cleft between rights and duties in contemporary American culture.

In Paul rights entail duties. I drew the inferences above that to have equal rights is to have them *toward other human beings* and at the same time to be *obliged to God* in the exercise of those rights, including the obligation to treat all human beings with equal dignity. Where all rights are from God, all rights entail duties to God. Where rights are equal rights, they entail equal duties to others.

Speaking of his own apostolic rights, Paul declares "I am free with respect to all," but "I have made myself a slave to all" (1 Cor. 9:19). Paul's freedom is based on God's call, which removes him from every human loyalty or obligation. At the same time the call makes him servant of all, on new terms. This makes sense only if Paul becomes slave to all as *God's slave*, living under "God's law" (v. 21) and "for the sake of the gospel" (v. 23). Hence, Paul's duty to others derives from the divine call that sets him free from every human authority. He interprets his right to receive support for his apostolic work within this framework. He exercises or forgoes this right on the basis of his duty to God in a particular situation. His rights are in service of the duties entailed by his divine calling.

All Christians have a call from God. This implies that the same structure of freedom, rights, and duties that we find in Paul's conception of his apostleship applies to each believer. In baptism Christians die to every worldly authority (Rom. 7:1-6; Gal. 2:19; 6:14); they are given a new identity (Gal. 3:26-28) and a call in Christ (1 Cor. 1:26; Phil. 3:14-15; 2 Thess. 1:11), with spiritual gifts (1 Cor. 12; Rom. 12:3-8); they become slaves of Christ (Rom. 6:22; 1 Cor. 3:23; 6:20; 7:23) who now owe nothing to anyone except "to love" (Rom. 13:8). That is, their freedom through baptism means that they now owe everyone everything, since love is an all-encompassing obligation. But it is God who determines the contents of this debt, the aims of this love.

A close connection between rights and duties also exists in the early American tradition, especially eighteenth- and nineteenth-century American individualism. The severing of rights from duties belongs to late American individualism; it has become a dominant note only in the last forty years or so. The primary arenas in which rights have been severed from duties are in private life and voluntary association. Or, to put it another way, duty to *self* is now seen as a paramount duty. Our popular language reflects this. When we justify our freedom from an explicit or implicit obligation (leaving a relationship, reneging on a promise, etc.), our trump card is often a statement such as, "I have a duty to myself . . ." or "I owe it to myself. . . ."

Self-Realization and Duty-Free Individualism

In America today, rights are usually thought of as freedoms, including freedom from duties to people and institutions. What I will call "duty-free" individualism subordinates community obligations to individual rights and self-fulfillment. Our current language of self and rights is now thick with this brand of individualism, even though older traditions continue to compete with it. The authors of *Habits of the Heart* speak of "expressive individualism."[31] Their phrase points to a key element, namely, the priority that duty-free individualism places on individual self-fulfillment. The primary project of the late-modern self is to become its true and unique self beyond all roles and obligations. This notion of the self is epitomized in Gail Sheehy's description of midlife passage as a journey out of the roles, standards, and expectations that society, family, and friends impose on us to discover and affirm our own true, unique selves.[32] The same note is struck at the end of the acclaimed American film *My Dinner with André,* set in a New York restaurant, where André, champion of the quest for authentic existence and true selfhood, has the last word about identity:

31. Bellah, et al., *Habits of the Heart,* 32-35, 73-74. The authors correctly find antecedents for expressive individualism in the nineteenth century, but I do not think this form of individualism becomes common until the twentieth century and probably not until the post–World War II period.

32. Gail Sheehy, *Passages: Predictable Crises of Adult Life* (New York: Bantam, 1977), 242-51, 351-54.

> . . . people hang on to these images of father, mother, husband, wife . . . because they seem to provide some firm ground. But there's no wife there. What does that mean? A wife. A husband. A son. A baby holds your hands, and then suddenly there is this huge man lifting you off the ground, and then he's gone. . . .[33]

This film portrays André as exactly the type of "other-directed" autonomous individuals that David Riesman saw on the horizon of American society in 1950 (in his influential book *The Lonely Crowd*) and hoped would complete their journey of self-discovery and become the dominant form of American individualism in the future.[34] The contrast with Paul is striking. I find no concept, much less any advocacy, of self-realization in Paul. There is Christ-realization in us (Gal. 4:19; 2 Cor. 3:17-18), but not self-realization. Salvation is in an important sense an escape from self and the tyranny of one's passions (Rom. 7:14-25).

Duty-free individuals may be very social and highly committed, but their sociality is voluntaristic and they remain sovereign over their obligations, reserving the right to retract them at will. Americans remain a "nation of joiners," but voluntary association increasingly means involvement along with a right of imminent *dis*association, seeing oneself as free to leave club, church, league, community organization, etc., whenever one chooses, often with no notice or explanation.[35] This implies that personal dissatisfaction with the group supersedes loyalty or duty to the group.

Popular conceptions of church membership exhibit the shift to duty-free or expressive individualism in American society. Americans display a propensity to switch denominations and many "surf" without joining any particular congregation.[36] Choice of church membership is based to a large

33. Wallace Shawn and André Gregory, *My Dinner with André: A Screenplay* (New York, Grove, 1981), 112-13.

34. David Riesman, with Nathan Glazer and Ruel Denney, *The Lonely Crowd: A Study of the Changing American Character* (New Haven: Yale University Press, 1950, abridged edition with new preface, 1961), 19-31, 304-7.

35. The phrase "a nation of joiners" is one of the memorable characterizations of America coined by Bellah, et al., *Habits of the Heart* (167).

36. On denomination switching, see Phillip E. Hammond, *Religion and Personal Autonomy: The Third Disestablishment in America* (Columbia: University of South Carolina Press, 1992), 73-74; on "surfing," see Robert D. Putnam, *Bowling Alone: The Collapse and Revival of American Community* (New York: Simon and Schuster, 2000), 74, and the studies cited there.

extent on a consumer mentality (church as provider of services), and churches themselves "market" their "products." Decisions to participate in, join, and remain in a particular Christian community are based to a significant extent on personal judgments about how far that involvement promotes self-fulfillment and other practical considerations about meeting individual and family preferences. We find nothing comparable in Paul. In his day, the churches were fledgling groups dotting the Mediterranean world, not established institutions competing with each other for membership. The corporeal metaphor in 1 Corinthians 12 suggests that believers are like body parts, not club members. That is, Christians are not interchangeable units but integral parts of the community to which they belong. The disciplinary action Paul lays down for the Corinthian church in 1 Corinthians 5 rests on similar assumptions about how believers belong to their community. His proposed discipline is a bodily excision. The offending member is not to be sent out in freedom to find a new church home but is to be delivered over to Satan (1 Cor. 5:2, 5, 13), a chilling image that may point to the man's ultimate salvation but above all has the health of the church in view.

Moreover, the purpose of being a part of the body of Christ is service to God and others, not personal self-fulfillment or family well-being as ends in themselves. Of course, Paul believes that being in Christ is rewarding: "I regard everything as loss because of the surpassing value of knowing Christ" (Phil. 3:8). But this value is not personal self-fulfillment. It is generated not from within as a completion of the self but externally as freedom from the self (selfishness) and conformity to Christ. Paul speaks of this in many ways: as sharing Christ's sufferings and having the hope of resurrection (Phil. 3:10-11; Rom. 8:17-25), as "being transformed into the same image [of God in Christ] from one degree of glory to another" (2 Cor. 3:18), as liberation from the enslaving passions of the flesh to live a life pleasing to God (Rom. 7:14–8:8). He tells the Philippians, "Let each of you look not to your own interests but to the interests of others. Let the same mind be in you that was in Christ Jesus . . ." (Phil. 2:4-5). What follows these words is the "Christ-hymn" of Philippians, which describes Christ's servanthood and obedience to God.

Expressive individualism has also reshaped conceptions of marriage and divorce in America. The way people talk about the purpose of marriage and the rationale for divorce reflects a tension between traditional duty-based conceptions of marriage and newer duty-free self-understandings. Justifications for divorce based on judgments about the failure of the marriage to foster individual happiness and self-realization are common (and accommodating them is probably the main reason for no-fault divorce laws). Many Americans now eschew the term "duty" when talking about marriage and divorce. They may speak of commitment but not duty. This is probably because duty signifies an external obligation, transcending our immediate desires or purposes, calling for self-sacrifice, while commitment is something we see as largely subjective, dependent to a significant degree on feeling, and therefore as less permanent. A commitment lies within our prerogative to retract when we no longer "feel" it sufficiently.

Duty-free American individualism does not touch all obligations equally. Americans generally affirm that being a citizen entails obligations that are simply given, like Paul's "[pay] taxes to whom taxes are due, revenue to whom revenue is due, respect to whom respect is due, honor to whom honor is due" (Rom. 13:7). It is not such legal obligations or even social conventions that no longer hold their traditional force as common duties for Americans; it is *private* duties that have lost much of their claim on us. As noted above, an individual right to engage and disengage at will now exceeds duties in the private world of friends, voluntary associations, and family.

To the extent that private life is the place where Americans seek meaning, authentic selfhood, happiness, and fulfillment, the erosion of the power of duty in private life is a natural consequence. Individualism in America has become for many a project of the solitary self, entailing therefore a primary duty to self-development (or self-expression). This brand of individualism began as a social movement with the Baby Boomers and coincides with the ascendance of therapeutic models of the self.[37] The popular therapeutic model sees the self as a kind of chrysalis, inherently good and needing nurture for proper development. Moreover, in the therapeutic worldview, each chrysalis is most essentially itself in its uniqueness and therefore has a moral obligation to develop its unique potential. Since the private world is the primary arena in which this project takes place, it is also the primary scene of the attack on duty because the project of becoming one's own unique self comes into conflict with traditional duties, particularly those emanating from the nuclear and extended family.

I have already indicated some ways in which duty-free individualism is at odds not only with Paul's cultural environment but also with basic

37. A landmark study of this phenomenon is Philip Rieff, *The Triumph of the Therapeutic: Uses of Faith after Freud* (New York: Harper and Row, 1966).

tenets of his theology. For Paul, the individual is not the highest value (God is), the self is not inherently good but rather divided, the cure for what ails the self is not to trigger or enhance the self's own inner curative powers but liberation through Christ, the purpose of a human life is not the realization of the self's secret goodness and beauty but a transformation of the self to serve God and God's new creation. This last idea, *the purpose of a human life,* gets at the core conflict between American individualism and the Pauline gospel.

The Purpose of a Human Life

For Paul, the purpose of freedom is obedience to God expressed in service to others in accord with God's aims in the gospel. In the dominant American conception, freedom is the right not to be interfered with and the prerogative to renounce duties when we perceive them as impeding self-fulfillment. The fundamental difference between Paul's understanding of freedom and the dominant American notion of it lies in a basic difference over the purpose of a human life.

The Pursuit of Happiness and Personal Self-Realization

In its famous second paragraph, the American Declaration of Independence specifies "the pursuit of happiness" as a basic human right. The phrase "pursuit of happiness" holds a special charm for Americans, who have attached it to the loftiest and the most mundane endeavors, and much in between. In American legal history, Justice Field's influential dissenting opinion in the 1872 slaughterhouse cases lodged the right to pursue happiness in the U.S. Constitution, which inspired the Supreme Court in later years, notably during the so-called Lochner era, to mine the pursuit of happiness doctrine for various specific rights, among them "opium smoking, carrying a pistol, the sale of liquor by municipalities, the use of trading stamps, the sale of contraceptives, the spraying of citrus fruit, the sterilization of imbeciles, and the licensing of plumbers."[38] This bit of arcane his-

38. Howard Mumford Jones, *The Pursuit of Happiness* (Ithaca: Cornell University Press, 1953), 47.

tory reflects the American tendency to see the pursuit of happiness as a matter of individual decision and preference, the job of the law being to protect this pursuit. (I hasten to add that the ideology of the Lochner era was also laissez-faire capitalism, which means that the doctrine of an individual right to pursue one's chosen interests was part of a larger legal movement that consistently took the side of employer interests in cases involving worker health, safety, unionizing, the right to strike, and like concerns.)

In contemporary America, pursuing happiness has come to mean an individual quest for personal success, self-fulfillment, or "self-actualization." The popularity of M. Scott Peck's book *The Road Less Traveled* shows how deeply the idea of a journey of self (and *to* self) resonates with Americans.[39] In its most extreme form, this journey is highly individualistic, an autonomous path that intersects the lives of other people but is not undertaken *with* others. Hence, any meaningful connections between stages of the journey exist, if at all, only in the self. Moreover, the stages of the journey may not be integrated even in the self, especially for those who see only the present moment as defining who the self really is. Related to this is the amoralistic way in which self-identity and self-fulfillment are often defined. For some Americans, moral relativism means radical doubt about whether it makes sense to adopt any moral code or principles. For others, moral convictions compete with the pursuit of happiness, operating as a kind of limitation on what one ought or ought not do in pursuing happiness. For most, whether they are morally skeptical or morally confident, the pursuit of happiness is not *itself* a moral quest.

If most Americans do not understand the pursuit of happiness as a moral quest, they do typically see the right to pursue happiness in one's own way as a moral right that gives a moral sheen to the pursuit of happiness. In a chapter titled "The Pursuit of Happiness," the authors of *Habits of the Heart* identify what amounts to one of the few non-relativistic moral principles in a society that otherwise sees moral values primarily as shifting sets of preferences. "The ultimate ethical rule is simply that individuals should be able to pursue whatever they find rewarding, constrained only by the requirement that they not interfere with the 'value systems' of others."[40] Americans tend to equate political rights with moral

39. M. Scott Peck, *The Road Less Traveled: A New Psychology of Love, Traditional Values, and Spiritual Growth* (New York: Simon and Schuster, 1978).

40. Bellah, et al., *Habits of the Heart,* 6.

rights. Legally regarded, political rights are social permissions sanctioned by law and backed up by the power of the state. In our society they enjoy a special moral dignity thanks to the almost sacred status of the Declaration of Independence and the Constitution, where we think of our rights as primordially enshrined. Legally, these social permissions are not moral affirmations of the choices or behaviors that the rights protect; they are affirmations only of the freedom of individuals to make their own choices. Nevertheless, what is permitted tends to acquire, within the common sense, a status of moral good. Hence, a typical American attitude to, say, Sally's use of her substantial personal wealth might be that it is morally good if she devotes most of it to worthy causes and that it is also morally good (perhaps not *as* good but still morally positive) if she uses her wealth effectively for her own happiness and personal fulfillment because she has the right to do so.

To summarize, the contemporary idea that moral values are preferences rooted in desire and that rights are not just social permissions but implicit moral affirmations of preferences means that the American rights creed lends moral dignity to the preference approach to the moral life. Since Americans understand these rights in a quasi-religious sense (as divine or sacred rights), the rights creed now carries the sense of cosmic moral command: it is your right and duty to devise or choose your own values and pursue them for your own happiness, individual happiness being the ultimate purpose of sacred human rights.

The Way of Christ

There is nothing equivalent in Paul to the American idea of "the pursuit of happiness" as a life preoccupation. Paul almost never uses the conventional Greek language for happiness, words such as *eudaimonia* (happiness, well-being), *hilarotēs* (cheerfulness), *makaria* (happiness, bliss, blessedness), *olbos* (happiness), *euphrosynē* (good cheer), and their cognates. He does speak frequently of *chara* (joy, happiness) and *chairein* (rejoicing), words that express a specific kind of happiness from God.

More significantly, Paul does not define the purpose of a human life as happiness (or joy or self-fulfillment), even though he attaches joy to the pursuit of a human being's right purpose: there is a joy that comes from faith (Phil. 1:25). Some Pauline contrasts to the notion of life as a pursuit of happiness are the following: "to those who by patiently doing good work seek glory and honor and immortality, [God] will give eternal life; while for those who are self-seeking . . . there will be wrath and fury" (Rom. 2:7-8); "Do not seek your own advantage but that of the other" (1 Cor 10:24); "Since you are eager for spiritual gifts, strive to excel in them for building up the church" (1 Cor. 14:12); "Love does not seek its own interests" (1 Cor. 13:5, my translation); "Let each of you look not to your own interests but to the interests of others" (Phil. 2:4); "So then, whenever we have an opportunity, let us work for the good of all, and especially for those of the family of faith" (Gal. 6:10). These formulations show that for Paul the purpose of a human life is eternal life pursued through obedience to God, who calls us to live for others. There is an element of self-interest here, as shown by Rom. 2:7 and the other promises and warnings in Paul that appeal to human self-interest. But the pursuit of one's own interest is tied to the interests of others, which are to be paramount. Christians are to make love their aim (1 Cor. 14:1) and in so doing "fulfill the law of Christ" (Gal. 6:2). Or, to put it another way, *salvation* is the purpose of a human life, and salvation is a process that has conformity to Christ's self-giving way at its heart (Phil. 2:1-13).

Christ's way is the "law of Christ" for Christians, Christ himself the paradigm of the moral life. Paul's letters offer three decisive clues to the nature of Christ's life as a rule for us. In Romans 15 Paul says of Jesus that "he did not please himself" (v. 3). In 2 Corinthians 8 Paul says that Jesus "became poor" so that his followers "might become rich" (v. 9). In Gal. 2:20 he describes Christ as the one "who loved me and gave himself for me." Each of these descriptions characterizes Christ as exemplifying sacrificial love.

We can understand living according to the law of Christ as the core meaning of sharing the sufferings of Christ in Paul. Christ suffered because "he loved me and gave himself for me" (Gal. 2:20), because "he became poor" that "you might become rich" (2 Cor. 8:9), because "he did not please himself but, as it is written, 'The insults of those who insult you have fallen on me'" (Rom. 15:3). It follows that sharing Christ's sufferings happens when his followers risk themselves in love, as he risked himself. The cross — in its many forms — is the price the world exacts from those who live by the law of love.

In Phil. 3:14, Paul urges the Philippians to imitate him in his pursuit of "the prize of the heavenly call of God in Christ Jesus." For Paul, this divine call involves sharing Christ's sufferings, "becoming like him in his death" in order to "attain the resurrection from the dead" (Phil. 3:10-11; cf. Rom. 8:17). How is suffering with Christ a "condition" for attaining resurrection? In Paul's thinking, Christ is the way to resurrection and his followers attain resurrection by being in him. This means that the connection between suffering and resurrection is the same for them as for him because it is *his* death and resurrection that absorbs them. For Jesus, the resurrection is the vindication and restoration of his suffering love. God rescues Jesus' sacrificial love from the destruction of death. Apart from God's act, Jesus is weak. "He was crucified in weakness but he lives by the power of God" (2 Cor. 13:4). His life counts no more than any other life under the sentence of death. In that case, Paul's words in 1 Cor. 15:19 apply to Jesus himself. "If for this life only," we might say, "Christ gave himself in sacrificial love, then he is of all people most to be pitied." The resurrection is God's way of giving victory to Christ's suffering love, saving it from the futility to which all of creation is otherwise subject (Rom. 8:20-21). Those in Christ have the same hope that their labors will not be for nothing (1 Cor. 15:58).

We might call Paul's self-description in Phil. 3:10-11 a christomorphic statement of the gospel in which Paul, in effect, states the true purpose of a human life through his own example: "becoming like him [Christ] in his death if somehow I might attain the resurrection of the dead." Other gospel statements in Paul also express this purpose in their "final clauses." Some pertinent examples are the following: "who was handed over to death for our trespasses and raised *for* our justification" (Rom. 4:25); "*so that,* just as Christ was raised from the dead . . . we too might walk in newness of life" (Rom. 6:4); "*so that* the just requirement of the law might be fulfilled in us, who walk not according to the flesh but according to the Spirit" (Rom. 8:4); "who gave himself for our sins [*in order*] *to* set us free from the present evil age" (Gal. 1:4); "Christ redeemed us from the curse of the law . . . *in order that* in Christ the blessing of Abraham might come upon the gentiles, *so that* we might receive the promise of the Spirit through faith" (Gal. 3:13-14); "For our sake he made him to be sin who knew no sin, *so that* in him we might become the righteousness of God" (2 Cor. 5:21). These statements belong to a larger pattern, a gospel story in Paul, that might be summarized as follows:

> God has acted in Jesus' life, death, and resurrection to fulfill the promises to the patriarchs and to show redemptive grace to all creation by

> offering the blessing of Abraham to all human beings, both Jew and gentile, giving the Spirit as the first installment of that blessing, in order to free us from the present evil age, to establish us as a new community in a new creation, bestowing on us the status of children of God, calling us to a new way of life, under the law of Christ, and giving us the hope of the kingdom of God, when the church will join with God's people Israel in fulfillment of the promises to the patriarchs, when creation will be set free from bondage to death, and when God will be all in all.[41]

The purpose of a human life resides, for Paul, within the framework of this larger redemptive work of God. It means accepting God's gifts and living out the law of Christ in the pursuit and hope of God's new creation (which God has already begun to create among us). The framework is a *story* and the human actors in this story are not autonomous individuals but a new *community* whose ultimate hope is a kind of unity beyond human imagination: God all in all (1 Cor. 15:28).

Individual human purpose is found in God's call, which draws the individual into a communal purpose (the life and mission of the church) whose goal lies both within and beyond the world. That purpose can be summed up as love itself. "Make love your aim," Paul says (1 Cor. 14:1). Love is one of the enduring goods (13:8) and is "the greatest of all" (v. 13). This is not love in general, but the love of God perfected in human experience as knowing as we are fully known (vv. 11-12) and finding ourselves integrated into God's perfect wholeness (15:28). This kind of love is realized provisionally, in limited ways, in the body of Christ.

Learning to Hope

For Paul, the aims of love lie finally beyond present earthly life. The purpose of love attaches to what are ultimately unseen goals beyond human control. As we have seen, the resurrection rescues suffering love from the futility it otherwise suffers in the present age. The purpose of a human life is "to be saved," an idea that Paul sees as a present process to be completed beyond

41. This summary is based primarily on the following passages in Paul: Rom. 14:8; 8:19-21; Gal. 3:13-14; Rom 8:23; 2 Cor. 1:22; Gal. 1:4; 2 Cor. 5:17; Gal. 6:14-15; Gal. 6:2; 1 Cor. 9:23; 1 Cor. 15:25-28; Rom. 11:25-31.

life in the present age. From Rom. 8:18-25 and 1 Cor. 15:20-57, it is clear that to be saved is to be incorporated into God's transforming work of new creation, which will fully appear when death, the last enemy, is destroyed.

Americans live in a "this-worldly" culture that crowds out any positive role for otherworldly hope. Some Americans reject traditional "otherworldliness" as fanciful. But even those who accept otherworldly hope on faith find it difficult or even impossible to orient their lives to that hope. It is not simply that few American are apocalypticists expecting the end of the world at any moment and therefore renouncing all worldly tasks and plans. Paul himself was not that kind of apocalypticist, one proof being that he saw his mission to the gentiles as a long-term project involving considerable planning. Yet he constantly sought to motivate his churches by referring them to their ultimate hope beyond this life. Why is it so difficult for contemporary Americans to live for that kind of hope? Is it simply that we find it hard to imagine the sort of survival beyond death that we associate with traditional Christian teaching? In fact, this kind of imagining is not so difficult for many Americans. The problem lies not so much in *conceiving* a life beyond but in *living* for it.

Perhaps one way to link Pauline hope with American experience is by beginning with the anticipations of the future that Paul sees at work in the present. Paul thinks we should live not only for the future but for the unseen presence of God's hope in our lives right now.[42] This is one way of putting the famous "already but not yet" in Paul. Almost everything Paul affirms of the future, he also affirms in some way of the present. This has encouraged some to interpret Paul's gospel as "this-worldly" (as opposed to "otherworldly") in orientation. Rudolf Bultmann's demythologizing is one approach of this kind. For Bultmann, every day is the "last day," every hour the hour of final judgment, of decision, of resurrection, understood in existential terms. Nevertheless, demythologizing by itself does not make the Pauline gospel relevant to Americans. The problem of connecting Paul's eschatology — demythologized or not — with American life lies primarily with the competing religious and secular forms of what might be called American "realized eschatology."

By American realized eschatology I mean the perception that this-worldly bodily comfort, economic well-being, and the various freedoms

42. In 2 Cor. 4:16-18, for example, Paul speaks of an unseen hope that is already at work in believers ("our inner person is being renewed day by day").

now enjoyed by the majority of Americans are in some way a fulfillment of biblical eschatology, literally or by analogy. A striking anecdote illustrating a secular version of American realized eschatology is Anthony Grafton's report that some of his Princeton students demur from reading about utopias because, in their view, they already "live in a perfect society."[43] It is easy to associate the comforts of American life with traditional biblical images of earthly and heavenly blessing, which typically feature bodily health and material bounty. Utopian tendencies in the American ethos encourage this sort of identification, whether in the form of American civil religion celebrating America as the Promised Land or in personal life stories of economic blessing from God (most extremely in current "health and wealth" gospels). We affirm our comfort almost religiously.[44]

The achievement of so much general human comfort in contemporary American society and our quasi-religious affirmation of comfort have two effects: they alienate us from Paul's understanding of Christian hope at the same time that they encourage us to see our comfort as divine blessing. Christian interpretations of American prosperity have often led to the judgment that God has graced us and affirmed us in our prosperity, security, and leisure.

In America today, earthly existence is not, for most people, the painful physical trial it was for many of our ancestors and for humankind through most of history. Viewed in terms of Christian eschatology, American bodily comfort and well-being are seen as a present sample of heavenly happiness. Moreover, the suppression of death in our culture fits with American religious views of the transition from life to afterlife as a kind of seamless passage, a continuity from present life to more and better of the same, not a release from lifelong suffering.

Paul's letters offer little foothold for the view that American material bounty and comfort are a divine blessing. For Paul, God's blessing for life in this age is the Spirit. The present realization of future glory is often a hiddenness of glory in suffering. And even though Paul teaches his

43. Anthony Grafton, "Over the Rainbow," *New York Review of Books* 47/19 (November 30, 2000): 6. I assume he is talking about some of his own students when he refers to our time as "an age whose besetting errors include self-satisfaction, when some students ask why they should read about utopias when they live in a perfect society. . . ."

44. On the sources of this ideology of comfort, see John E. Crowley, *The Invention of Comfort: Sensibilities and Design in Early Modern Britain and Early America* (Baltimore: Johns Hopkins University Press, 2000).

churches to care for material needs, he sees the purpose of a human life as lying beyond the material, beyond this world, beyond all bodily life as we know it.

One could say, speaking within the framework of biblical theology, that the concrete this-worldly hopes of the Hebrew prophets for social justice, peace, and material prosperity provide a balance or corrective to any form of Christian hope that takes its cues solely from Paul's otherworldly eschatology. At the same time, the accent in Paul on a divine glory that transcends everything earthly and material is a challenge to any eschatology that makes earthly social justice, peace, and material prosperity *ultimate*, even when these social goods are seen as God's work and gift. Paul holds that there is something more important than happiness, conventionally understood. He calls for the pursuit of love — love as way and goal, love as the acceptance of suffering in sacrifice, love as conformity to Christ's death.

This way of suffering love opens one to gifts in the present that cannot be found in the pursuit of comfort. Paul puts it this way:

> We boast in our sufferings, knowing that suffering produces endurance, and endurance produces character, and character produces hope, and hope does not disappoint us because God's love has been poured into our hearts through the Holy Spirit that has been given to us. (Rom. 5:3-5)

Talk like this is quite alien to American sensibilities. What Paul says seems downright illogical to us. To see Paul's point, we have to keep in view from the outset that the entire passage is about *acquiring hope.* For Paul, the task of a human life is learning to hope. This poses an extraordinary challenge for people who are used to getting what they want now, or at least to demanding it now, and who therefore tend to define their life goals in terms of what they think they can reach by their own effort in the relatively near future. It strikes us as extraordinarily odd, or beside the point of life, to see life's journey as a process aimed at producing character in us so that we can finally learn to hope. Hence, the American self-reliance dogma would lead us to rewrite Paul's words something as follows: We boast in our self-reliance, knowing that self-reliance produces character and character makes it possible to work hard, endure hardship, and win the prize of success. Character in this scheme comes early in the process, as the first product of self-reliance, which puts everything in motion. In fact, character must spring immediately into being, since the path to success depends on the individual's own sovereign effort. "Just do it!" as a recent American presidential candidate liked to say, himself a self-styled self-reliant man, maker of his own way from rags to riches.

By contrast, for Paul character is not the starting point; suffering is. The individual is part of a "we," a community of those who share Christ's sufferings. This naturally involves decision on their part, but the focus of Rom. 5:3-5 is on how God is at work in suffering to produce things that do not come automatically through either suffering or human decision or self-reliance. Character comes at the end of this process and produces hope, not worldly success or even spiritual peace and security. Peace is already given as God's gift (Rom. 5:1). Hope is patient, expectant waiting for what God will do in the future. This shows that even the "inward life" is not a "success story." What spiritual peace and security we enjoy, we have as a gift in the form of hope (see also Rom. 8:24-25).

It is, of course, possible to paint these contrasts too sharply. Certainly the American tradition knows something about the importance of virtues in the classical sense, those habits acquired through practice. While many Americans seem to think that adopting the right creed (or acquiring the right information) is the key to success, others know better. There is also a noble tradition of sacrifice and generosity in the American heritage. It is not that the American tradition knows nothing of the kind of sacrificial service and other-centeredness that Paul advocates; it is not that American churches have no notion of Paul's teaching about being in Christ and living for the new creation. The problem is that we also have strong competing traditions — traditions of individualism that are so powerful that they tempt us to suppress our knowledge of authentic Christian discipleship or persuade us to recast Paul and the rest of the New Testament in terms compatible with the basic assumptions and goals of American individualism.

CHAPTER 3

Paul's Theological Ethic and the Chinese Morality of *Ren Ren*

K. K. (Khiok-khng) Yeo

Christianity has entered China from the West through various avenues: missionary envoys, political treaties, military aggression, and social welfare to the poor, the illiterate, and victims of the wars. As has often been pointed out in recent decades, in these encounters, Western Christians were often not able to differentiate their theology from the wider cultural context of world politics and Western imperialism, with the result that the Chinese were often confused or suspicious about the intentions of Christian proclamation from the West.

But on another level we cannot expect any Christians to neatly separate their culture from their Christianity, as if Christian faith were timeless and abstractable from culture. I do not assume that when I read Paul I do so by transcending culture. We always understand out of our own cultural knowledge. While we can achieve some critical distance on our culture, we cannot transcend culture altogether. Instead we can enter into a cross-cultural dialogue. For me this dialogue involves reading the ancient Paul out of cultural understandings that are both Western and Chinese, since I am Chinese, grew up in Malaysia, and have been educated in both a Chinese and an American context. These two cultural traditions shape my reading of Paul. Western critical scholarship enables me to understand the ancient Paul, who was neither Western nor modern but a Hellenistic Jew who translated his theology into non-Jewish contexts within a larger Greco-Roman cultural setting. At the same time, I am aware as a Chinese how certain Western assumptions do shape Western readings of the ancient Paul. This is not all bad.

Unless otherwise indicated, all translations from Chinese and biblical texts are my own.

We can ask Western questions of Paul and receive fruitful answers that do not simply impose a Western grid on Paul. But we can also ask Chinese questions of Paul. And from a Chinese perspective we may see some things about the ancient Paul that are more difficult for Westerners to see.

This cautions us against assuming that the ancient Paul can be described in a purely objective way. Not only do we bring our own lenses to Paul, we also meet a Paul who wrote in ways that are open to more than one interpretation (and were so for ancient readers as well). Hence, when I make assertions about what Paul thinks and says, I do not want to be interpreted as claiming that my interpretations are the only defensible ones or get us to the "real" Paul better than those of anyone else. Instead I am giving my best interpretation of Paul, which means Paul as I see him from my dual Chinese and American perspectives.

I begin with an examination of Chinese church history to show some of the dynamics and consequences of the interaction between Christian faith and Chinese culture, focusing on the encounter of biblical interpretation with Chinese culture. Then I present a cross-cultural comparison of Paul and Chinese classical texts with the following themes in mind: cosmology, ethics, theology, community, love, and anthropology (what it means to be human).

Cross-Cultural Hermeneutics in Chinese Church History

Christianity reached China as early as the seventh century and the encounter has engendered a number of significant efforts at cross-cultural interpretation of the Bible. Interpreting Christian faith in an authentically Chinese way remains a challenging task for Chinese Christians today. In this effort we can learn from past attempts to sow the seeds of Christian faith in a Chinese context. This history will set the stage for looking at Paul from a Chinese perspective.

The Superficial Contextual Hermeneutic of the Seventh-Century Nestorian Mission

The first attempt at Christian mission to China for which we have record was an effort by Syrian Nestorians who came to North China (then known as Cathay) at the height of the Tang dynasty. Because of the Tang's open and tolerant foreign policy, Emperor Tai Tsung received the Syrian Christian Alopen and his envoys and issued an edict in 638 CE permitting them to spread the faith.

In 1625 a nine-foot Nestorian tablet was found in Hsianfu (near Sian), capital of Shensi. This famous tablet suggests an attempt to contextualize Syrian Nestorian Christianity in a Chinese form. The top of the tablet shows a carving of two monsters holding a pearl, a cross that surmounts a lotus (emblem for Buddhism), and a cloud (emblem for Daoism or Islam).[1] Below these emblems is a heading that reads, "A Monument to the Diffusion throughout the Middle Kingdom [China] of the Illustrious Teaching of Ta Chin [Syria]." The combination of Christian faith with indigenous Chinese religious symbols points to an accommodationist hermeneutic. Most Chinese scholars interpret this accomodationist approach as a strategy of self-preservation, a survival tactic of a group seeking identity and security in a largely hostile environment. Cary-Elwes observes that the inscription "is quite orthodox in its terminology" but has "one strange omission, namely, all mention of the Crucifixion and Death of Christ."[2] Nevertheless, there is the symbol of the cross at the head of the tablet, but it is difficult to know how it was understood. If Cary-Elwes is correct that this early Nestorian brand of Chinese Christianity had no real theology of the cross, then our first evidence for Christian faith in China shows a faith significantly removed from Pauline patterns of thought.

The Nestorian monument is also interesting because it narrates Chinese history as if to suggest that the Christian mission had an important and honored place in that history, probably in order to give a favorable impression of the Nestorian Christians in a cultural setting that showed little interest in Christian faith. The syncretistic and seemingly indigenous hermeneutic of the Nestorian Christians in China had little hope of affecting the Chinese dynasty and soon disappeared from Chinese history, leaving behind only this intriguing stone.

The Nestorian experience in China reveals the perennial issue of Christian faith encountering Chinese imperial and religious power. The

1. The cloud is probably a reference to Daoism. It seems unlikely that Syrian Christians fleeing Islamic persecution would use the cloud as a symbol for Islam.

2. Columbas Cary-Elwes, *China and the Cross: Studies in Missionary History* (London: Longman, 1957), 34-35.

Nestorians did not come to China with the motive of foreign expansionism. Rather, they came to China as diplomatic envoys or religious refugees. The glorious Tang dynasty (known especially for its artistic accomplishments in literature, painting, poetry, china, etc.) needed nothing from this foreign religion. Even though the Christian theology was expressed in idiomatic Chinese and the laborious translation of Adam Thing-ching was impressive, Christianity was merely a foreign religion. The non-Chinese names on the monument indicate that the church leaders were foreigners. This suggests that one reason for the failure of the Nestorian mission was that its cross-cultural hermeneutic was not carried out by Chinese Christians and therefore lacked the cultural depth and authenticity to make it a genuinely indigenous faith.

Proselytizing Christian Hermeneutics in the Yüan Dynasty (1280-1367)

The thirteenth century was an age of political and religious imperialism. Both China and Europe were threatened by the Mongols during this time. Ogodei, the son of Genghis Khan, aimed to conquer the world from the Yellow Sea to the Atlantic Ocean. Kublai Khan, the grandson of Genghis Khan, brought China under Mongol rule in 1260. The Mongol Yüan Dynasty was the first foreign rule in China. During that same period, the Franciscan and Dominican missionaries of that era were committed to converting the Mongol Empire for the sake of Christ. They held a great council at Lyons in 1245 with the agenda of countering the threat of the Golden Horde of Genghis Khan. Innocent IV sent Friar John of Pian di Carpina (Giovanni de Plano Carpini) to Karakorum with a letter to Ogodei, advising the Khans to become Christians. Friar John and his entourage were not well received. Güyük Khan, whose mother was a Nestorian Christian, replied in defiance against the Pope, the emperor, the Roman Empire, and against the God of the Franciscans.[3] Yet because of the *Pax Mongolica* that made it possible for China and foreign traders to have direct contacts by land via the silk route, Christianity came to China from foreign lands through international trade and science.

In 1265 two Venetian brothers, Niccolo and Matteo Polo, arrived in

3. Cary-Elwes, *China and the Cross*, 42.

China. Kublai Khan sent a letter with them on their return in 1269, requesting that the pope send a hundred men "wise in the Christian law and acquainted with the seven arts."[4] Only two Dominicans were sent, and they gave up halfway along their journey.[5] In 1289 Pope Nicholas IV sent Franciscan John of Montecorvino (1247-1328) to meet Kublai Khan. Friar John tried to persuade the Khan to become a Catholic. The emperor remained unconverted but authorized John to build a church in Beijing. John's missionary efforts in China were largely successful. By 1305 he had baptized 6000 Chinese. In 1307 Pope Clement V appointed John Archbishop of Beijing and Patriarch of the East. John was evidently also an able diplomat. As a result of the good relations he fostered with the Great Khan, the Catholic Church and the Chinese imperial court had many favorable exchanges of gifts and honors until 1367, when the Yüan dynasty fell in the Red Turbans Revolt led by Chu Yüan-chang. In the wake of this political upheaval, Christian missionary activity in China ceased for the second time. Christian communities were persecuted and Catholic bishops killed.

The reasons for the extinction and failure of the Franciscan mission in China are many. I will mention only three. First, the Franciscans did not adequately understand and deal constructively with Chinese veneration of ancestors, the Confucian ethics of family, and the Chinese worldview. Second, the Franciscans failed to work with Chinese converts to devise patterns of Christian faith sensitive to Chinese customs and expressed in the indigenous Chinese languages. Instead, Chinese converts were taught Greek and Latin.[6] Third, the Franciscans took the side of the foreign merchant class in the wake of the Mongol conquest.

Contemporary missiology stresses that contextual theology is a necessity; anything less is a form of cultural imperialism. The Franciscan mission failed to engage Chinese culture in a constructive, dialogical way and therefore never took root in China in forms that could withstand the stress of political and social change. In some respects, the Syrian Nestorian mission looks like an effort at indigenization, but historical scholarship suggests that even the Syrian impulse to accommodation was

4. Cary-Elwes, *China and the Cross,* 48.

5. The Polos, together with Niccolo's son Marco, returned to China, arriving in Beijing in 1275, but they did not carry out any missionary work. Marco became a minor civil servant in the Khan's Mongol Empire.

6. Cary-Elwes, *China and the Cross,* 70-71.

primarily for the sake of political self-preservation. The Nestorians curried the favor of the Chinese royal court but failed to reach the common people.

The Accommodationist Hermeneutics of the Jesuit Mission in the Ming Dynasty (1368-1643)

The first sincere accommodationist mission did not appear until the arrival of Jesuit missionaries during the Ming dynasty. The Jesuits imitated Paul's apostolic style of "becoming all things to all people" (1 Cor. 9:19-23). They entered Chinese history during a time of momentous restoration. For years, many Chinese felt oppressed under the Mongolian rule of the Yüan Dynasty. Native Chinese secret societies were formed, brotherhoods bent on resistance and overthrow of the regime. Their aim was to supplant the khans and restore Chinese rule. Chu Yüan-chang, a leader of one of the secret societies, finally toppled the Yüan government and set up the Chinese Ming Dynasty. During the Ming dynasty Sino-centrism developed in the form of Confucian orthodoxy. The intellectual vitality of Confucianism was restored in the revival of Wang Yangming (Wang Shou-ren, 1472-1529). Wang's brand of Confucianism argued for unity of self and society, knowledge *(chih)* and action *(xeng)*, mind *(xing)* and principle *(li)*. Innate knowledge of right and wrong in every individual should lead one to public life driven by love *(ren)*. Wang criticized the twelfth-century Confucianist Zhu Xi (1130-1200) for his emphasis on self-cultivation to the neglect of social and political involvement.

The Wang revival posed a challenge to the Jesuit missionaries. They faced the alternative of offering a Christian message that rejected Confucianism, presenting itself as more persuasive and attractive to the Chinese than Confucianism, or working out an accommodationist hermeneutics that integrated Christian faith with the Confucian worldview. In his first expedition to Asia, St. Francis of Xavier (1506-52) dressed in Western ecclesiastical clothes and was despised by the Japanese. Soon he learned the lesson of accommodation and wore Japanese dress in his second expedition. But he failed again because the Japanese claimed to possess superior wisdom from China — Confucianism. St. Francis decided to convert China, the mentor of Japan. On his way to China to win over the Chinese emperor in 1552 he died of fever on the offshore island of Shangquan (Sancian).

Nevertheless, his accommodationist policy set the course for the mission work of later Jesuits in China.

The Jesuits dominated the mission scene in China from 1582 onwards. The most famous missionary of that order was Matteo Ricci (1552-1610), Li Matou, whose tactic was to supply the needs of China, as he discerned them, and to reach out to the most influential groups in the Chinese society. He introduced Western mathematics, science, and cartography, and he reached out to the emperor and the elite official class.

Ricci spent considerable time learning how to read and write Chinese. Within a few years he was able to translate the Four Books of Confucianism into Latin. In 1594 Ricci turned to a serious study of the classics of Confucianism. He wrote, "I have noted in the Canonical [Confucian] Books many passages which are favorable to the things of the faith, such as the unity of God, the immortality of the soul, the glory of the blessed."[7] Ricci interpreted Confucius as a moralist and not a superstitious idolater. Confucianism, Ricci believed, "was not formally a religion but only an academy."[8] Ricci was so adept in Confucianism and the classical texts that he was welcomed by the Eastern Grove (Tongling) Academy of Wang Yangming to engage in discussion with eminent literati. Many Chinese were converted to the Catholic faith, among them Xu Guangqi (a Confucian scholar), Li Chih-tsao (an expert in Chinese literature), and Yang Tingyun. These three became the pillars of the Catholic Church in China.[9]

Ricci's hermeneutic of accommodation had two important aspects. First, on the issue of compatibility between Christianity and Confucianism, Ricci understood history in a progressive movement of promise to fulfillment. Ricci was convinced that the earliest Confucian teaching about *Tian* and *Shangdi* referred to a personal supreme Being. In other words, the fuller revelation of Christianity did not annul but supplemented and fulfilled the original Confucian teachings.[10] Second, on the issue of religion and ethics, Ricci thought that one could make positive connections between the self-cultivation practices of the Confucian rites and Christian discipleship through the spiritual exercises of Ignatius of Loyola. He attempted to reconcile the Christian and Confucian traditions by arguing

7. Cary-Elwes, *China and the Cross*, 97.

8. Cary-Elwes, *China and the Cross*, 99.

9. See Bob Whyte, *Unfinished Encounter: China and Christianity* (Glasgow: Collins, 1988), 62.

10. Whyte, *Unfinished Encounter*, 71-72.

that Christian discipleship was about self-cultivation in virtue, uprightness of heart, and sincerity of will. Ricci interpreted the Christian doctrine of sin as humanity deformed by passion, which weakened the will's propensity for virtue and love. Ricci's hermeneutic was genuinely cross-cultural.

The Rites Controversy of the Early Ching Dynasty (1644-1721)

The period between Ricci's death (1610) and the fall of the Ming dynasty witnessed a turn in the cross-cultural hermeneutic of the Christian missionaries. Not all the Jesuit fathers agreed with Ricci's view on the Rites of Confucius. Catholic resistance to accommodation evoked intermittent persecutions during the first decades of the seventeenth century. In 1615 Shen Ts'ui of Nanjing obtained a decree from the Board of Rites in Beijing expelling the Jesuit fathers, and two years later the emperor issued a decree expelling all missionaries.

The Rites Controversy reveals how basic Confucianism is to Chinese culture. The fate of Christianity in China has long depended on how it interacts with Confucian ethics. Two major issues in the Rites Controversy concerned the veneration of Confucius and ancestors and the naming of God. The question of how to name God in the Chinese language focused on the words *Tian* (Heaven) and *Shangdi,* both of which have been used as names for the highest personal being and have also been used to translate "God" in the Bible. *Shangdi,* in its earliest usage (probably during the Zhou dynasty), referred to the Shang emperor ancestor as a divine figure. Hence, the archaic meaning of *Shangdi* is "God-Emperor on high." It could be assumed that ancient Chinese believed in a supreme being and that *Shangdi,* when used to name a transcendent being, meant the supreme being. For the most part this issue has been resolved. The standard Chinese Bible in use today employs *Shangdi* for God, but other Bibles use other names, as we will see below, including *Tian.*

The accommodationist Jesuit fathers, following Ricci's view, held that reverence toward Confucius and ancestors was not worship but acts of honoring and remembering; these practices did not involve treating the ancestors as gods. But some Jesuit fathers and most Dominicans and Franciscans argued that among the common people the practices of ancestor veneration did involve idolatrous acts and belief. For example, Nicholas Longobardi (1556-1654), the successor of Ricci, warned that the Church might be condoning pagan elements in Chinese Christian life. The most forceful argument came from a Dominican, Friar Morales, who argued before Pope Innocent X in 1643 that the Chinese rites were superstitions. The Pope condemned ancestor veneration that same year.

The controversy remained alive, however. For example, in 1693 when Charles Maigrot, Vicar-Apostolic of Fukien, published a booklet against ancestor worship, a group of Jesuit fathers defended the practice as nonreligious and interceded with Emperor Kang-hsi (1662-1721), assuring him that Chinese Christians could practice the rites. The emperor was reassured, but the opponents of the Jesuits continued their attack. In 1701 Pope Clement XI sent a papal legate to China to resolve the issue; the legate concluded that the rites were idolatrous. In 1704 the famous decree of Clement XI and the Congregation of Rites allowed only one name for God in Chinese, that is, *Tian-zhu,* which means literally "the Heavenly Lord." The decree also prohibited ritual acts in honor of Confucius and veneration of ancestors. In 1715, Clement XI published the encyclical *Ex illa die,* pronouncing excommunication on Catholic missionaries who disobeyed the rules of the Holy See regarding Chinese Rites and the name of God. The same year, Emperor Kang-hsi issued a famous edict outlawing Christianity, banishing the missionaries, and calling for the destruction of the churches. The edict aimed to eradicate Christian faith from the soil of China.

But Christianity did not die out and the Rites Controversy continued. A papal bull issued by Benedict XIV made some compromises from the Roman side. The bull permitted the use of ancestral tablets, so long as all "superstitious" words were corrected and ambiguous words explained. It also allowed ritual offerings of food and *kow tow* (kneeling and bowing with head touching the ground) in ceremonies honoring ancestors. But in July 1742 Benedict issued *Ex quo singulari providentia factum est,* reversing the permissions of the earlier bull.[11]

As an outcome of the Rites Controversy, Christianity became an alien religion because of its anti-Chinese, anti-Confucianist stance. It was not until 1939 that the Holy See reversed its position on the Rites Controversy. The Congregation of Propaganda issued a decree rescinding the 1715

11. Cary-Elwes, *China and the Cross,* 157-60.

decision embodied in *Ex illa die*. By then, however, the situation was much different. China had abolished the Confucian educational system, and the Chinese government insisted that honoring Confucius was not a religious act. Nevertheless, two hundred years of anti-Chinese Christianity could not be erased in a single ecclesiastical pronouncement. The anti-Chinese missionary legacy continues to shape Chinese perceptions of the Christian faith.

The relationship between a foreign religion and an indigenous culture is especially acute when the religion is not well accepted by the dominant culture. Ever since the Rites Controversy, the crucial hermeneutical concern has been the relation of Christian faith to Chinese culture. To rephrase the ancient church father Tertullian's question "What has Athens to do with Jerusalem?" we might ask "What has Jerusalem to do with Beijing?"[12] The issues of the Rites Controversy still divide the Chinese churches. Even today a majority of Protestants see the ancestor rites as idolatrous, while Catholics are more open.[13] If Jerusalem has nothing to do with Beijing, then to speak of Chinese Christianity is a contradiction. Indeed, many Chinese Christians find it difficult to be faithful Christians and filial pietists or Confucianists. Many live in the unresolved tension of embracing the teaching of Confucius and Christ without knowing how to unite the two.

Church, Society, and Denominationalism

In the eighteenth century, Protestant Christianity came to China not by bringing scientific technology or seeking an intellectual encounter with the literati but through missionary efforts to reach the common people and also in connection with the opium trade. During the years of the opium war, Western traders, politicians, and missionaries found a place in China to expand their interest and calling. While the Catholic missionaries of the past had focused their work on the emperor and the official literati,

12. The ancient church father Tertullian asked, "What has Athens to do with Jerusalem?" See my *What Has Jerusalem to Do with Beijing? Biblical Interpretation from a Chinese Perspective* (Harrisburg: Trinity Press International, 1998).

13. I have attempted to deal with this issue in my Chinese book *Ancestor Worship: Rhetorical and Cross-Cultural Hermeneutical Response* (second edition, Hong Kong: Chinese Christian Literature Council, 1996). See also the conclusion of this chapter for a fresh look at the question.

the Protestant missionaries reached out to the rank-and-file. Many of the Protestant missionaries focused on social needs of Chinese society such as education (Morrison) and medical services (Peter Parker).[14]

The first English missionary, Robert Morrison (1782-1834), a Presbyterian, was committed to bringing about a social transformation of Chinese culture through Christian education, which meant socialization to the culture of the Christian West. In 1814 Morrison converted a Chinese Buddhist, Liang Fa. Liang was baptized in 1816 and became the first Protestant Chinese clergyman in 1827. Liang's writings inspired Hong Xiuquan's apocalyptic vision of national salvation in the Taiping Rebellion. Liang was attracted to Christianity because, like many commoners of his day, he was looking for a path of moral power for himself and his nation. The Confucian ethical imperatives were dominant in Chinese culture at all levels, since the education system was still based on Confucianism. But Liang was not one of the literati; the philosophical perspective of Confucianism on self-cultivation and the governance of an empire was not part of his intellectual makeup. Nor did he find the rituals of folk religion effective for moral transformation. It was the Reformed gospel of repentance, regeneration, and sanctification that captured his soul.

One significant issue that arose in modern Protestant missions to China was whether the Christian gospel calls for social transformation or is concerned primarily with individual salvation. This familiar debate in modern Western Christianity was replicated on the mission field. The dispute itself is ill-suited to traditional Chinese ways of thinking about the relation of the individual to society. Hence, the importation of the Western controversy about "personal salvation" over against "social gospel" made little sense to most Chinese and hindered missionary efforts to make Christian faith intelligible in the Chinese context. This is not to say that all Chinese theologians were immune to the distinction between a personal and a social gospel. As we will see, Watchman Nee fell under the spell of largely individualistic pietism.

A second issue was how the gospel of reconciliation could be persuasive to Confucianist Chinese when the Christian mission was represented in China by competing denominations that disagreed on matters of doc-

14. In 1835 Peter Parker opened a hospital in Guangzhou and founded the Medical Missionary Society in 1838. For more on medical missionary efforts in China, see Whyte, *Unfinished Encounter*, 134-36.

trine and did not cooperate with each other. Traveling great distances and risking their own lives at all cost, committed missionaries were creating schism in China. This motif would resurface again and again in Chinese church history. The Christian witness is undermined by a Western denominationalism that flies in the face of both the Christian message of unity and the Confucianist values of concord, community, and harmonious interpersonal relationships. For example, when the 1850 New Testament was published, two editions were printed because Chinese Christians could not agree on the common term for God.[15] The Bible societies printing the Protestant Bible have continued to issue two versions.[16] Since the Catholic Bible used *Tianzhu* (Heavenly Lord), the Catholic Church today is called *Tianzhujiao* in Chinese, meaning Church of the Heavenly Lord. But the Protestant churches have also been referred to as *Jidujiao*, meaning the Church of Christ. The point is that Chinese — Christian or non-Christian — often think of Catholic and Protestant not as one Christianity but as two different world religions.[17]

Biblical Interpretation in the Modern Era: The Bible and Chinese Culture

Chinese biblical hermeneutics in the modern era has taken a number of forms, from approaches indebted to the West that tend to neglect the task of theological indigenization to forms of accommodation that take seriously the importance of recontextualizing the teaching of Scripture in Chinese terms.

15. I served as a translation consultant for the United Bible Societies in 1993 and noticed the impasse on a common term for God in the "Common Version" Chinese Catholic and Protestant Bible.

16. And in the old days of typesetting, the Chinese printer simply had to exchange the two-character block of *Shangdi* for the one character-block of *Shen*, leaving a blank space in front of Shen to keep it with the next word. But most Chinese Christians interpret the *Shen* format with a space in front as a more sacred and honorable way of addressing God. It is a typical style to address an elder with respect by simply leaving a space before his or her name. Though it is true that Chinese formal writing often leaves a blank space before the honorable addressee's name, the *Shen* version of the Bible was not printed with that intention.

17. The burgeoning post-denominational movement of the "Three-Self" Churches (churches of the official Three-Self Patriotic Movement) is a Chinese response to the pain of denominationalism.

The Little Flock, founded by Watchman Nee (Ni Duosheng, 1903-72), appears in certain respects to be an effort at establishing an indigenous Chinese Christian polity and ecclesiology. However, the Little Flock owes much of its theological insight to Western dispensationalism (John Nelson Darby and the Plymouth Brethren, the Scofield Bible) and Keswick "victorious life" teaching. In *The Spiritual Man*, an exposition of Paul's theology, Nee adopts the Western Greek and Gnostic view of a body-soul dualism. Saving souls became his only concern. Helping the poor and victims of the war was not part of his prophetic calling. He was preoccupied with sanctification concerns such as the "second blessing," "baptism of the Spirit," and "spiritual illumination." He distinguished the spiritual Christian from the "carnal Christian" who spent time in the world.

Wang Mingdao, in his widely circulated *Spiritual Food Quarterly*,[18] also promoted a dualistic cosmology and anthropology. He emphasized pursuing a sanctified life in preparation for the coming of Jesus. He understood evangelism exclusively as spiritual conversion for the spiritual community of the elect. The political ethics of Confucianist teaching did not influence Nee and Wang at all.

Moreover, Nee and Wang assumed that to be Christian was to transcend culture. Although one can appreciate many positive elements in their invigoration of Chinese Christianity in the twentieth century, their biblical interpretation did not achieve depth as an indigenous appropriation of Scripture for Chinese Christians. In their effort to transcend culture, they adopted Western cultural Christianity instead of working out a Chinese form of the faith.

Greater hermeneutical sensitivity to the demands of indigenization is found in the hermeneutics of Wu Leichuan, T. C. Chao, Y. T. Wu, and Bishop Ting. We will focus on Wu and Chao.[19]

The modern intellectual and national reform of the May Fourth movement in Chinese history, which got under way around 1916, was a reaction not only to feudalism but also to Christian theology. Operating out of the spirit of the May Fourth movement, with its critique of traditional Chinese society *and* Western imperialism, Wu Leichuan (1870-1944) ar-

18. Here and elsewhere I give the titles of Chinese books in English.

19. For a good introduction to Wu's life and theology, see Chu Sin-Jan, *Wu Leichuan: A Confucian-Christian in Republican China* (New York: Lang, 1995); for Chao, see Winfried Glüer, *Christliche Theologie in China: T. C. Chao, 1918-1956* (Gütersloh: Mohn, 1979).

gued that Chinese theology must address the question of the national salvation of China. According to Wu, the Chinese people were already in search of a new direction; hence, it would be "only futile for Christianity to identify itself with traditional Chinese culture."[20] Wu argued that the perfect personhood of Jesus, who exemplified unity in his words and deeds, reveals to humanity a radically new and holistic form of existence. This new way of being truly human is what the "kingdom of God" means. Wu found common cause between the new impulses toward socialism in China and what he saw as socialist dimensions in Jesus' teaching. For Wu, Jesus' kingdom is a combination of idealism and materialism, a prototype of the socialist society, the communal sharing of property.[21] Jesus, according to Wu, offers a socialist kingdom of freedom, justice, and equality.[22] Jesus' kingdom message is a basis for the "national salvation" of China.

Wu found affinities between Jesus' vision of the kingdom of God and Confucianist ideals.[23] In Wu's view, Jesus was concerned for the peace of the whole universe, including social justice for the poor and the outcasts. Wu saw a connection here with the Confucianist ideal of *ren* (love), and he thought that Jesus' kingdom ethic could therefore be positively linked with the Confucian idea of self-cultivation for the purpose of maintaining a harmonized family, ruling a nation, and bringing about peace to the universe.

T. C. Chao (Zhao Zichen, 1888-1979) also sought a new accommodation of the Bible and Chinese culture, but took a very different approach from Wu to the teaching of Jesus. Chao is a fascinating figure. Trained at Union Theological Seminary in New York, Chao early on sought to reject his Confucianist culture and fell in love with the Western reading of the biblical witness to Christ. Later he developed a more indigenous Chinese approach. In his 1935 book *The Biography of Jesus,* Chao rejected the idea that Jesus' message is political, much less revolutionary.[24] Although he sought to work out a Christian social ethic that was not individualistic, he rejected socialism. He lamented that so many of the youth of his time were

20. Whyte, *Unfinished Encounter,* 179.

21. Wu Leichuan, *Christianity and Chinese Culture* (in Chinese; Shanghai: Youth Association Bookstore, 1936), 71-72.

22. Wu Leichuan, *Christianity and Chinese Culture,* 90-92.

23. Wu Leichuan, *Christianity and Chinese Culture,* 97.

24. T. C. Chao, *The Biography of Jesus* (in Chinese; Hong Kong: Christian Literature Publisher, 1965 [original edition 1935]). In his preface (pp. 6-8), Chao does not see Jesus as eschatological or apocalyptic. See also his critical view of socialism on pp. 674-75.

attracted to Communism; he also attacked the individualistic "selfish" gospel of much popular Christian faith.[25] Chao struggled with the question of how to reconcile the Confucian impetus to transform society through self-cultivation with a Protestant soteriology based on accepting the free grace of God. He seems to have rejected the Confucian teaching about self-perfection as well as the liberal Protestant idea of the atonement as moral example. Chao's ethic was based on dying and rising with Christ as found in Romans, a mystical interpretation of the Christ-event of death and resurrection. Chao opted for an interpretation of Christian faith through a Pauline lens that is at odds with Confucian ethics. The mystical dying and rising with Christ of Chao's Pauline theology has little, if anything, to do with the Confucian idea of the "kingly outside and sagely inside" that makes a person adept at doing good for society through self-cultivation.

But there may be an influence of Confucius in Chao's rejection of eschatology. It is unnatural for a Confucianist to believe in eschatology, since the golden age *(Datong)* is not a future age but the past age of the Zhou Dynasty, which people are called to imitate.[26] For Chao, Paul's statement of future hope and promise have to do with union with Christ via God's Spirit as a way of recovering in one's present life the original vision of being truly human, as we have that true humanity in Christ. If "eschatology" is the right word for this, it is "realized" eschatology.

Critical Reflections

My conviction is that the hope and future of Chinese theology depend largely on the development of specifically Chinese approaches to biblical hermeneutics and the working out of contemporary biblical-theological perspectives that do justice to the specific cultural textures of Chinese life. Unfortunately, most Chinese commentaries and other forms of Chinese biblical interpretation today present themselves as "culturally neutral,"

25. See T. C. Chao, "The Christian Spirit Tried by War," in *Christian Voices in China*, ed. Chester S. Miao (New York: Friendship, 1948), 17, quoted in Whyte, *Unfinished Encounter.*

26. See my essay "Messianic Predestination in Romans 8 and Classical Confucianism," in *Navigating Romans through Cultures: Challenging Readings by Charting a New Course,* ed. K. K. (Khiok-khng) Yeo (Romans through History and Culture; Edinburgh: Clark/New York: Continuum, 2004), 259-88.

which turns out to mean tacitly Western (European and North American).[27] Chinese biblical interpretation today is still dominated by and large by Western scholarship. This means either traditional historical-grammatical exegesis or radical postcolonial interpretation, which seeks to deconstruct the Bible and Western culture in the interest of promoting purely Chinese culture. But what is Chinese culture? And what is Chinese cultural interpretation? Is Chinese interpretation simply an interpretation given by someone who is Chinese? This begs a further question. Who is Chinese? What is the cultural characteristic of being Chinese?

Every culture changes over time. One way that cultures evolve is through interaction with other cultures. A given culture at any moment in time is always a hybrid of cultures. It is therefore a mistake to imagine that cultures have homogeneous, unchanging identities. It is important to be clear about what one means by "Chinese," but also to be cautious and not claim too much for one's definition. In our time, an emerging modern (largely Western) global culture transmitted through trade, travel, technology, communication, and education (especially non-Westerners receiving higher education in the West) threatens traditional cultural identities and values. Thus, a modern "Chinese" might identify more with the global culture of Hollywood romance, watching CNN in Canton, drinking Coke, eating pizza, and studying Jacques Derrida than with speaking Mandarin, listening to Chinese classical music, or reading the *Classic of Change*. A modern Chinese may be like any non-Chinese, unfamiliar with the traditional Chinese classics such as *The Dream of the Red Chamber*, the writings of Confucius. A modern Chinese may dislike Chinese opera, rice, and the longevity noodle. A modern Chinese of this kind, except for his or her ancestry and perhaps appearance, is a non-Chinese.

Allow me first to define Chinese culture in relation to "civilization." I believe Samuel Huntington is correct in speaking of Confucianist civilization as the cultural ethos of China and other neighboring countries in Asia.[28] Chinese culture is a distinctive pattern within this broadly Confucian civilization. As a Malaysian, my own Chinese identity is rooted in

27. Looking at various biblical commentaries and series of the last twenty years, one will be surprised to see how rarely Chinese authors deal with the biblical text in terms of Chinese culture.

28. Samuel P. Huntington, "The Clash of Civilizations?" *Foreign Affairs* 77 (Summer, 1993): 22-49, and his *The Clash of Civilizations and the Remaking of World Order* (New York: Simon and Schuster, 1996).

Confucianist (and Daoist) culture (rather than Buddhist). Before I knew Paul, I already knew Confucius.

I believe the perennial Chinese characteristic is found in the Chinese cosmology of *dao de* (the Way of Morality/Virtue). Even among those Chinese who intentionally want to reject the Confucianist ideal, the Confucian ethic often still plays a significant role in their thinking. For example, the Confucian ethic of knowledge and action is found in T. C. Chao and Maoism. Chao and Mao did not agree in their theological assumptions, yet both, despite their rejection of the Confucianist ideal of how to be fully human, in fact also held to Confucianist political ethics.[29]

Our discussion here raises the question of commensurability and interpretation. In other words, is there enough common ground between Chinese culture and Pauline theology to make conversation possible? Can Pauline theology be interpreted in Chinese terms without ceasing to be Pauline?

As an interpreter, I come to the Pauline corpus and the Chinese classics not as a detached, "objective" observer but as a subjectively engaged and interested interpreter, one who has already been shaped by Paul and by the Chinese tradition and has a stake in the outcome of the interpretive process. At the same time, I do not want to impose Paul artificially on Chinese culture or arbitrarily force Paul into a Chinese mold. My own identity is bound up in this tricky hermeneutical negotiation. I cannot separate the Chinese and Christian dimensions of myself.

The Chinese Cosmology of *Dao De* and Pauline Theology

Chinese Culture and "Religion"

In some Western understandings of Pauline theology or Christianity, it is quite acceptable to differentiate between and contrast theology and ethics, faith and works, doctrine and practice. In Chinese thinking, however, these sets of seemingly bipolar concepts are intentionally held in tension so that the fluidity between them is maintained.

29. On Chao, see his works mentioned earlier; on Mao, see K. K. (Khiok-khng) Yeo, *Chairman Mao Meets the Apostle Paul* (Grand Rapids: Brazos, 2002), 123-26. Interestingly enough, Chu observes of Wu Leichuan's hermeneutics that Leichuan, "[a]s a Confucian scholar, having little cross-cultural experience . . . unconsciously imposed Confucian values onto Jesus' life" (Chu, *Wu Leichuan,* 191, n. 24).

One origin of this fused relationship between theology and ethics is the development of Chinese religion *(chung-jiao)* out of the Chinese school/family *(jia)*. Religion as *chung-jiao* emphasizes the practicality and usefulness of one's learning from the wisdom of the past. *Chung* means ancestral tradition; *jiao* means teaching or education. The pictogram *jiao* portrays a teacher holding a staff giving instruction, thus stressing the authority of the instructor. Therefore, *chung-jiao* means ancestral teaching. Tradition and history have proven the teaching's credibility and usefulness. In short, the Chinese have a functional view of "religion," and they perceive truth as usefulness and practical wisdom.

Jia, which is an older term than *chung-jiao,* designates a grouping or school of thought or teaching that has authority. *Jia* stresses the familial structure and tradition of Chinese communities. The family is considered the basic unit of society. It is so basic that larger social groups are modeled after it. There is also an important connection with Confucianism here (as we will see below). The earlier forms of philosophy — Daoism, the yin-yang worldview — are ways of life practiced as schools of thought that only later become institutionalized as "religions." In their earliest forms, these schools of thoughts are lived-out reality, and the emphasis is always on the practical, ethical dimensions of *being human.*

Chinese Cosmology and Pauline Eschatology: The Dialectical Relationship between Dao and De

The intertwined relationship between cosmology and anthropology, theology and ethics, universe and family, is the essence of Chinese culture, which is commonly termed *dao de* ("the Way and the Morality"). *Dao* (like the Greek *logos*) is the creative principle and wisdom that generates the way of life, which in turn is a harmonious plentitude. While *dao* in Chinese is relationship with the cosmos, *de* signifies relationship with humanity. *Dao* denotes the actualization of the self in harmony with the cosmic and spiritual realms; *de* denotes the actualization of the self in wholeness within the social and ethical realms.

The intertwined relationship of *dao* and *de* in the Chinese worldview is evident especially, though not exclusively, in the Daoist and Confucianist concepts of *jia* ("family"). The Chinese traditionally understand religion as *jia,* meaning family, but family is not simply biological. Family is a microcosm of the universe; therefore family structure reflects *dao,* the logos of the universe. And family relationship exists in the structure of moral propriety and rules. Since *dao* and *de* are related in the classical Chinese assumption that there is a moral universe, *jia*/family expresses the relationship of *dao* and *de.* An example of the interrelationship between *dao* and *de* is seen in the Daoist school, where *dao de* is expressed in the harmony of self with nature. The oneness of self and nature engenders the undifferentiated cognitive and emotive process articulated by Zhuang Zi (369-300 BCE), who said in his tractate on the fusion of subject and object, titled *Cosmology,* that "[h]eaven and earth live with me; the ten thousand things and I are one."[30] In other words, we do not just observe *dao,* we participate in it. We do not contemplate nature and life but relate with and in them so that subject and object are one.

During the fifth and fourth centuries BCE, Lao Zi and Zhuang Zi attempted to solve the problem of cultural deterioration and conflict by saying that although reality *(dao)* exists, each person has his or her own limited perspective. Conflict arises because each one imagines that he or she possesses the whole truth but in fact has only a "lens" that gives a limited vision. According to Lao Zi, the solution is to understand "nothingness." For even truth comes from nothingness, and all will return to nothingness. Lao Zi, in *Dao De Jing ("The Classic of Dao De")* says that "[t]he *dao* that can be told of is not the eternal *dao.*" The best way to know *dao* is to meditate and keep silent. Nevertheless, Lao Zi used five thousand words to write about the *dao.* Why? Because the self-revealing *dao* invites interpretations. Lao Zi writes:

> There is Something undifferentiated, and yet complete in Itself. Soundless and Formless; Independent and Unchanging; Pervasive and Inclusive. It can be regarded as the Mother of the Universe. I do not know Its name. I named It "*Dao.*" Only I was forced to give It a name. I regard It simply [as] the "Great." For in greatness, It produces. In producing, It expands. In expanding, It regenerates.[31]

Dao is the ungraspable quality of the ultimate reality, a creative force that derives from timeless, unknown nothingness.

30. *Zhuang Zi New Translations* (in Chinese), trans. Hwang Ching Hung (Taipei: SanMin, 1985), 74. The English translation here is mine.

31. Milton M. Chiu, *The Tao of Chinese Religion* (Lanham: University Press of America, 1984), 6.

The Chinese understanding of *dao* sketched above is in many respects very different from Paul's understanding of God and especially Paul's *historicizing apocalyptic* interpretation that God can be known in Christ. Paul's Jewish eschatology points to the openness of the human condition and the hope of a transformative future. This aspect of Paul's theology (resurrection) differs significantly from Daoist cosmology. The Daoist cosmology acknowledges an open-endedness of *dao,* but does not look toward a consummation, a *telos,* of the cosmos. It only explains that to be a moral human being one needs to be open to the future. Paul envisions the imminent kingdom of God that speaks to the human condition in terms of a resurrection hope requiring openness to future transformation. The resurrection of Jesus is already the beginning of this future through which humanity will be saved as the purpose or *telos* of God's redemptive activity in history. Through Jesus' life and work, God reveals that human beings are granted community with God and participation in eschatological salvation; human fate is not death but resurrection from the dead.

In the Chinese understanding of *dao,* the cosmos has its own *natural* process of creation and redemption. Human beings can be morally responsible parts of that process. In contrast, the eschatological nature of truth, for Paul, requires "faith" from believers. "Faith" in the Pauline epistles is not a rigid subscription to certain religious ideology or dogma. Faith is trust animated by hope and love, by *being faithful just as the incarnated Christ was faithful.* The apocalyptic eschatology of Paul in Galatians gives the clearest example of how this framework shapes christology, soteriology, freedom, and ethics. For example, in Gal. 1:4, Paul refers to "the present evil *aeon.*" The idea here of a distinction between the present evil age and a future good age is not the Gnostic distinction between evil material creation and good spiritual matter. Rather, Paul's eschatology expresses hope for the present creation in a new creation, the redemption of the present creation from its suffering under sin and death (Gal. 1:4; 6:15; Rom. 12:2; 1 Cor. 1:20; 2:6; 2:8; 3:18; 2 Cor. 4:4). Paul's cosmological and apocalyptic eschatology is therefore grounded in Christ. Christ reveals the mystery and pattern of the cosmos and defines the end, the *telos,* the goal and purpose, of the cosmos. This revelation speaks of God breaking into the present *aeon* by sending his Son and Spirit: "when the fullness of time came, God sent his Son. . . . God sent the Spirit of his Son into our hearts" (Gal. 3:23-25; 4:4, 6, NRSV). Before

God broke into the confinement of the *aeon,* human beings were in helpless bondage, and after the apocalypse (revelation), human beings are set free through Christ.

Paul's ethic of freedom is based on Christ's liberation of those who are enslaved to the power of sin and death. The Chinese understanding of freedom from the perspective of *dao,* the order of things, is that individual and community ought to follow the right course in tune with how things are, as ordered by *dao.*

The Dialectical Relationship between Theology and Ethics: Transcendent and Immanent *Tian* (Heaven)

Dao is not just a total mystery but a Way. In fact, *dao,* understood as the Way in Chinese culture, often means the expression of the transcendent in a concrete manner, such as the moral order in the ethical realm. The dialectical relationship between *dao* (Way) and *de* (morality) in classical Confucianism is the union between theology and ethics, which depends on the union between *Tian* and humanity. For example, filial pietists seek the union of the *dao* and *de* in the actualization of selfhood in cosmic harmony. According to *Hsiao Ching (The Classics of Filial Piety),* "Filial Piety is the first principle of heaven, the ultimate standard of earth, the norm of conduct for the people."[32] Because of the unity between *dao* and *de,* Chinese people seek to follow the pattern of heaven and earth and hope that they will be led by the rightness of the heavens and the benefits of the earth to harmonize all under heaven.

Because of Confucius's preoccupation with political ethics, many have categorized him as a humanist with no awareness of religion. It is true that his understanding of *Tian* (heaven) is limited, but, besides his own religious life of offering prayers and sacrifices, Confucius does have the understanding that *Tian* is both a transcendent and an immanent cosmic principle. The transcendence is the creative *dao,* an elusive aspect of *Tian;* the immanence is the all-pervading life-force of *Tian.*[33] One stands in awe

32. Chiu, *The Tao of Chinese Religion,* 348.

33. Donald Alexander, "The Concept of *T'ien* in Early Confucian Thought," *His Dominion* 11 (1985): 14. Cf. *Mencius* 5.a.2. *Mencius, Chung Yung (Doctrine of the Mean), Analects,* and *Great Learning* are the four Confucian classics. The Chinese text I am using is *The Four Books* (Hunan: Hunan, 1995).

of the greatness and creativity of *Tian.*[34] For Confucius, transcendence is best known in immanence; in other words, ethics reveals one's relationship with *Tian.*

The Confucian *Tian* is not incarnated as a human being. In Confucius's understanding, human beings do not become *Tian*/divine; the Confucian goal is harmony between *Tian* and humanity. Human beings are to actualize in their moral lives the creativity and goodness of *Tian.* To be human as *ren ren* (loving others) fulfills the mandate of heaven, so that all may live in righteousness and orderliness in relation to others as a society of sacredness. In other words, the mandate of heaven is given to human beings so that they can be moral selves as the free expression of their oneness with *Tian.*[35]

The ancient classic *The Book of Odes,* which Confucius respected, says, "*Tian* gave birth to the multitude of people, where there is a thing, there is a principle; that is why people hold to rightness and like this natural, beautiful virtue."[36] Confucius does not mention this poem in the *Analects,* but a similar concept of this "transcendence/immanence" of *Tian* is expressed there. Confucius assumes that all humans come from *Tian* the Creator and that morality *(de)* is endowed from *Tian.* The mandate of heaven is given to all humanity for them to be moral selves as the expression of their oneness with *Tian.* Hence, Confucius believes that the ethical responsibilities of being human are concrete expressions of the transcendent *Tian.* He emphasizes that the sage-rulers are to be virtuous, providing an example for others to follow and thus bringing about the renovation of society (*The Great Learning* 1:1). *The Doctrine of Mean* likewise states that if a sage-ruler knows how to cultivate his own character, he will know how to govern other people (20:11). Confucius's genius is that he transforms the concept of the mandate of heaven from a highly political mandate for the ruling family to a universal responsibility of all human beings. Unfortunately, his legacy has often been reversed in ruler-cults where Confucianism is used to ritualize Confucius's ethics and subsume love under *li* (holy ceremonies). The result is the domination of the socially inferior by emperors who see themselves as sons of heaven and fathers of citizens.

34. *Doctrine of the Mean* 33; *Analects* 16:8; Alexander, "Concept of *T'ien,*" 15.

35. See Chen Chung-Ying, "Confucian Onto-Hermeneutics: Morality and Ontology," *Journal of Chinese Philosophy* 27 (2000): 35.

36. Chae-Woon Na, "Filial Piety in Confucian Thought," *North-East Asia Journal of Theology* 28/29 (1982): 40.

I find in Rom. 1:18-32 something similar to the Confucian understanding of *dao* and *Tian* and the dialectical relationship between transcendent and immanent *Tian* (and hence between *dao* and *de*). While the cultural contexts are different, it strikes me that Romans presents an argument whose logical structure has affinities with the Chinese traditions we have been considering. Paul argues that all humans are accountable before God on the basis of the knowledge they have of God.

The nature of the truth about God available to all is described in Rom. 1:19 and 32. This truth is not innate in humans but is rather revealed to them. All know the invisible qualities of God spelled out in 1:20 as the "eternal power" and "divine nature" of God. "Eternal power" refers to the witness to God in the power, mystery, and greatness of God in the awesome creation. "Divine nature" refers to God's supremacy over all deities. Although God is invisible, God is manifested indirectly in the effects of God's creative act and ongoing sustenance of creation. This manifestation of God calls for worship. Human creatures are to worship and honor God as the Creator. There is a structural similarity here with the Chinese concept of the *dao* as the Transcendent revealed to humanity and making human beings accountable for their response to the revelation of the *dao.*

The other aspect of the manifestation of God is the "moral oughtness" for humanity. This is referred to as "God's righteous decree" in Rom. 1:32, the righteous actions required by God. There are certain elementary ethical precepts that all human beings know. The human desire to do good rather than evil is evident in all cultures, even though different peoples (and individuals) disagree about the definition of the good. For Paul, the universality of human knowledge of the moral ought makes all "without excuse" (1:20). The knowledge or manifestation itself is clear and sufficient, Paul thinks, for all human beings to be held accountable before God. People have failed to live according to this knowledge of God and have instead "suppressed the truth" (1:18). "Knowing God, they did not revere God as God or give thanks" (1:21). They "exchanged the glory of the immortal God for images" (1:23), "exchanged the truth of God for a lie" (1:25), and "did not consider it worthwhile to retain the knowledge of God they had" (1:28). Thus, Paul's creation theology of the immanent ethic grounded in knowledge of God resembles the *dao de* or transcendent and immanent *Tian* of Daoism and Confucianism. The revelation of the *dao* makes human beings accountable to live the way of the *dao de.*

But there are also differences between Paul's understanding of God's general revelation and the Chinese conceptions of *dao de.* First, Paul takes a pessimistic view of humanity's moral condition and interprets it as slavery to sin, the only answer to which is liberation through God's redemptive work in Christ. Second, Paul understands that human moral failure makes humanity subject to God's wrath. By contrast, the *dao* is not a personal divinity who brings wrath on humanity or saves humanity through redemptive historical activity. The moral consequence for wrongdoing is not divine retribution but the negative effects of the wrong actions themselves, the way they disturb the harmony of relationships between human beings and heaven.

Confucian and Pauline Ethics

To Be Holy and Human

While the language systems used in Confucian and Pauline ethics are not the same (one is political, the other theological), Paul concurs with Confucius that ethics is theological in the sense that ethics is graced by God. Yet, there is a difference. According to Confucius, being human *is* being a holy person (being religious or pious). According to Paul, being sanctified (being holy) *is to become* authentically human (conformed to the image of the second Adam, Jesus Christ). Confucius approaches anthropology from a cosmological and social-political perspective. Paul approaches anthropology from a theological and christological perspective that views true humanity as the new human being created by God in Christ (Gal. 3:26-28; 2 Cor. 3:18; 5:17). By contrast, Confucius understands being human as the endowment of *Tian.*

While Paul's egalitarian notion of human beings is christologically grounded, the Confucian notion of equality of human beings is grounded in the order of heaven. *Doctrine of the Mean* (1.1) says, "What Heaven has conferred is called the nature." All persons are born equal with the same nature, which they receive from Heaven. Heaven is just in the sense that all are created morally equal. Mencius describes the universal feeling of commiseration that all have upon seeing a child fall into a well (2.a.6). Every person has that feeling of commiseration because every person has the same human nature, the gift of *Tian.* "Feeling of commiseration is the beginning of *ren* (love)." The universal *ren* is the ultimate goodness in the universe and is also found in human nature, the *"pen-shin"* (original nature), as Mencius sees it. To realize the moral ideal as a moral subject is the task of each individual as he or she participates in the ultimate good *(Tian* or *dao).*

Paul sees the life of holiness as the "obedience of faith" (Rom. 1:5; 16:26), humanity's faithful response to divine grace. The Pauline view assumes the enslaving power of sin and therefore the need of divine grace, enabling power, through "being in Christ." For Paul mercy, forgiveness, and reconciliation through Christ's work on the cross break the dominating power of sin and death, and believers are enabled to live a holy life before God and neighbor through the faith that incorporates them into Christ by baptism. In contrast, Confucius's cosmic-ethical conception of selfhood understands grace as *given to all in creation.* And because there is no fallenness of humanity, there is no need for a redemptive union in which human beings are drawn into a special divine grace.

Confucian ethics is based on *yi* (righteousness) and on the goodness of human nature *(xing),* while Pauline anthropology has to consider the reign of sin and then how God's work in Christ overcomes sin. But we can somewhat lessen the distance between Confucianism and Paul by adopting the Mencian interpretation of human nature and comparing it to Paul's idea of sin as an external force. Whether there is a sharp difference between Pauline and Confucianist anthropology is difficult to tell because Mencius, the greatest disciple of Confucius, interprets the "goodness of human nature" not in the sense that humans never sin or that human nature is entirely good. Mencius means that all human beings have goodness in their nature. Mencius also says that the normal or normative human nature is good, that humans sin because of circumstances and not because of their inborn created nature,[37] and that practical human goodness requires that human beings fully develop the "beginning" *(tuan)* of inherent *ren* (love), *yih* (righteousness), *li* (propriety), and *chih* (wisdom). Human nature is naturally good in the sense that water naturally flows downward (Mencius 6.a.2). But he would probably agree that many people live in an upside-down world, under circumstances that misdirect human goodness. Paul does not see human beings as naturally good, but he does view human wrongdoing as a result, at least in part, of spiritual forces operating contex-

37. "Just as barley will produce a good or bad crop depending on cultivation, soil, rainfall despite the fact that the seeds are the same" (*Mencius* 3.a.4).

tually on human moral agents. According to many scholars, Paul speaks of the human tendency to sin by considering sin an external force or power (e.g., in Romans 6–7).[38] Thus, sin is a power or spiritual context (lordship) in which human beings are trapped. Redemption is a transfer of lordship from the sphere of sin to the sphere of Christ.

A further question is whether Paul would agree with Confucius regarding law as a way to achieve the freedom to do good. If by "law" we mean a body of teaching about morally required behaviors, then the Pharisee Paul may have seen the Law as a way to freedom and righteousness, but the Christian Paul does not. Confucius holds that *li* (rites or holy ceremonies) are necessary to moral formation. And Confucius is more optimistic than Paul about the possibilities for human moral actualization because of his assumptions about the goodness of human nature and the activity of grace in all people through self-cultivation. Paul is pessimistic (and, I think, more realistic) about human moral incapacity because of his assumptions about the dominating power of sin and the necessity for redemption as a precondition of the moral life. Nevertheless, we should not paint these contrasts too sharply in view of some of the qualifications and alternative possibilities mentioned above.

Confucian ethics views the holy life (idealized as the life of the sage) as an attainment of virtues in community (self-cultivation through community). Paul sees the holy life (what many Christian traditions call "sanctification") as the fruit of freedom from the power of sin and new life in the Spirit (Romans 5–8, Galatians 5). This does not mean that there are no more temptations and that one enters into a life of perfection. Rather, it means that the power of sin is broken; sin loses its power to reign over believers who now participate in the liberating death and resurrection of

38. If Paul has a Jewish understanding of sin as the *yetzer hara'* (evil impulse) that incites human beings to choose sin, and if the *yetzer hara'* is conceived as an external power, then Paul's anthropology is somewhat closer to *Mencius's* understanding. However, there are also good reasons for seeing the *yetzer hara'* as a dynamic immanent within the human person, just as sin in Romans 7 may also be understood as a tendency of the human person (or what "dwells in the flesh"). It may be best to think of "sin" in Paul and the *yetzer hara'* in ancient Jewish thinking as dynamics that have both internal and external dimensions. On Paul's thinking in connection with ideas about the *yetzer* in Second Temple Judaism, see Joel Marcus, "The Evil Inclination in the Letters of Paul," *Irish Biblical Studies* 8 (1986): 8-21. On good and evil impulses within a person according to rabbinic traditions, see W. D. Davies, *Paul and Rabbinic Judaism* (second edition, London: SPCK, 1955), 24-26, 30-31.

Christ. Moreover, Paul understands this as a process that assumes the limitations of human moral nature even in Christ (Rom. 6:19). Confucian ethics would not go so far as Paul and say that the power of sin is broken, because Confucian ethics does not regard sin as enslaving, such that the one who wants to do the good cannot do it (contrast Rom. 7:15-20). Moreover, Confucian ethics does not speak of strength beyond that common grace given to every person and actualized in self-cultivation, a moral formation that takes place properly in community under the guidance of traditional morality.

The Mandate of Heaven and "Love Your Neighbor"

Both the Confucian and the Pauline ethical systems emphasize that the ethical life is relational. For Paul, the Christian belongs to the holy God in a new community under the obligation to "do good to everyone" — to the household of faith and to the world (Gal. 6:10). For Confucius, one belongs to the transcendent *Tian,* which expresses itself in harmonious moral relationships with family, society, and the wider human community. Both Paul and Confucius understand the process of moral formation as growing in love for neighbor. For Paul this growth is directed toward the ultimate goal of realizing the image of God in the believer. This life of love towards one's neighbor expresses a life of faith and love toward God. While Christians are not under law but under grace, they are under "the law of Christ" (Gal. 6:2) and are being conformed to the image of Christ (2 Cor. 3:18; Gal. 4:19). Confucius advocates that all are to actualize the mandate of *Tian* by committing themselves to *ren,*[39] because what makes human beings human is *ren.*[40] In other words, the will of God for any community is to practice a life of love.

Confucius regards *ren* as the fountainhead of all virtues. The word *ren* in Chinese characters is composed of two ideograms: "person," con-

39. Chiu, *The Tao of Chinese Religion,* 191-92.

40. Translated variously as "human-heartedness" (E. R. Hughes), "benevolence," "love" (Derk Bodde), "benevolent Love" (H. H. Dubs), "humane," "human-at-its-best," "goodness" (A. Waley), "humanity," "virtue" (H. G. Creel), "human-relatedness," "charity," "humanity" (W. T. Chan), "morality," "compassion" (Lin Yutang), "human-to-humanness" (F. S. C. Northrop), etc. See Fung Yu-lan, *A Short History of Chinese Philosophy,* ed. Derk Bodde (New York: Macmillan, 1948), 69-73.

noting self, and "two," connoting relation or "co-humanity."[41] Etymologically, *ren* is to be translated simply as human-relatedness, and human-relatedness is defined specifically as love, which is the cardinal principle of human relationships.[42] Fang Ying-hsien expresses this "in terms of two semiotic foci: *ren* is (1) the tender aspect of human feelings, namely, love, and (2) an altruistic concern for others. . . ."[43] In *Doctrine of the Mean,* "*ren* is human, and the greatest exercise of it is in loving relations" (20:5). Mencius says that "*ren* is the distinguishing characteristic of human" (7.b.16). He argues that filial love is the universal work of righteousness (7.a.15). *Ren* is to be empathic/conscientious *(chung)* and merciful/reciprocal (*shu, Analects* 4:15). *Ren* connotes all the moral qualities that govern the relationships between two or more human beings.[44] Therefore, the good society is one in which people treat each other as human *(ren)* out of the love in *chung* and *shu.*[45] Paul's reinterpretation of the Law makes the similar point that the new life in Christ means loving one's neighbors, which fulfills the Law (Gal. 5:13-15; Rom. 8:4; 13:8-10). Thus, just as *ren* is for Confucious the animating principle and goal of *li,* so love for Paul is the animating principle and goal of the Law. But for Paul there are also dangers in the Law. Sin can use the good Law to incite those who want to please God by doing the Law to do the opposite (Romans 7). Moreover, the Law can become an occasion for ethnic boasting (Rom. 2:17-28; 3:27-31).

To Be Fully Human by Differentiation and Socialization

In the Confucian worldview, the complex interrelationship of human affairs is to be the scene of differentiation and strengthening of personhood in *ren* and *li.* Personhood in individuation is practiced in

41. Tu Wei-ming says, "Etymologically *ren* consists of two parts, one a simple ideogram of a human figure, meaning the self, and the other with two horizontal strokes, suggesting human relations." See Tu Wei-ming, *Confucian Thought: Selfhood as Creative Transformation* (Albany: SUNY Press, 1985), 84. Cf. Wing-tsit Chan, "Chinese and Western Interpretations of *Ren* (Humanity)," *Journal of Chinese Philosophy* 2 (1975): 108-9.

42. Fung, *Short History of Chinese Philosophy,* 69-73; Chan, "Chinese and Western Interpretations of *Ren,*" 109.

43. As quoted in Tu, *Confucian Thought,* 84.

44. Fung, *Short History of Chinese Philosophy,* 69-73; Chan, "Chinese and Western Interpretations of *Ren,*" 109.

45. Chiu, *Tao of Chinese Religion,* 77-78.

ren (love) and *li.* Individuation and the actualization of personhood take place in dyadic social relations that make us fully human.[46] The Confucian notion of the human being is essentially that of a social person who learns the science and art of adjusting to the world.[47] In other words, Confucius sees liberal education not only as book-learning but also as ritual and cultural practice, which reinforce the interaction of self with the larger community (from self to home to society to nation to the world). This constant reinforcement serves as a process of self-cultivation if it is practiced in the spirit of loyalty, reverence, brotherhood, discipleship, and so forth.

We authenticate our being, thus becoming fully human, not by detaching ourselves from the world but by making sincere attempts to harmonize our relationships with others. With regard to the social dimension of self-cultivation (as the process of becoming fully human), Confucius says, "Virtue does not exist in isolation; there must be neighbors" (*Analects* 4:25).[48] Elsewhere he says, "In order to establish oneself, one helps others to establish themselves; in order to enlarge oneself, one helps others to enlarge themselves" (6:28). The human person is transformed by participation with others in ceremony, which is communal. And that is the mandate of heaven, that all may live in righteousness and orderliness in relation to others in and as a society of sacredness. Human nature is to be cultivated as individuation and socialization. To be a *ren ren* (a loving person) is to participate in the holy as a dimension of all truly human existence. Fingarette writes, "Human life in its entirety finally appears as one vast, spontaneous and Holy Rite: the community of man [humanity]."[49] To be a *ren ren* is to be courteous, diligent, loyal,

46. Tu Wei-ming observes this Confucian understanding of self-cultivation in the social dyad. Tu argues that "a social dyad is not a fixed entity, but a dynamic interaction involving a rich and ever-changing texture of human-relatedness woven by the constant participation of other significant dyadic relationships." See Tu, *Confucian Thought,* 237.

47. M. Weber, *The Religion of China: Confucianism and Taoism,* trans. H. H. Gerth (Glencoe: Free, 1951), 235.

48. In the first instance, this link is to the general reciprocal good faith and respect among people *(shu* and *chung);* in the second instance this reciprocal good faith is given a specific content: it is that set of specific social relationships articulated in detail by *li.* In short, where reciprocal good faith and respect are expressed through the specific forms defined in *li,* there is *ren*'s way. See Herbert Fingarette, *Confucius: The Secular as Sacred* (New York: Harper and Row, 1972), 42.

49. Fingarette, *Confucius,* 17. See *Analects* 3:17; 4:5; 6:8. For a different interpretation of

brave, broad, and kind (*Analects* 13:19; 14:5; 17:6), displaying these virtues in the public, social sphere.

Paul never treats the question of society per se. Nevertheless, his discussions of the relations of Jews and gentiles in God's saving purpose and his descriptions of the church provide clues to how he thinks about sociality. Paul insists that the gospel is God's revelation that gentiles are not to be absorbed as Jewish proselytes into the new people of God in Christ; the uncircumcised and the circumcised have Abraham as their father through faith (Rom. 3:30; 4:12, 16). Likewise, God bestows the Spirit on gentiles as gentiles, on those who share the faith of Abraham, not because they are Law-keepers or Jewish proselytes (Gal. 3:1-5). Thus, in addressing the question of the social distinctions between Jews and non-Jews, Paul argues for a preservation of difference in a commonality of faith: unity in social diversity.

Li *and Torah in Confucian and Pauline Theological Ethics*

The primary difference between Confucian and Pauline ethics concerns the use of rules/law to attain a sanctified life or life of perfection. According to Confucius, *li* (holy ceremony) is the structure of love, the ritual that makes one human. Etymologically, the ideograph *li* symbolizes a sacrificial act. Wing-tsit Chan points out that it originally meant "a religious sacrifice." However, the earliest available dictionary meaning of *li* is "treading" or "following." Specifically, it points to the act or ritual whereby spiritual beings are properly served so that human happiness is obtained. To live a life of *li* is to be in a cultured yet natural pattern of interpersonal relationship that "works through spontaneous coordination rooted in reverent dignity."[50]

According to Confucius, "[w]hen a person is born, his nature is straight" (*Analects* 6:19), and "human nature is closely similar, but the habits of people are widely different" (17:2). All are endowed with the same "seed of humanity," but whether every person will cultivate the seed to its full potential is another matter. In other words, the equality of human beings is equal possibility for actualization. Confucius also affirms an equal-

ren and *li* in Confucius's thought, see Fung, *Short History of Chinese Philosophy,* 72-72, 94; also Tu, *Confucian Thought,* 81-92.

50. Fingarette, *Confucius,* 8. See *Analects* 2:3; 13:3.

ity of the value of a human qua human.[51] Confucius and Mencius do not attribute a full human nature to the person; they often talk of the "seed" or "beginning" of human nature or *ren*. This perspective led Confucianism to develop an ethical system aimed at helping people to actualize themselves, a system based on rules of propriety.

Paul argues that Christian sanctification can*not* be attained by means of the Law (Rom. 7:14-25) but only by means of "the law of the Spirit" (8:2). Speaking of his past self under the Law, Paul says that he wanted to do good but did evil (Romans 7), just as his zeal for the Law led him to become a persecutor of the church, God's people (Galatians 1). As a Pharisee Paul wanted all to be the people of God through obedience to the Law (which was good), but he persecuted the church (which was evil). Paul's strong desire, will, intention, or zeal to conform to the Law as a Pharisee was at odds with his performance. Despite his delight in the Law (Rom. 7:22), his approval of it as good (7:16, 23), and his desire to keep it (7:18, 19, 21), he was defeated by sin, by "another law at work in my members" (7:23). He became a wretched or miserable person, a man in despair (7:24). Freedom comes through the Spirit's deliverance. The Spirit liberates believers from the tyranny of sin's misuses of the Law (compare Rom. 7:13-20 with 8:1-4).

Paul thus knew from personal experience that piety may result in violence against one's neighbor. His call (Gal. 1:13-14) involved a personal transformation. He realized that his perfection and faithfulness to the Law led him to persecute Christ's own. In those moments when he thought he was showing zealous love for God, he was doing violence to others in God's name. The conundrum of any religion is that zealots use holy swords and the faithful hate infidels.

Confucius does not speak of sin as a power that misuses *li*, but he is aware of the danger of ritualism and legalism. That is why he wants to ground *li* in *ren*. For it is possible that one loves another merely for the sake of doing the commandment (as a religious achievement and a noble task). Loving for the sake of filial piety can be superficial. For example, "Merely to feed one's parents for the sake of piety without reverence . . . even dogs and horses are fed" (*Analects* 2:7). Merely doing what *li* expects is

51. Hsieh Yu-Wei, "The Status of the Individual in Chinese Ethics," in *The Chinese Mind: Essentials of Chinese Philosophy and Culture*, ed. Charles A. Moore (Honolulu: University Press of Hawaii, 1967), 310.

superficial; what is essential is a higher principle than that structure, and that is *ren*. Therefore, *li* must be grounded in *ren*.[52] In a similar vein, Paul says that the whole Law is fulfilled in the command to love one's neighbor as oneself (Gal. 5:14; Rom. 13:8-10). Whatever obligation Christians have to the Law is to be carried out with love as its guiding principle.

Freedom and Community

Both Paul and Confucius lived in cultures that valued community. The Chinese understanding of the human self as a social entity strikes a harmonious chord with Paul's understanding of community. Family is important to both, and just as Confucius thought of the family as part of a virtually seamless web of expanding networks, encompassing society, nation, and cosmos, so people in Paul's day thought of the family as a microcosm of the universe, which was ordered in the same (patriarchal) way. Paul inherited this view from his culture, but also radically modified it by speaking of a new creation in which the church as the family of God becomes the fundamental unity of sociality, a new community for the new creation.

Throughout his letters, Paul assumes the priority of community over individuality. His metaphor of the body of Christ in 1 Corinthians 12 shows that, while he calls for the Corinthians to value the contribution of each member, the purpose of the gifts bestowed on the individual by the Spirit are for the upbuilding of the whole body. Likewise, Confucian ethics regards communal edification as the ultimate goal of being human. In the words of Confucius, the aim of Confucian ethics is "to demonstrate illustrious virtue, renovate the people, and rest in the highest excellence."[53] Re-

52. This is what Tu Wei-ming means by "the primacy of *ren* over *li* and the inseparability of *li* from *ren*." See Tu Wei-ming, "*Li* as Process of Humanization," *Philosophy East and West* (1972), 188.

53. *The Great Learning* 1:1. The naming of that way of life as philosophy, ethics, or spirituality is itself an intellectual controversy. T'ang Chün-I, for example, explains that "love and respect for one's parents is not biological but is moral, being based upon a sense of obligation or a debt of gratitude, and is therefore spiritual" (Moore, ed., *The Chinese Mind*, 186). Also note the autobiography of Confucius: "At 15, I set my mind on learning; at 30, I stood firm; at 40, I had no doubts; at 50, I knew the mandate of Heaven; at 60, I was at ease with whatever I heard; at 70 I could follow my heart's desire without transgressing moral principles" (*Analects* 2:4).

lationships are essential to the practice of Confucian ethics, as the Five Cardinal Relations show. The relations are worked out in pairs with corresponding virtues: ruler to subjects (human-heartedness and reverence), father and son (compassion and filial piety), husband and wife (righteousness and obedience), older and younger brothers (mutual respect), and friends (affection, loyalty, and trust).

This is not to imply that Confucius and Paul have no concept of individual rights. It only means that individual rights are understood from the standpoint of communal obligations. For example, Confucius understands freedom as directed toward others; once others are free, I will be free as well. Freedom is directed to a moral purpose. Hsieh Yu-Wei says, "The freedom advocated in Confucian ethics is the freedom to do good or the freedom to choose what is good. It is ethical freedom of choice."[54] This freedom depends on community: "When I walk alone with two others, they may serve me as my teachers. Choose what is good and follow it, but avoid what is evil" (*Analects* 7:21). "The superior person is an ecumenical and not a sectarian" (2:14).

The Confucian notion of choosing the good means to choose *ren* because *ren* is the objective principle. Thus, freedom is also self-mastery. "Yen Yüan asked about *ren*. The Master said, 'To subdue one's self and return to propriety is *ren*. If a person can for one day subdue himself and return to propriety, all under Heaven will ascribe *ren* to him'" (*Analects* 12:1). Chen Chung-Ying writes, ". . . once one can do right things without reliance on outside authority, one may be said to achieve moral autonomy and moral maturity. This inner transformation with larger and deeper moral freedom and social responsibility speaks to Confucius's notion of 'self-cultivation' of virtues one finds originating from oneself."[55]

Cruciform Love

For Paul the freedom of the Spirit is freedom for love in community (Gal. 5:1–6:10). The positive goal of freedom through Christ is to be "enslaved to one another through love" (5:13). This positive purpose has its equalizing effect of changing the object of freedom from carnal self-existence to love

54. Hsieh Yu-Wei, "The Status of the Individual in Chinese Ethics," 310.
55. Chen, "Confucian Onto-Hermeneutics," 35.

and service to others, "doing good to all, especially those of the household of faith" (6:10). Love or *ren* is intentional action that reaches out and relates to others with the purpose of sharing and building up relationships (cf. 1 Cor. 8:1).

By sending his Son and his Spirit to humanity, God reached out to humanity in the most intimate, personal, and worthy manner to create new community. God showed love to humanity in the cross of Christ, even while we were God's enemies (Rom. 5:10). Christ's faithfulness reveals that God's righteousness is made available to all according to the principle of faith (trust) rather than in strict conformity to a cultural or religious system. God's love in Christ makes room for all to be fully human through love, conformed to the image of Christ, who is the expression of God's love. This love is defined by God's love in Christ. God in the crucified Christ voluntarily limited the divine infinity through an incarnation of love and servanthood that exhibits full trust in God and radical vulnerability and service to others (Phil. 2:5-11; Gal. 1:4; 2:20). God's love in Christ pursues humanity through such deep humiliation and lowliness that Christ became "a curse for us" (Gal. 3:13). The sovereign God above all things is the God who in Christ becomes the ultimate outcast, the cursed one, the marginalized neighbor.

As the manifestation of cruciform love in Christ shows and as Paul's hymn to love in 1 Corinthians 13 teaches, love is not self-centered but other-centered. It does not require equal reciprocity of reward or justice of payment in return. It does not manipulate others to its own ends or put others at risk in order to minimize the risk of self. To be human, conformed to the image of the new humanity in Christ, is to be bound to God and bound to love for our neighbors. The test of faith and piety comes when our neighbors are our enemies. While sometimes our enemies turn out to be good neighbors, cruciform love will continue even if neighbors are enemies. Cruciform love is the law of life in God's sovereign rule because the reign of God is the reign of love. Love is the greatest of the great virtues that survive into eternity (1 Cor. 13:13), the power and purpose of God's own vocation to become "all in all" (15:28).

From Confucius I learn that *ren ren,* being a loving person, makes us fully human and at one with the ultimate good *(Tian).* From Paul I learn that *ren ren* is cruciform love leading us toward God's "all in all."

A Practical Example of Chinese Christian Piety in Pauline Perspective: Ancestor Veneration

I will conclude this study by illustrating some of the practical implications of the dialogue between Paul and Confucius for Chinese Christian life, focusing on the institution of ancestor veneration or worship.[56]

Ancestor worship is rooted in the ethics and spirituality of *hsiao* (filial piety). The word *hsiao* is made up of two radicals, an old person and a child, denoting the responsibility of the child to support the older person. According to *Hsiao Ching (The Classics of Piety)* "the relation and duties between parent and child belong to the Heaven-conferred nature."[57] Confucianism emphasizes filial piety as a way of life ordained by heaven, a path to right relations between heaven and humanity and among human beings.

The virtue of filial piety is rooted in the cosmic and spiritual value systems of *li* and *ren ren*. As *Hsiao Ching* declares, "It is filial piety that forms the root of all virtues, and with it all enlightening studies come into existence."[58] Hence, ancestor veneration, as an expression of filial piety, contributes to the moral formation of the individual and the community. It also promotes the continuity of identity through lineage and family and has the memorial value of preserving the stories of the past, as well as the creative function of envisioning the future of the family. Finally, ancestor veneration provides for times of family reunion and for care for bereaved family members.

The practice of ancestor veneration involves a domestic shrine, typically containing a photograph of deceased parents or grandparents. Sacrifices and prayers are regularly offered before this shrine.[59] On special occasions, notably the birthday of the ancestor, the family shares a meal before the shrine, which is understood as a meal with the dead, a communion be-

56. The term "ancestor *worship*" can be misleading, since not all who practice ancestor veneration engage in acts of worship toward their ancestors or think of their ancestors as divine beings. The term "veneration," which I have adopted here, is softer and broader, covering both attitudes and actions of worshipful reverence and attitudes and practices of respect. Indeed, many Chinese prefer to speak simply of honor and respect for ancestors rather than of worship. Nevertheless, in many contexts "worship" is apt, as will become clear below.

57. *Hsiao Ching* 9. I use a Chinese text of the *Classics of Filial Piety* published in Taiwan. The Chinese title, publisher, and author are difficult to render into English, so I will not include them here.

58. *Hsiao Ching* 1.

59. Candles, incense, and paper money are used in these ceremonial acts. The money is buried with the deceased (or on certain days burned) to assure the prosperity of the deceased.

tween the living and the departed. Among Chinese Christians, the sharing of meals before the ancestral shrines is very rare, but it can be understood spiritually as an expression of the communion of saints in anticipation of the future resurrection of the dead.

There is a common Chinese belief that gods are the ghosts *(kui)* of departed human beings who dwell in the *yin* ("shady") world of *im-kan* ("prisons of earth"). Living human beings inhabit the *yang* ("sunny") world. In this cosmology, ancestors are seen as mediators between human beings and the supernatural. If the living family does not care for the deceased's soul, the soul degenerates into *kui,* a ghost or demon. But if sacrifice and prayers are offered, the soul of the ancestor can be elevated to the status of a spiritual being or *shen* (a god or *yang* soul). Hence, in addition to the motive of devotion to parents, many Chinese also practice ancestor veneration as a way of placating demons,[60] cursing enemies, and securing blessings from the *shen.*

The value of filial piety expressed in ancestor veneration is in some ways compatible with Paul's understanding of the moral life as a practice of the love we owe to every human being (Rom. 13:8-10). Nevertheless, Paul nowhere singles out parents for special devotion, and he elevates the spiritual family in Christ above all other relations: "So then, whenever we have an opportunity, let us work for the good of all, and especially for those of the family of faith" (Gal. 6:10, NRSV). Furthermore, the idea that the departed acquire spiritual powers to bless or hurt the living and must therefore be treated well in order that the living may prosper and avoid harm contradicts Paul's theology in fundamental ways. Paul proclaims that Christ has been exalted above all the powers of the world. All blessing comes through his death and resurrection and cannot be obtained through any kind of human "work," whether "works of the Law" or "*li*," including acts of ancestor veneration.

Another point of tension is the strongly hierarchical nature of the Confucian worldview, which casts women and children as inferior persons. Ancestor worship reinforces this assumption of filial piety. By contrast, Paul celebrates the equality of male and female in Christ.[61] Not only

60. In addition to prayers and offerings, another way of pleasing the ancestors and avoiding harm from them is *fung sui,* a form of geomancy. The technique is to curry the favor of the ancestor by locating the grave at a good site and invoking the help of shamans who can mediate between the living and the dead.

61. I do not mean to claim that Paul is a thoroughgoing egalitarian in the modern sense. Nevertheless, there are important ways in which Paul undercuts the patriarchy of his

Gal. 3:28 but also Paul's recognition of a woman apostle (Rom. 16:7), among other things, reflects this. Paul's anthropology is also more pessimistic than that of Confucianism. Chinese Christians can learn from Paul that *li*, including its expression in acts of filial piety, does not have the power to break sin's grip over humanity. Moral formation through *li* animated by *ren ren* needs something more than the right social context and good intentions. It requires death to self and the world through the cross of Christ (Romans 6; Gal. 2:20; 6:14).

This suggests that Paul's theology calls for Chinese Christians to abandon the assumptions and practice of ancestor veneration or to reshape them in the light of the Pauline gospel so that they express, rather than conflict with, that gospel of the crucified and exalted Christ, who is lord of the powers and who creates a new spiritual family in which old relationships are brought to an end and love reaches out not just to one's biological family and one's friends but to all, even to outsiders and enemies.

My extended family in China is not Christian and does practice ancestor veneration. My immediate family does not, but I advocate a "mild" form of veneration (most Chinese Christians prefer to say "respect" or "honor"). Nevertheless, this evokes considerable resistance in Chinese churches. I think Chinese churches are overly cautious and strongly Westernized on this issue. I advocate a strong enculturation of the Confucian ethic for the Chinese family in the modern age, so that the virtues of honoring ancestors and elders are restored in a critically appropriated and thoughtfully informed manner. I also advocate that Chinese churches help families to claim their Chinese Christian identities as we come up with creative ways of honoring, communing with, and extending care to our ancestors and elders. "All Saints Day" can serve as the ritual whereby we relate to our ancestors within the context of the Christian hope that they exist in the memory of our God. But more can be done. The *li* (propriety) of ancestor veneration is about realizing the moral and spiritual aspirations of our ancestors. It is not simply about burning incense and asking for blessings, but loving our neighbors, helping the poor, contributing to the welfare of a community, and the like, all done in the name of our God and surrounded by our "cloud of witnesses."

---

own time in view of the gospel of Jesus Christ. This point has been made by many, e.g., my *What Has Jerusalem to Do with Beijing?* 262-308.

CHAPTER 4

Paul and Peoplehood in African American Perspective

Charles H. Cosgrove

Many avenues suggest themselves as ways of approaching Paul from an African American perspective. I have chosen to write on "Paul and peoplehood" because this topic requires engagement with two very important impulses of the African American tradition: integrationism and nationalism.

The question of peoplehood concerns identity and raises the complex question of names. There is a long history of names for Americans of African descent — names chosen by "whites," the same names rejected, modified, or embraced by African Americans, who have also invented new names for themselves as acts of self-definition against outsider definitions and who continue to debate the question of names for themselves. Some of this history is suggested by the following sampling of names used by African Americans as self-designations — all used at various times during the nineteenth century: Black (capitalized or lower-case), Afro-American, Anglo-African, Black Saxon, Negrosaxon, Afric-American, men or people of color, sable. In what follows I use the now largely dominant "African American" except where I am describing an aspect of African American history to which another name closely attaches. Notable examples include nineteenth-century "black abolitionists," nineteenth- and twentieth-century forms of "black nationalism," twentieth-century "black power" and "black theology," and twentieth-century uses of "Negro" as a term of dignity. I should point out that "black" is still used by many Americans of African descent as a self-description (especially by the generation shaped by late 1960s consciousness) and hence is often a synonym for African American in current usage. From time to time I also use the term "black" in this general way.

History of Interpretation

Over the past twenty years or so, African American scholarship on Paul has entailed efforts not only to read Paul with African American concerns in mind but also to examine critically the history (and ruling assumptions) of Eurocentric interpretation of the Bible. One widely shared critical tenet of African American biblical scholarship is that every interpreter works out of a tradition of interpretation that gives his or her approach a distinctive shape and direction. There is no disinterested, neutral interpretation of the Bible. Hence, African American biblical scholarship appropriately includes, among other things, examination of the history of culturally dominant biblical interpretation for its racist ideology, including racist uses of Paul, and recovery of the history of African American biblical interpretation in order to engage that history as a *usable past*, a rich tradition inviting both critical and constructive engagement.

Retrieving that usable past for the interpretation of Paul means mining the record of a long history of religious and political appropriations of Paul in the African American tradition: references and allusions to Paul in spirituals, abolitionist speeches and writings, preaching, poetry, fiction, political analysis, and other forms of ecclesial and public discourse. Over the course of its history, African American interpretation of Paul has often shared features with dominant Anglo-American interpretation. Typically it has also been at odds with Anglo-American interpretation or given that interpretation a fresh slant or stamp.

Figurations of Paul in African American Discourse

I will use the term "figuration" to denote images and uses of Paul in the African American heritage. Paul has figured in a variety of roles in the some 200 years of African American interpretation of the Bible for which we have record. Eight notable figurations are Paul as pro-slavery advocate, Paul as prisoner, Paul as traveling missionary/apostle, Paul as preacher, Paul as convert, Paul as charismatic, Paul as quotable biblical authority, and Paul as sermon text. Space does not permit a detailed description of every one of these, but two — "pro-slavery Paul" and "quotable Paul" — deserve further comment in preparation for what follows.

Pro-slavery Paul is the Paul whom slaves encountered in the preaching and catechesis of the Southern plantation. In what has become a famous anecdote, Howard Thurman reported that his grandmother refused to read anything from Paul's letters except 1 Corinthians 13 because all her plantation master ever quoted from Paul was "Servants, obey your masters" (Col. 3:22; Eph. 6:5).[1] Similar testimony about the use of Paul is found in many nineteenth-century witnesses. Lewis Hayden, a black abolitionist, related how he used to attend a so-called "church" where he heard "that Gospel which is so peculiar to the South — '*Servant, obey thy master!*'" which is "the sum total of the Gospel which slaves have preached unto them."[2] This kind of preaching and teaching to slaves in Paul's name accounts for an understandable antipathy toward Paul among many African Americans, including twentieth-century intellectuals and leaders such as Howard Thurman, James Baldwin, James Cone, and Albert Cleage.[3]

Paul the quotable biblical authority is Paul in brief citation or allusion (phrase or sentence) to prove, illustrate, or ornament a point. In older African American discourse, passing quotations from Paul (and other parts of the Bible) are sometimes a type of ornamental literary device, like the literary quotations that grace so much refined discourse in the eighteenth and nineteenth centuries. Nevertheless, in African American discourse, most passing quotations from Paul's letters are one-sentence invocations of Paul's epistolary voice that illustrate, illumine, epitomize, judge,

1. Today, New Testament scholars doubt that Paul himself wrote Ephesians and debate whether Paul wrote Colossians. The words to slaves in these two letters probably express a later development of the Pauline tradition.

2. C. Peter Ripley, ed., *The Black Abolitionist Papers, 1830-1865*, 5 vols. (Chapel Hill: University of North Carolina Press, 1986-92), 4:266. For similar reports, see Daniel Payne, *The Voice of Black America: Major Speeches by Negroes in the United States*, ed. Philip S. Foner (New York: Simon and Schuster, 1972), 71; David Walker, *Walker's Appeal, in Four Articles, Together with a Preamble to the Colored Citizens of the World, but in Particular, and Very Expressly to Those of the United States of America* (second ed., 1830; reprint: New York: Arno, 1969), 51; an ex-slave in Clifton H. Johnson, ed., *God Struck Me Dead: Religious Conversion Experiences and Autobiographies of Ex-Slaves* (Cleveland: United Church Press, 1969), 134-35; Edward Scott in *The Black Abolitionist Papers*, 4:367; the court, pronouncing sentence, in the trial of Denmark Vesey in Robert S. Starobin, ed., *Denmark Vesey: The Slave Conspiracy of 1822* (Englewood Cliffs: Prentice-Hall, 1970), 34. See further Milton C. Sernett, *Black Religion and American Evangelicalism: White Protestants, Plantation Missions, and the Flowering of Negro Christianity, 1787-1865* (Metuchen: Scarecrow, 1975), 73-76.

3. See Allen Dwight Callahan, "'Brother Saul': An Ambivalent Witness to Freedom," *Semeia* 83/84 (1988): 247; Amos Jones, Jr., *Paul's Message of Freedom: What Does It Mean to the Black Church?* (Valley Forge: Judson, 1984), 5-7.

inspire, ironize, and comfort. Paul's words and authority are used to defend a position or to clothe some action, undertaking, or event in the mantle of Paul's language of faith. This style of quotation reflects a time when the Bible was the nation's book and formal public speech often contained familiar quotations from the Western literary canon. African Americans adopted this rhetorical tradition and used it to their own purposes, often turning the tradition against itself. In examining Paul in African American perspective, I have given such one-sentence quotations and allusions close attention.

Reading Paul: Contemporary African American Hermeneutics

A number of African American New Testament scholars have addressed themselves to hermeneutical questions regarding the significance and use of Paul. I will focus here on contributions by Abraham Smith, Vincent Wimbush, and Brian Blount.

In a paper dealing with slavery and Pauline hermeneutics, Abraham Smith discusses strategies of anti-slavery biblical interpretation that black abolitionist William Wells Brown uses in his novel *Clotel* to disarm pro-slavery interpretation of Paul.[4] One tack is to question and expose the motives of the pro-slavery interpreters. Another approach is to quote Paul against the pro-slavery position. A third strategy is to interpret Paul in a wider biblical context, including the witness of Jesus.[5] Smith uses the hermeneutical slogan "There's more in the text than that" (adapted from one of the characters in the novel) to express possibilities for emancipatory interpretation of Paul when Paul is read by those with a commitment to black liberation and when his letters are approached through a broader biblical tradition of emancipation and social justice.

4. Abraham Smith, "'There's More in the Text Than That': William Wells Brown's *Clotel*, Slave Ideology," in *Society of Biblical Literature 1997 Seminar Papers* 36 (Atlanta: Scholars, 1997), 618-36.

5. Smith treats these same themes in "Putting 'Paul' Back Together Again: William Wells Brown's *Clotel* and Black Abolitionist Approaches to Paul," *Semeia* 83/84 (1988): 251-62. In this essay, Smith stresses the importance of reading particular passages in Paul in the light of the broader Pauline corpus. In "There's More in the Text Than That," Smith also notes Brown's reading of Paul within the wider biblical canon, which strikes me as an especially important hermeneutical approach.

Smith offers Brown's hermeneutical approach as a useable tradition for contemporary African American interpretation of Paul. Here I draw (and affirm) two hermeneutical implications from Smith's essay: First, moral character shapes interpretation, such that interpretive decisions are also moral decisions (between competing interpretations). Second, the church's interpretive decisions in appropriating Paul for Christian faith and practice should be guided by the biblical witness as a whole, especially the social justice witness of the exodus, the prophets, and the life and teachings of Jesus.

Vincent Wimbush tackles questions regarding the interpretation and use of Paul through the lens of ancient ascetic formations. The ascetic impulse is a form of world-renunciation, typically motivated by a group's discovery of a new ideal.[6] Wimbush finds three forms of ascetic behavior in 1 Corinthians 7: (1) the asceticism of spiritual elites whose slogan is "all things are permitted," a stance toward bodily life that rejects worldly norms and conventions;[7] (2) an asceticism of non-elites (the so-called "weak"), whose orientation is "eat not, touch not," a stance that rejects a world in which the abstaining (who may be Jewish Christians) feel alien and estranged;[8] and (3) Paul's own "as-if-not" stance, a mediating position that calls for accepting the world "as the *sphere* of Christian existence" but not "the *source* of value and identity."[9] Wimbush further characterizes Paul's "as-if-not" stance as engaging the world through "rational critique of the structures and dominant order of the day," working out "differently ordered individual and group priorities, challenges, and social formations, all in the pursuit of the ideal of living out one's devotion to the Lord in the context of the city."[10]

The idea of Paul as a worldly ascetic has special affinities with what Wimbush calls *marronage:* the state of being socially "marooned" and constructing an alternative world in response. The concept of *marronage* de-

6. The perception of "a fundamental tension between the world and the new ideals inspired asceticism, behavior signifying a new critical attitude of resistance, a refusal to orient the body, indeed, the self, in the world in traditional or socially acceptable ways." See Vincent L. Wimbush, "The Ascetic Impulse in Early Christianity," *Theology Today* 50 (1993): 420-21.

7. Wimbush, "Ascetic Impulse," 422-24.

8. Wimbush, "Ascetic Impulse," 424-25.

9. Wimbush, "Ascetic Impulse," 425-28.

10. Wimbush, "Ascetic Impulse," 428.

rives from runaway slaves being called maroons (French *marron*). Wimbush uses *marronage* to denote flight from "white-world" and the establishment of an alternative world.[11] He identifies three stages of *marronage:* "(1) flight or marronage (de-formation), (2) settlement and building on a site of marronage (formation); and (3) self-making, self-naming and negotiation with the outside world from the site of marronage (reform[ul]ation)."[12] The entire history of African American life in America is one of *marronage,* expressed in these basic formations, which succeed each other without canceling each other. The Bible figures in these stages as a diverse fund of stories, prophetic speeches, visions, poetry, exhortation — "all of which have reflected and continue to reflect some parallel phases in African American formation and strivings."[13]

Wimbush does not spell out the connections between Paul's this-worldly asceticism and *marronage,* but his work as a whole suggests to me that Paul can be fruitfully interpreted via the concept of *marronage,* that he can be appropriated by Christians today as a biblical example of an ascetic response to the world through rational cultural critique, and that one way to interpret African American uses of Paul is to ask how a given figuration of Paul serves flight (de-formation), settlement (formation), and self-making (reform[ul]ation). Wimbush stresses that Paul's particular form of worldly asceticism is tied to his own cultural context and should not be adopted as a model today. Rather, the Pauline (and other early Christian) ascetic responses to the world serve as a challenge to Christians today to work out in their own cultural contexts ways of being in the world without selling out to the world.[14]

Marronage in its various formations can be seen as a way of describing and analyzing what has often been called black nationalism, an assortment of practices and values adopted by black people in their quest for freedom, political enfranchisement, and self-determination. At the same time it is useful to consider how black nationalism is related both posi-

11. Vincent L. Wimbush, "Introduction: Reading Darkness, Reading Scriptures," in *African Americans and the Bible: Sacred Texts and Social Textures,* ed. Vincent L. Wimbush and Rosamond C. Rodman (New York: Continuum, 2000), 5 and 31, n. 12.

12. Wimbush, "Introduction: Reading Darkness," 23.

13. Wimbush, "Introduction: Reading Darkness," 27.

14. This is how I interpret Wimbush's comments at the end of *Paul, The Worldly Ascetic: Response to the World and Self-Understanding According to 1 Corinthians 7* (Macon: Mercer University Press, 1987), 97-98.

tively and negatively to another impulse in the African American tradition, namely, integrationism. The two — nationalism and integrationism — are sometimes in opposition to one another, but they also exist in a dialectical relation, interpenetrating each other. The links between nationalism and integrationism are explored by James Cone, one of the founders of the black theology movement. In a revealing comparison of Martin Luther King and Malcolm X, Cone observes that "Malcolm and Martin illuminate the two roads to freedom that meet in the African American search for identity in the land of their birth."[15] King symbolizes "integrationism" and Malcolm "nationalism." Nevertheless, Cone argues, a kind of nationalist strain — or at least some of the important concerns that typically arise in black nationalism — appears in King and becomes more pronounced in the latter part of his life. Likewise, Malcolm X eventually embraces — or at least appears to have embarked on a path toward embracing — some of the integrationist values of King.

The African American experience in America was described poignantly by the pioneering African American sociologist W. E. B. Du Bois as a "double consciousness," a conflict in identity about whether one is African or American or somehow both.[16] The effort to be American or dialectically both African and American leads to integrationism. The effort to be distinctively African or black, even if also American, leads to nationalism.[17] Cone stresses that the integrationist and nationalist impulses can be distinguished but are not to be neatly separated. Nationalism and integrationism are interdependent values, and no significant African American thinker has supported purely one or the other.[18] Hence, Cone shows, it is important to conceive the range of African American forms of nationalism in ways that do not simply polarize nationalism and integrationism but show significant overlap between various forms of each.

In the African American Christian tradition, integrationism is the affirmation of universal human unity and equality and a hope of political striving to bring social reality into conformity with God's creation of all peoples "of one blood" (Acts 17:26, KJV). Integrationism is epitomized in the old slogan of the black abolitionists, "Am I not a man and a brother?"

15. James H. Cone, *Martin & Malcolm & America: A Dream or a Nightmare* (Maryknoll: Orbis, 1991), x.

16. W. E. B. Du Bois, *The Souls of Black Folk* (New York: New American Library, 1969).

17. Du Bois, *Souls*, 3.

18. Cone, *Martin & Malcolm & America*, 4.

in the motto of the African Methodist Episcopal Church ("God our Father, Christ our Redeemer, man our Brother"), in the concept of the "beloved community," in Howard Thurman's mystical sense of foundational human unity, in a 1960s black poet's longing to "forget my Otherness," and in myriad other expressions of African American claims to full and equal participation in the life of the nation.[19] African American ethicist Peter Paris speaks of the "prophetic principle" of the black church tradition based on "the parenthood of God and the kinship of all peoples."[20] As an expression of this prophetic principle, integrationism rejects all forms of racism, projects various ideals of interracial community, and calls for a wide range of strategies to gain equal participation in the various spheres of American life, from civil rights to cultural expression.

Joining Cone's interpretation of nationalism with Wimbush's understanding of *marronage,* I suggest that African American "flight" (from white-world), "settlement," and "self-making" have often involved a dialectic of integrationist and nationalist impulses. This will prove significant for interpreting Paul in African American perspective.

Finally, I wish to mention the work of Brian Blount, particularly his treatment of the relation between the so-called "indicative" and "imperative" in Paul. In Pauline scholarship, these terms refer to the apostle's theological assertions about what God has done/does and what we are to do as a matter of ethical response in obedience to God. Blount advocates an interpretation of "theology" and "ethics" in Paul that closely integrates the indicative and imperative: "In Paul, then, ethics do not stand alone as a separate theoretical category. They presuppose a relationship where the one is an integral part of the other. *Theology enables ethics.* Ethics establishes theology in the living reality of a community's loving and liberating existence."[21]

19. "Am I not a man and a brother?" (an oft-repeated slogan; see Foner, *Voice of Black America,* 25, for an early example). For Thurman's conception of human unity, see, for example, Howard Thurman, *The Search for Common Ground: An Inquiry into the Basis of Man's Experience of Community* (New York: Harper and Row, 1971). Naomi Long Madgett's poem "The Race Question" speaks of respite from Otherness in *Black Voices: An Anthology of Afro-American Literature,* ed. Abraham Chapman (New York: New American Library, 1968), 477.

20. Peter J. Paris, *The Social Teaching of the Black Churches* (Philadelphia: Fortress, 1985), 10.

21. Brian K. Blount, *Then the Whisper Put On Flesh: New Testament Ethics in an African American Context* (Nashville: Abingdon, 2001), 125-26 (also the larger discussion in 125-

Reading Blount's discussion, with which I deeply resonate, I could not help but think of a hermeneutical axiom that seems to pervade traditional African American appeals to Scripture (on slavery and other questions). It is the assumption — usually unstated but everywhere presupposed — that to describe God (that is, to make any statement about God's action or identity) *is to imply a corresponding human moral obligation in imitation of God.* This means that biblical statements about God entail a moral *imitatio Dei,* a summons to live in conformity to God's character. Henry McNeal Turner, a nineteenth-century bishop in the African Methodist Episcopal Church, epitomizes the practice of this hermeneutic when he declares, "Always take sides with the weak, the frail and impotent, especially when in the right. God does it."[22]

The Focus and Approach of This Study

The following examination of Paul and peoplehood in African American perspective unfolds under the following aspects: (1) freedom and slavery; (2) the necessity, especially under conditions of racism, for at least some forms of self-chosen separation and independence to ensure the survival and practices of cultural or "national" identity; (3) the beauty and dignity of "blackness" (African heritage, African American bodies, the distinctive forms of African American culture); (4) the unity and equality of all peoples; and (5) suffering and the cross of Christ. In developing these themes I have looked for possibilities for an emancipatory interpretation of Paul, following Abraham Smith's suggestion that there is "more in the text" than traditional interpretations have often suggested. I have also paid special attention to the dialectic of "integrationism" and "nationalism" within the *marronage* formations that Vincent Wimbush describes, seeking to interpret the themes of nationalism and integrationism by taking cues from African American interpretations of Paul. With Brian Blount I have aimed to

49). Blount stresses that in practice (including Paul's own practice) this ideal integration of theology and ethics is not always faithfully achieved.

See also Blount's earlier study in hermeneutics, *Cultural Interpretation: Reorienting New Testament Criticism* (Minneapolis: Augsburg/Fortress, 1995).

22. Henry McNeal Turner, *Respect Black: The Writings and Speeches of Henry McNeal Turner* (New York: Arno, 1971), 46.

view theology and ethics in Paul as an indissoluble unity in which statements about God's character and actions carry ethical implications.

A People Bound for Freedom

African American Christians have historically seen themselves as *a people bound for freedom.* This conception of peoplehood, linked with hopes of liberation and "uplift" (to use an older term for advancement in society), derives from biblically-shaped understandings of peoplehood and hope. According to Abraham Smith, African American theological approaches to Paul properly proceed from a commitment to liberation informed by the liberating voices of the Bible (see above). Scripture's witness to God's liberating actions and purpose is part of what might be called, in traditional terms, a "rule of faith" of the African American hermeneutic, a guide for how to let Scripture interpret Scripture.[23] This hermeneutic takes a variety of forms. For example, the traditional African American narrative sermon treats the Bible as a single grand story in which each part has its place. Thus, the African American Bible is a story of liberation in which Moses and Jesus are the central witnesses and orientation points. Sometimes African Americans have set Moses and Jesus against Paul; other times they have found in Paul an ally alongside Moses and Jesus.

We cannot approach "freedom" in Paul from an African American perspective without seeing that freedom as a biblical concept is linked above all with the story of liberation from Egypt. In the history of African American interpretation of the Bible, the exodus story has pride of place.[24] For at least two hundred years and probably longer, African Americans have invoked the exodus as a symbol of this-worldly deliverance. As Cone puts it, "almost all blacks in America — past and present — have identified

23. On the history and concept of "rules of faith" as hermeneutical norms, see my *Appealing to Scripture in Moral Debate: Five Hermeneutical Rules* (Grand Rapids: Eerdmans, 2002), chapter five.

24. Recently, however, some African American scholars have been reexamining the role of the exodus in black faith and theology, asking whether it may harbor an anti-Egyptian and therefore anti-African bias. See Randall C. Bailey, "Is That Any Name for a Nice Hebrew Boy? Exodus 2:1-10: The De-Africanization of a Biblical Hero," in *The Recovery of the Black Presence in the Bible,* ed. Randall C. Bailey and Jacquelyn Grant (Nashville: Abingdon, 1995), 25-36.

Egypt with America, Pharaoh and the Egyptians with white slaveholders and subsequent racists, and blacks with Israelite slaves."[25] The exodus motif appears in a variety of voices from African American history — in John Marant's sermons from the 1780s, in the accounts of slave-revolt conspiracies (Gabriel Prosser in 1800, Denmark Vesey in 1822, and Nat Turner in 1831), in Robert Alexander Young's *The Ethiopian Manifesto* (1829), in David Walker's *Appeal* (1829), in the secret language of the Underground Railway, in Sojourner Truth's lobbying efforts for free black settlements in Kansas, in post–Civil War migrations to northern states and western territories ("exodusters"), in yearnings to leave America altogether (including various colonization movements from the 1850s to the 1920s, also conceived as forms of African Zionism), in the Depression-era Great Migration to northern cities, and in later civil-rights era rhetoric of the South or America as Egypt. Examples could be multiplied.

One can fruitfully interpret the exodus as a central symbol in African American Christianity via Wimbush's concept of *marronage.* The biblical people of God appear for the first time as God's people in slavery in Egypt. Egypt, which African Americans early on equated with America, is a *marronage* site in slavery because Egypt is a place of alienation and social death for the Hebrew people. Exodus is flight from Egypt or *marronage* to a new place, the site of formation in the wilderness on the way to the Promised Land. For African Americans, flight from American-Egyptian slavery has often taken the form of literal exodus: the underground railroad, the great northern migrations, movement to free black settlements in the American West, and nation-building ventures in West Africa (Liberia). Flight or *marronage* has also taken the from of ascetic resistance and renunciation of white-world (America as Egypt) through separatist movements within America or through integrationist projects that nonetheless seek to establish and preserve African American identity.

In African American interpretation of Paul, the exodus/*marronage* hermeneutic pays special attention to Paul's language about slavery and freedom. Some kind of freedom from chattel slavery seems implied by Paul's famous declaration in Gal. 3:28: "There is no longer Jew or Greek, there is no longer slave or free, there is no longer male and female." A disputed question in Pauline studies is whether the end of the slave-free dis-

25. James H. Cone, *For My People: Black Theology and the Black Church* (Maryknoll: Orbis, 1984), 63.

tinction has present social implications. Since Paul treats the end of the Jew-gentile distinction as having social implications, we might assume that the same holds for "slave or free." However, it is not clear that "slave-free" and "male-female" have the same egalitarian social implications for Paul that he presses in the case of relations between Jews and gentiles.

According to one longstanding interpretation of Paul's teaching about social relations, Paul does not challenge the institution of slavery. Advocates of this interpretation have typically stressed that he nowhere calls for any general emancipation of slaves in the churches of his mission, that in 1 Corinthians 7 he tells slaves not to seek freedom but to remain in the state in which they were called, and that in Philemon he sends a runaway back to his master. They have also pointed to the household codes in Col. 3:22-25 and Eph. 6:5-8, which instruct slaves to obey their masters. This traditional interpretation was somewhat modified in twentieth-century critical scholarship by those who regarded Colossians and Ephesians as letters stemming from a later generation of Paul's disciples. Nevertheless, some scholars have continued to see Paul adopting a socially conservative stance toward slavery in Philemon and 1 Corinthians 7.

Pro-slavery use of Paul led to antipathy or at least ambivalence toward Paul among slaves and their descendants.[26] However, as African American New Testament scholar Allen Callahan points out, there have always been efforts by African American interpreters (lettered and unlettered) to demonstrate viable alternatives to the traditional socially conservative interpretation of Paul.[27] These stretch from abolitionist claims in the 1850s that Philemon is emancipatory to Amos N. Jones's more recent argument in the 1980s that Paul is an apostle of freedom in a social as well as a spiritual sense.[28] A starting point for discovering that there might be "more in the text" than the traditional interpretation allows is to recognize that Paul was in no position to call for, much less to mobilize for, change in the wider society. Orlando Patterson, an eminent authority on the history of slavery, is emphatic on this point, insisting that "[i]t is preposterous . . . to criticize Paul for not calling for abolition of

26. This observation has been made many times. For a recent survey and analysis by an African American New Testament scholar, see Clarice J. Martin, "'Somebody Done Hoodoo'd the Hoodoo Man': Language, Power, Resistance, and the Effective History of Pauline Texts in American Slavery," *Semeia* 83/84 (1998): 203-34 and the literature cited there.

27. Callahan, "Brother Saul"; also Smith, "There's More in the Text Than That."

28. Jones, *Paul's Message of Freedom.*

slavery."[29] This point has special force when we consider that, unlike biblical prophets such as Amos, Paul did not operate with a "prophetic" consciousness (focused on historical, this-worldly social and political change in which human beings themselves are the change agents), but was an apocalyptic thinker who expected the near end of the world and with it a radical cosmic change brought about directly by God. Paul's primary purpose was to complete his mission to the gentiles in preparation for the imminent appearance of Christ and the consummation of history. It would be highly anachronistic of us to expect him to translate the egalitarian vision of the gospel into a social program. On the other hand, some have found a self-conscious if subtle challenge to Roman hegemony in Paul's gospel, and we do see him shaping communities that are in some sense counter-cultural. Certainly, we can appropriately pose the question of how Paul thought the end of the slave-free distinction (Gal. 3:28) was to be expressed in the Christian communities. I will focus here on recent African American interpretation of 1 Cor. 7:21-23 and Philemon.

Paul's directive to slaves in 1 Cor. 7:21 poses an intractable puzzle for translators. The RSV and the NRSV illustrate the problem. The RSV rendered v. 21, "But if you can gain your freedom, avail yourself of the opportunity." The NRSV has the opposite translation: "Even if you can gain your freedom, make use of your present condition [of slavery] now more than ever."[30] Amos Jones, an African American minister who wrote a Doctor of Ministry dissertation on Paul and the black church, which he later revised in book form, sides with the translation choice represented by the RSV. According to Jones, 1 Cor. 7:21 calls slaves to seek their freedom and presents us with the foundation for a liberative reading of Paul for the black church.[31]

Appreciative of Jones's work but doubtful that his exegesis rules out other interpretations, another African American scholar has recently argued very persuasively that 1 Cor. 7:21-24 is inherently ambiguous and open to more than one plausible interpretation.[32] In *The Tyranny of Reso-*

29. Orlando Patterson, "Paul, Slavery, and Freedom: Personal and Socio-Historical Reflections," *Semeia* 83/84 (1998): 269.

30. The RSV and NRSV also have marginal notes suggesting the possibility of alternative translations.

31. Jones, *Paul's Message of Freedom*, 27-68.

32. Brad Ronnell Braxton, *The Tyranny of Resolution: 1 Corinthians 7:17-24* (Society of Biblical Literature Dissertation Series 181; Atlanta: Society of Biblical Literature, 2000).

lution Brad Braxton criticizes efforts to "prematurely resolve" the "complexity and ambiguity" of the passage[33] and proposes that Paul was deliberately unclear because he had not fully worked out an answer to the question about slavery and Christian identity.[34] At the end of his erudite demonstration of these points, Braxton briefly distinguishes between our knowledge that a biblical text is inherently ambiguous and our decisions to resolve ambiguity because the "ethical exigencies of our lives" and the need to "get on with the business of living" call for choosing exegetical sides and promoting one interpretation against others.[35] We can do both — remain honest about textual ambiguity and also opt for what we think is the theologically and ethically best interpretation — by being clear about what we are doing, recognizing and acknowledging that our resolutions are "fictions."[36] I conclude from this that for Braxton moral and theological considerations may appropriately lead us to opt for an emancipatory interpretation of 1 Cor. 7:21-24, so long as we do not claim that this is the only reasonable way to interpret the passage. In *The Tyranny of Resolution*, Braxton does not offer a resolution of 1 Cor. 7:21 on ethical or other grounds, but he does practice emancipatory interpretation of Paul in a later book, *No Longer Slaves*.[37] There he embraces a form of reader-response criticism that calls for recognizing that readers are co-constructors of textual meaning and that an African American hermeneutic (as well as approaches from other perspectives) should therefore seek relevant possibilities in the text without purporting to possess the one correct interpretation.[38]

Braxton's take on 1 Corinthians 7 calls for confronting the ambiguity of this passage, its resistance to neat resolution, but also embracing, on moral grounds, the emancipatory interpretative possibilities of the text. This strikes me as in tune with a more general African American hermeneutic for interpreting authoritative icons in the often hostile American context in which African Americans find themselves. Many black Americans have chosen to relate to ambiguous dominant American traditions by

33. Braxton, *Tyranny*, 1, 234, and passim.

34. Braxton, *Tyranny*, 228.

35. Braxton, *Tyranny*, 274.

36. Braxton, *Tyranny*, 274.

37. Brad Ronnell Braxton, *No Longer Slaves: Galatians and African American Experience* (Collegeville: Liturgical, 2002).

38. Braxton, *No Longer Slaves*, 18, 28-44.

embracing, on one hand, the possibilities for emancipatory potential and being suspicious, on the other hand, about potentials in those same traditions for unfreedom and oppression, recognizing that the meaning of American symbols depends on how they "read." For example, Blacks have appealed to the Declaration of Independence, the Constitution, and other American icons when arguing for black freedom and equality, but have also criticized these same symbols, recognizing their susceptibility to racist interpretations. A similar approach to Paul by African American Christians makes sense in the light of the use of Paul's letters on all sides of the freedom debate, whether the question is freedom from chattel slavery, as it was in antebellum days,[39] or various forms of *social* equality and freedom, including issues such as "affirmative action" that are being debated today in America's unfinished dialogue about "race."

We turn now to Philemon. In a contribution to Cain Felder's anthology of recent African American biblical scholarship, Lloyd Lewis points out the pervasiveness and strategic use of familial language in Philemon.[40] Lewis argues that when we reconstruct the sense of this language from Paul's other letters (notably Galatians), we discover that the letter to Philemon implements an argument for Onesimus's emancipation. Moreover, Paul's appeal also harbors broader liberationist implications. Especially striking is the language in vv. 10 and 16: Paul has *fathered* Onesimus (v. 10), making Onesimus Paul's *child* and a *brother* in Christ to Philemon (v. 16). All of this is gospel language, the language of the new creation/new family established by God in Christ. When Paul requests that Philemon receive Onesimus back "no longer as a slave but as a beloved brother . . . both in the flesh and in the Lord," this appeal rests on warrants found in a gospel that has put an end to the distinction between slave and free (Gal. 3:28). Thus, the new family in Christ is to be concretely embodied by the church in its social relations ("in the flesh and in the Lord"). In other words, Paul is asking Philemon to emancipate Onesimus.

Admittedly, Paul does not explicitly generalize this request to apply to other slave-master relations in the church, perhaps because the politics of his mission would not have allowed it or perhaps because he did not see it

39. Braxton provides an extended discussion of competing interpretations of 1 Cor. 7:17-24 in antebellum debates over slavery. See *The Tyranny of Resolution*, chapter 5.

40. Lloyd A. Lewis, "An African American Appraisal of the Philemon-Paul-Onesimus Triangle," in *Stony the Road We Trod: African American Biblical Interpretation*, ed. Cain Hope Felder (Minneapolis: Fortress, 1991), 232-46.

as crucial for the advancement of that mission. Nevertheless, more general emancipatory implications are present in Philemon to the extent that we give force to the "kinship in Christ" as the ultimate basis of Paul's appeal. Whether we *should* give general force to the kinship language by reading Philemon through the lens of Galatians is more than a purely exegetical question. Braxton's caution about 1 Corinthians 7 holds for Philemon as well. Presumably, Braxton would say that if we wish to resolve the ambiguity of Philemon in the favor of freedom, we must first frankly acknowledge that Philemon is ambiguous — ambiguous in a way that historical-critical exegesis cannot overcome, ambiguous probably for the very recipients of this letter. It should not be surprising that not all interpreters — and not all African Americans — have seen the letter to Philemon as a request for Onesimus's emancipation. Not only what Paul says but also his silences in Philemon invite competing interpretations. That he says nothing about other slaves in the church or about slavery in general could be taken as intentionally limiting. Or perhaps he is being politically cautious, but in a way that leaves a door open. One wonders what debates about the meaning of the letter ensued at Colossae among masters and slaves in private. Did the masters muster arguments favoring a very narrow construal of Paul's request (the way pro-slavery advocates did in North America)? Did slaves see emancipatory implications? If so, did any of them have the courage to share their emancipatory readings in the community assembly? And, if Paul did manage to make his promised trip to Colossae, how did he clarify his meaning when he got there? We have no answers to these questions, but we can reasonably imagine that in its original setting the letter evoked a range of competing interpretations. Nevertheless, the witness of the later letter to the Colossians indicates that the church (and the Pauline tradition) did not adopt an emancipatory interpretation of the gospel. Hence we are faced with a hermeneutical choice: whether to use Colossians and Ephesians as the decisive clues to the meaning and scope of Philemon or whether to use Galatians as the decisive guide. Lloyd Lewis commends this second approach to us, and Braxton's hermeneutic calls for frankness about the nature of such a decision — acknowledging that it is a reader's choice in the construction of the meaning of the text, not a mere discovery of what is demonstrably the correct original meaning of the text.

I have focused on the question of chattel slavery and socioeconomic freedom in African American interpretations of Paul. But there is also a long history of African American hope for freedom beyond this life. In an essay on Paul and the African American community, Michelle Venable-Ridley draws attention to this. She observes that although Pauline texts were often used (and in her judgment misinterpreted) to support black acquiescence to slavery, leading to a tradition of black antipathy to Paul, the eschatological hopes of black Christians have a parallel in Paul.[41] One could add that the Christian hope embraced by African Americans was certainly influenced at least indirectly by Paul, whose letters have always been a primary witness of Christian faith. And perhaps one can interpret Paul as Venable-Ridley interprets the spirituals, namely, as having a bifocal eschatology that looks simultaneously to this-worldly liberation and future liberty in the resurrection from the dead.[42]

Before leaving this theme of freedom through the future hope, I want to mention Theophilus Gould Steward's interpretation of Pauline eschatology. In *The End of the World; or, Clearing the Way for the Fullness of the Gentiles* (1888), Steward, a prominent theologian of the African Methodist Episcopal Church, proposed a historicizing interpretation of biblical eschatology, arguing that the "end of the world" spoken of in biblical prophecy refers to the end of a worldly age, not to the end of history.[43] By giving New Testament eschatology a this-worldly interpretation, Steward was able to construe Rom. 11:25 (together with other eschatological passages) within the framework of a then popular Christian philosophy of history according to which God superintends a process of electing nations in history to further the gradual march of civilization toward its perfection in the kingdom of God on earth. Steward's version of this process has four great epochs: the patriarchal age, the Jewish age, the present age (which he calls the Roman age — the age of empire), and the future age, whose dawn he expects to appear soon. In working out this interpretation of history, Steward explicitly attacked the political ideology of Josiah Strong's popular book, *Our Country*

41. C. Michelle Venable-Ridley, "Paul and the African American Community," in *Embracing the Spirit: Womanist Perspectives on Hope, Salvation, and Transformation,* ed. Emily M. Townes (Maryknoll: Orbis, 1997), 212-33.

42. Venable-Ridley, "Paul and the African American Community," 226-27.

43. T. G. Steward, *The End of the World; or, Clearing the Way for the Fullness of the Gentiles, with an Exposition of Psalm 68:31 by James A. Handy* (Philadelphia: A.M.E. Church Book Rooms, 1888). Steward was influenced by nineteenth-century adventism and relied in part on Henry Alford's distinction between two future comings of Christ — one to set up an earthly kingdom in which Christ may be visibly or invisibly but "effectually" present and a later coming to bring about the final end of history (Steward, *The End of the World,* 20).

(1885), which set forth an ideology of manifest destiny based on the idea that white America is God's chosen instrument for a special mission in history, namely, the spread of Anglo-Christian civilization to the world.[44] In Steward's scheme white America is not the elect people destined to be the new Adam of the age of perfection. Rather, the end of the world will spell the demise of Anglo-Saxon rule, signaling the advent of the era of Afro-Asiatic peoples. These are the "fullness of the gentiles" to be brought in according to Paul's prophecy: "I want you to understand this mystery: a hardening has come upon part of Israel, until the full number of the Gentiles has come in" (Rom. 11:25). This ascendance of the Afro-Asiatic peoples to political dominance belongs to God's plan for humanizing the world.[45] The idea that Afro-Asiatics are a chosen race with a special historical vocation is a variation on a popular nineteenth-century philosophy of nations or "races" in history. According to this view, each people or race has its own peculiar "genius." By developing that genius in its time, each group makes its own distinctive contribution to the progress of humanity.

The Afro-Asiatic future did not arrive as Steward expected, and his exegesis has significant problems. Nevertheless, one can appreciate his engagement with Strong in a reversal of Strong's racist vision, and one can also ask whether Steward was perhaps on to something in looking for prophetic-political guidance in Paul's eschatological vision in Romans 11. While I cannot affirm Steward's interpretation, I think there is a basis for a political theology in Romans 11 that serves the freedom of the oppressed (see below).

Separatism

Closely linked with exodus as freedom in the black tradition are various forms of black nationalism. Some 150 years ago black activist Martin Delany described African Americans as "a nation within a nation."[46] Born out of "slave culture,"[47] black nationalism is a rich tradition of modula-

44. Josiah Strong, *Our Country: Its Possible Future and Its Present Crisis* (New York: Baker and Taylor, 1885).

45. At least Steward can be read this way.

46. Martin Delany in Herbert Aptheker, ed., *A Documentary History of the Negro People in the United States,* vol. 1 (New York: Carol, 1951, 1979), 327-28.

47. See Sterling Stuckey, *Slave Culture: Nationalist Theory and the Foundations of Black America* (Oxford: Oxford University Press, 1987).

tions on Delany's perception. As a collection of sentiments and values, black nationalism stands for peoplehood, corporate self-determination in history, the dignity and beauty of black selfhood, and the preservation of black identity and culture(s). As a program, black nationalism has meant everything from Booker T. Washington's agenda for independent, self-powered Negro uplift to the militant activism of Black Power in the 1960s.

As a way of defining peoplehood, "nationalism" is an elastic term with many connotations and associations, including negative ones such as imperialism and ethnocentrism.[48] It is important to stress that some forms of nationalism are diametrically opposed to imperialism, ethnocentrism, and the use of violence to extend the interests of a people or state. The German historian Johann Gottfried Herder, who coined the term nationalism *(Nationalismus),* conceived the nation as a "people's culture," the unique way of life of a particular folk, bound by kinship ties and links to place (land), defined by a unique history.[49] Isaiah Berlin has credited Herder with discovering "belonging" as a basic human need. In Berlin's words, "Just as people need to eat and drink, to have security and freedom of movement, so too they need to belong to a group."[50] For Herder, Berlin writes, "[t]o be human meant to feel at home somewhere, with your own kind."[51] Herder's conception of national identity distinguished the nation from the state. Herder also rejected the Enlightenment idea of grading cultures, judging them by a rational, universal standard of the ideal civilization (which always turned out to look quite European). He celebrated human variety and grieved the destruction of cultures by aggressive European states.

"Nation," as I will use the term here, means corporate identity through culture and kinship, a form of identity and belonging that we take

48. Bracey, Meier, and Rudwick describe seven meanings of "black nationalism": racial solidarity, cultural nationalism, religious nationalism, economic nationalism, political nationalism (reformist and revolutionary), emigrationism and territorial separatism, and pan-Negroism and pan-Africanism. These meanings combine in various ways to form distinctive patterns of nationalism in a given thinker or group. See John H. Bracey, Jr., August Meier, and Elliott Rudwick, eds., *Black Nationalism in America* (Indianapolis: Bobbs-Merrill, 1970), xxvi-xxix.

49. See Isaiah Berlin, *Three Critics of the Enlightenment: Vico, Hamman, Herder,* ed. Henry Hardy (Princeton: Princeton University Press, 2000), 168-242.

50. Isaiah Berlin as quoted in Nathan Gardels, "Two Concepts of Nationalism: An Interview with Isaiah Berlin," *New York Review of Books* 38 (November 21, 1991): 19.

51. Berlin, quoted in Gardels, "Two Concepts," 19.

for granted and scarcely notice when it is not threatened but recognize as a vital part of ourselves when it is challenged or endangered. African Americans are keenly sensitive to the values of black culture and kinship because slavery and racism in America have been a direct and persistent threat to these values.[52]

Nations are not simple and distinct entities. They are always compounds of diverse influences and ancestries. This has been true of Israel since ancient times. It is true of African Americans, who are biologically descended from various African peoples and from various white ancestors and are cultural products of equally diverse African and American heritages. The complex nature of their identity is expressed in the compound name "African American"; it has been analyzed under W. E. B. Du Bois's concept of the "double consciousness"; it involves the story of white violence against Africans through separation of family members at slave auctions, white rape of slave women and children, cultural policing, cultural imposition, and cultural deprivation. It is also the story of African American resistance to white racism, struggle for freedom and civil rights, preservation of cultural heritages from Africa, and the creation of new forms of African American culture in America.

Black nationalism developed in response to white racism. Sometimes it involved an assertion of black racial superiority, but more often black nationalism has been egalitarian, often holding out the harmony of peoples (or "races") as its ideal. Eugene Genovese argues that "[t]he black variant of Christianity [in slave religion] laid the foundations of protonationalist consciousness and at the same time stretched a universal offer of forgiveness and ultimate reconciliation to white America."[53] Sterling Stuckey sees both elements — black nationalism and a gospel of universal reconciliation — already coming together in the old "ring shout" of slave religion.[54]

52. One can define nationalism more narrowly as a separatist program that always involves more than valuing and nurturing one's own ethno-cultural identity. See, for example, Cornell West in Michael Lerner and Cornell West, *Jews and Blacks: Let the Healing Begin* (New York: Putnam, 1995), 92-93. But the history of the use of "nation" and "nationalism" in African American history suggests that a broader, more flexible interpretation of the concept is also appropriate.

53. Eugene D. Genovese, *Roll, Jordan, Roll* (New York: Vintage, 1976), 284.

54. Stuckey, *Slave Culture*, 31 (building here on the work of Marshall Stearns, *The Story of Jazz* [New York: Oxford University Press, 1956], 12-13).

As Paris and others have observed, African Americans have long pursued various forms of *separatism* in their quest for *integration*. Paris quotes an 1896 declaration of African Methodist Episcopal bishops affirming the sentiments of human unity and equality and avowing that "[w]hen these sentiments are universal in theory and practice, then the mission of the distinctive colored organizations will cease."[55] Paris refers to these separatist African American projects of racial self-development as "soft nationalism."[56] They are "soft" because they do not involve aspirations toward national political independence.

Martin Luther King eventually adopted a kind of soft nationalism. Cone sees an evolution in King's thinking that led him eventually to link his integrationist ideals and his moral philosophy of nonviolence with certain values and aims of black nationalism. Disenchantment with white moderates and a fear that some forms of white integration meant "being integrated out of power" convinced King that it is sometimes necessary to choose "segregation as a temporary way-station to a truly integrated society."[57] King also began substituting the term "black" for "Negro," embraced the "black is beautiful" slogan, and began emphasizing black pride and black cultural achievement in his speeches.[58] All of this may seem quite mild and passé now, but it was radical in the 1960s.

While King never thought of himself as a black nationalist, the preceding shows that he advocated three important elements of the black nationalist tradition: the value, beauty, and pleasure of African American identity, culture, history, traditions; the importance of certain forms of separatism; and the conviction that African Americans have a vocation in history (a long-standing theme of King's philosophy). In King's understanding these themes were positively related to his vision of the beloved community based on the unity and equality of all peoples in God's sight, and his theology of the cross as divine reconciliation expressed through the power of suffering love. Without adopting the term "black nationalism," King eventually affirmed all the elements of this list. African American intellectuals James Cone, Gayraud Wilmore, and Joseph Washington

55. Paris, *Social Teaching*, 13.

56. Paris, *Social Teaching*, 45.

57. Cone, *Martin & Malcolm & America*, 234.

58. See, for example, Martin Luther King, Jr., "Where Do We Go from Here?" (Atlanta, August 16, 1967), in Foner, *The Voice of Black America*, 1068-77; also Cone's discussion in *Martin & Malcolm & America*, 229.

also show strong sympathies with the vision of vocational black nationalism, its way of uniting integrationist ideals with certain critical emphases and values of Black Power.[59]

Is there any basis for self-chosen political separation in Paul? At first sight this looks like an odd question, since we do not often associate Paul with politics. However, the Pauline mission was fraught with politics and Paul shows himself to be keenly sensitive to the complexities of power relations and their implications for the gospel mission. A strong Pauline argument can be made against separatism by appealing to Paul's theology of gentile inclusion and the pains to which he goes in his letters and missionary activities to defend the rights of the gentiles to full *social* inclusion in the church (see Galatians 2). But there is another side to the question of political separation in Paul. We find it in Rom. 11:17-20, where Paul tells the gentile Christians at Rome that Jewish "branches" were "broken off" the "olive tree" of promissory lineage from Abraham. The divine pruning of Israelite branches is Paul's way of interpreting the fact that the vast majority of Jews exposed to the gospel of Christ have not accepted it. God has "them hardened" (11:25) against the message about Jesus. This "breaking off" of Jewish "branches" through divine "hardening" is "so that" gentiles might be grafted in (11:19), which suggests that the hardening of Israel *makes room* for gentiles.

When I first read Cone's *Martin & Malcolm & America,* it struck me that the dialectic of integrationism and nationalism, as Cone analyzes its inner logic, provides a sociopolitical way of understanding Paul's theology of Israel in Romans 11. Hence, I came to understand Paul's idea of God "making room" for the gentiles as a theo-political idea having to do with power relations in Paul's time between God's people Israel and the new community of gentile believers.[60] The idea that some branches must be broken off before others can be grafted in makes good sense if Paul has in view some form of actual community where room for outsiders requires a removal of dominant insiders. Hence, we might construe Paul as follows.

59. For Cone, in addition to *Martin & Malcolm & America,* see *For My People,* 42, 189-207. See Joseph Washington, *Black and White Power Subreption* (Boston: Beacon, 1969), 185; *The Politics of God* (Boston: Beacon, 1967); Gayraud S. Wilmore, *Black Religion and Black Radicalism: An Interpretation of the Religious History of Afro-American People* (second ed., Maryknoll: Orbis, 1983), 192-240.

60. I eventually developed these ideas in *Elusive Israel: The Puzzle of Election in Romans* (Louisville: Westminster/John Knox, 1997), 86-89.

God has temporarily pruned the vast majority of Israelites to create what we might call "political space" for the gentiles. Paul is aware of the pressure on his gentile mission from Jewish Christian quarters, the conviction of many Jewish Christians that gentiles who accept the gospel must be circumcised and keep the Law at least minimally. Paul can well imagine what would have happened to his gentile mission if Israel as a whole had embraced the gospel and every synagogue had become a congregation of the Messiah Jesus. There would have been no political room for a mission like Paul's to flourish. The circumcision-free gentile mission would have been overrun and co-opted by well-meaning Jewish Christian Judaizers intent on maintaining the old traditions about the terms for incorporating gentiles into Israel. In the end there would have been no gentile church. But Israel as a whole did not embrace the gospel. Paul interprets this as God's own work to create ecclesial space for the gentiles. For a period of time the tiny gentile mission can flourish and its communities can become established before "all Israel" is grafted back into the olive tree: "a hardening has come on part of Israel until the full number of the Gentiles comes in. And so all Israel will be saved . . ." (Rom. 11:25-26).

God's "hardening" of Israel is thus a temporary strategy to ensure that gentiles enter and remain in the olive tree as *gentiles*. The separation of the two missions — one to the circumcised and one to the uncircumcised (Gal. 2:7-8) — also gives the gentile churches political room to grow and establish their own forms of life apart from the aegis of their older brother Israel. Ultimately, these two wings of the church belong together and must come together. Already there are mixed churches (Antioch) as signs of that unity. In the meantime, however, there is an important place for the separation of the gentiles from Israel, so that the gentiles can make their own way in the gospel.

This interpretation suggests that Paul was sensitive in his own way to questions of ethnic identity and the politics that jeopardize minority identity. But we must be cautious here. Braxton finds in Gal. 3:28 a warrant for diversity, freedom from the "tyranny of sameness" as he puts it,[61] but he qualifies this by noting that when Paul defends gentile equality with Jews he "does not appear to be encouraging the Galatians to say 'yes' to Gentile culture *per se*."[62] There is in fact no "gentile" culture, nor even a word "gen-

61. Braxton, *No Longer Slaves*, 94.
62. Braxton, *No Longer Slaves*, 70.

tile" as an adjective in the Greek of Paul's day. The English noun "gentiles" translates the Greek word for "nations" or "peoples," a term that Jews used to refer to non-Jews.[63] Hence, "Paul's assessment of cultural distinction," Braxton suggests, "could be described as a 'negative' understanding, namely one that defined Gentile identity by what it was not."[64] In other words, as a Jew who thus thinks of ethnic identity in Jewish categories, Paul aims to preserve *non-Jewish identity* and in this sense "Paul preached a law-free gospel among the gentiles in order to ensure ethnic diversity in the church."[65] As I have already mentioned, my own reading of Romans 11, informed by Cone's analysis of the dialectic between integrationism and nationalism in the black tradition, proposes that for Paul, God works out this Law-free gospel in history in a way that provides a space for the non-Jewish church to flourish free from domination by the Jewish church. If this perspective casts Paul's allegory of the olive tree in a fresh light, then perhaps reciprocally it also offers black theology further possibilities for thinking about questions of separatism and racial unity from a Pauline perspective.

Black Is Beautiful

A central meaning of peoplehood in the African American tradition is the assertion of black dignity in the teeth of American racism. In the 1960s this assertion took the memorable form "Black is beautiful," a celebrative slogan with a prophetic edge.

It might be argued that Paul's theology rules out all forms of ethnic pride as antithetical to the gospel. Rom. 3:27 comes to mind. Speaking as a Jew, Paul says, "Then what becomes of our boasting? It is excluded." Paul has in view the Jewish boast in the Law, which is tantamount to pride and confidence in Jewish identity, an identity defined by election and possession of the Law. When Paul undermines this Jewish boast by suggesting that it amounts to treating God as "God of the Jews only" (3:29), the implication seems to be that any ethnic boast is excluded by the gospel. Further-

63. The word *ethné* is not a proper noun (that is, not an ethnic name like Jew or Greek or Ethiopian) but a generic term, which is why I do not capitalize the word we use to translate it ("gentiles").

64. Braxton, *No Longer Slaves*, 70.

65. Braxton, *No Longer Slaves*, 94.

more, Paul's overall teaching about the human condition removes any basis for moral or spiritual pride, and this might be interpreted as excluding, by implication, any and all forms of human pride. Does "Black is beautiful" fall under this Pauline negation?

I have already noted that Braxton points to Gal. 3:28 as a basis for affirming not only racial unity and equality but also the value of distinctively African American identity. Braxton argues that we should not take Gal. 3:28 as a basis for abolishing social distinctions since it proclaims "not the obliteration of distinctions but rather the obliteration of *dominance*."[66] Hence, oneness in Christ does not mean "an amalgamated or undifferentiated identity" but rather practices of equality and mutuality "in the midst of our many differences."[67] The miracle of unity becomes evident only when "the social distinctions that define us are present and even accentuated."[68] Hence, Gal. 3:28 expresses God's gift of freedom in Christ "to say 'Yes' to blackness."[69] Many of my African American students also interpret Gal. 3:28 as supporting the concept "Black is beautiful" and as providing a basis not only for individual equality but also for valuing diverse cultural and ethnic identities in Christ.

Martin Luther King's understanding of Paul is also relevant here and representative of a widespread way of thinking about racial self-affirmation in the black church. For King, Paul's teaching about human unity and equality is part of the foundation on which a Christian theology of the dignity and honor of African American identity is built. King argues for black self-affirmation ("I'm black and beautiful")[70] as an inference from the theology of liberation based on moral ideals of human freedom, unity, and equality that he finds in Paul and Jesus. Black pride is a step toward freedom and equality because, "As long as the mind is enslaved [to the ideology of demeaning racial prejudice], the body can never be free."[71] Hence, Paul's theology of full human emancipation is a foundational presupposition of King's embrace of Black Power's celebration of black dignity. Related to this is King's acceptance of the assumption that racial pride (or cultural pride) is a basic human need, necessary for optimal function-

66. Braxton, *No Longer Slaves,* 94.
67. Braxton, *No Longer Slaves,* 94-95.
68. Braxton, *No Longer Slaves,* 95.
69. Braxton, *No Longer Slaves,* 95.
70. King, "Where Do We Go From Here?" in Foner, *Voice of Black America,* 1070.
71. King in Foner, *Voice of Black America,* 1070.

ing, an aspect of what it means for a human being to flourish and have a sense of well-being. For King it simply follows from this that the God of Jesus and Paul, the God whose whole being toward humanity is love, seeks and affirms black self-esteem. Divine love is the implicit link in King's theology between Paul and the beauty of blackness in God's eyes.

Black evangelist Tom Skinner has also argued that Paul's gospel does not exclude ethnic difference as an irrelevant category but preserves and affirms it. Skinner objects to those who use Gal. 3:28 ("There is neither Jew nor Greek . . .") to ask others to give up their culture. He maintains that this text means the end of the worldly, discriminatory connotations that get attached to ethnic and other differences but not the end of those differences themselves. Skinner adduces Paul as an example of someone who did not give up his cultural identity but was so passionately Jewish that he was willing to be cursed for the sake of his own people. The allusion here is to Rom. 9:2-3, where Paul calls on the Holy Spirit as witness to his love (anguish) for his people according to the flesh. A first-century audience, no less than a twentieth-first-century one, would have recognized this comment by Paul as an expression of what Josephus called *erōs patridos* — natural love of country.[72] Hence, Skinner's reference to Rom. 9:2-3 as an angle on Gal. 3:28 seems appropriate. He does not mean that Paul, in affirming his Jewish identity, was being ethnocentric but that Paul's ethnic self-affirmation has a place within his universalism. He sees Paul living out the gospel of divine impartiality by being ethnically self-affirming without being discriminatory or thinking his own group superior to others.[73]

72. In *Antiquities* 1.317, Josephus attributes the following sentiment to Jacob (who is explaining why he needs to return home): "Jacob replied in self-defense that he was not the only one in whose heart God had planted a love of native country, that it was innate in all, and that after so long a time it was right that he should return to his own." Josephus, *Jewish Antiquities,* Books I-III, trans. H. St. J. Thackeray (Loeb Classical Library; Cambridge: Harvard University Press, 1930), 153. Thackeray's "love of native country" renders *erōs patridos.*

73. The preceding description of Skinner's interpretations of Gal. 3:28 and Rom. 9:2-3 is based on *Tom Skinner: The New Community* (Tracy's Landing: Tom Skinner Associates, n.d.), videocassette.

The Unity and Equality of All People: Divine Impartiality and the Beloved Community

The concept of peoplehood in the African American tradition has often rested on the affirmation that all peoples are equal parts of the human race, created as one human family, destined by God for unity, and called in the present to forms of unity and respect for one another. African Americans have expressed the principle of human unity and equality through a number of biblical passages. One is Paul's assertion, to which we have already given considerable attention, that "there is no longer Jew or Greek, there is no longer slave or free, there is no longer male and female, for all of you are one in Christ Jesus" (Gal. 3:28).[74] Martin Luther King emphasized this Pauline definition of the new humanity that God aims to create through Christ. Appealing to Paul's words in an attack on segregation, King paraphrased, "for in Christ there is neither Jew nor Gentile, bond nor free, Negro nor white."[75] As we have noted, King also believed that in another sense there was "Negro and white," that is, in the sense of identities not placed in a discriminatory hierarchy but celebrated in equality. In the end, Gal. 3:28 symbolized for King both the end of racism and the affirmation of humanity in its ethno-cultural variety.

Two other frequently quoted biblical passages in African American discussions of racism are ascribed to Peter and Paul respectively in Acts: "Of a truth I perceive that God is no respecter of persons" and "[God] hath made of one blood all nations of men for to dwell on all the face of the earth" (10:34; 17:26). I have quoted these statements from the King James Version because that is the language in which they have been passed down as theological slogans in the African American church. In the African American tradition, Paul's pronouncement in Acts stands for the essential unity and equality of all "races," and Peter's statement of divine impartiality stands for God's own attitude in honoring that unity and equality. The implication is that human unity and equality are more fundamental than racial differences and that all human beings (and nations) should be imitators of God by showing no partiality on the basis of race, color, etc. This in

74. James Cone remarks that the words of Gal. 3:28 are "deeply ingrained in the Negro church tradition." See *Martin & Malcolm & America*, 31.

75. Martin Luther King, *Stride toward Freedom: The Montgomery Story* (New York: Harper and Row, 1958), 205.

turn is a warrant for social integration, the equal participation of all, together, in the rights, opportunities, and duties of society, regardless of "race, color, or creed."

Peter's words in Acts 10 express a teaching about divine impartiality that appears also as a basic theme of Paul's writings. In recent years, New Testament scholars have become especially attentive to the importance of this theme in Romans.[76] Hence, the idea of divine impartiality offers an important point at which contemporary New Testament scholarship can connect with traditional African American biblical interpretation in mutually enriching ways. Paul appeals to God's impartiality to show that God judges and saves Jew and non-Jew on the same terms (Rom. 2:11; 10:11-13). The idea of divine impartiality is also implicit in Paul's teaching that God regards Jews and non-Jews as being on the same level as sinners (3:9) and in Paul's argument that the "oneness" of God is a warrant for a circumcision-free mission to the gentiles (3:27-31). The confession "God is one" (3:29-30) means that God is equally the God of Jews and gentiles. Justification "by faith" and "apart from the Law" is an expression of God's impartiality because it vindicates the right of the gentiles to be part of God's people without requiring that they become Jews (v. 30).

Paul applies the concept of divine impartiality to judgment (Rom. 2:9-11) and salvation (10:11-13). It is clearly also the bedrock for his conception of the church in Jesus Christ, as the oneness (or reunification) declaration of Gal. 3:28 shows: "There is no longer Jew or Greek . . . for all of you are one in Christ Jesus." Divine impartiality is also rooted in Paul's vision of the oneness and allness of God, two ideas that I take to be intimately linked as a profound and mysterious conception of an all-encompassing divine unity. This oneness of God is deeper and greater than the revelation at Sinai, as Gal. 3:20 suggests in an enigmatic assertion about the mediation of the Law. The oneness of God is nevertheless also the deepest meaning of the Law and as such the foundation for the justification of Jews and gentiles alike (Rom. 3:27-31). God's all-encompassing oneness is also the deepest and final unity of the world: a unity on which all things depend (Rom. 11:36) and toward which all things are heading (1 Cor. 15:28). The church of Jew and gentile, male and female, slave and free, united in and beyond their differences, is a present manifestation in Christ of the origin

76. See in particular, Jouette M. Bassler, *Divine Impartiality: Paul and a Theological Axiom* (Society of Biblical Literature Dissertation Series 59; Chico: Scholars, 1982).

of all creation in God and the destiny of all creation in God's will to be "all in all" (1 Cor. 15:28). Here is a foundation in Paul for thinking about what "beloved community" means.

The concept of the beloved community, so closely associated with the Civil Rights Movement and Martin Luther King's vision for America,[77] is part of a quest for racial unity that has deep and diverse roots in African American thought. The concept reaches back to the antebellum period, for example, in Frederick Douglass's argument that racial heterogeneity produces a higher form of humanity in a nation, in Joseph Holly's claim that "the indivisibility of the human race" under God's providence means "an identity of their interest," a call for racial amalgamation in accord with the doctrine of unity in Christ ("one blood"), and in the argument of a black separatist that having "institutions of a complexional character" is a temporary expedient on the way to "human brotherhood."[78] It is important to note that these are expressions of different conceptions of the way to fulfill the ideal of human unity, including the nationalist approach of black separatism.

Although he does not work with Paul's theology, the thought of African American philosopher Howard Thurman is especially suggestive for discovering and exploring connections in Paul between the cosmic meaning of God's all-encompassing oneness and the moral life. For Thurman, the mystical unity of all things in God is not a speculative philosophy or an invitation to retreat from the world. It is a basis for ethical existence with others.[79] The power of Thurman's claim depends on our willingness to embrace with him a deep but often unspoken assumption of the African American religious tradition to which I referred at the beginning of this chapter: to grasp something about God's true nature is to be confronted by

77. The concept of the beloved community was central to the mission of the Southern Christian Leadership Conference, founded by King in 1957. See the early 1960s version of the leaflet "This Is SCLC," which lays out the organization's nature and program (see Francis L. Broderick, ed., *Negro Protest Thought* [Indianapolis: Bobbs-Merrill, 1965], 269-73). The concept but not the term "beloved community" is also clearly outlined in a 1942 "memorandum" by James Farmer regarding the formation of a Congress on Racial Equality (see Broderick, *Negro Protest Thought,* 215, 217).

78. See Frederick Douglass, *The Life and Writings of Frederick Douglass,* vol. 2, ed. Philip S. Foner (New York: International, 1950), 306-7; Ripley, *The Black Abolitionist Papers* 2:328-29; 4:18 (also 4:339); Bracey, *Black Nationalism in America,* 55.

79. On Thurman's mysticism, see Mozella G. Mitchell, *Spiritual Dynamics of Howard Thurman's Theology* (Bristol: Wyndham Hall, 1985), 30-36.

a summons to live life in a way that conforms morally to God's nature. Likewise in Paul, references to God's oneness and allness appear in contexts that lay a foundation for a way of living responsibly in the world. In Romans 12–15 Paul sets forth moral instruction in the light of the gospel he has unfolded and defended in the first twelve chapters of his letter. That gospel expresses the oneness and all-inclusiveness of God (see 3:27-30 and 11:36), and Paul's ethical instructions culminate with a corresponding call for unity, for "welcoming one another" (15:7-13). Many Pauline scholars have argued that this call for "welcoming" addresses conflicts in the churches at Rome between Jews and gentiles. Moreover, one can interpret the whole letter as Paul's effort to shore up and heal the relations between the Jewish and gentile wings of the church — from Jerusalem to Rome — symbolized by the gentile "offering" that Paul fears the Jerusalem church will refuse (15:30-32). Seen in this light, Paul is calling Christians divided by what we now call "race" to live according to the moral and spiritual implications of the knowledge that God is one, the God of Jews and gentiles, the One from whom all things have their existence and toward which all things are headed. Thus, Jews and gentiles already belong to one another by origin and destiny. Hence, they cannot be true to their calling without finding a way in the present to overcome their estrangement. By analogy, in our time, blacks and whites must be one because God is one. This is the most fundamental theological basis for the beloved community. As King and Thurman taught, at the deepest level we already belong to one another, are part of one another.[80] Every journey to the other is also a journey to ourselves.

African American Suffering and the Cross of Christ

The history of African American peoplehood in America is a story of struggle in which suffering is a near constant theme. In African American Christian faith, suffering is often interpreted by reference to the suffering

80. In *The Luminous Darkness* Thurman wrote: "[A] strange necessity has been laid upon me to devote my life to the central concern that transcends the walls that divide and would achieve in literal fact what is experienced as literal truth: human life is one and all men are members of one another." See Howard Thurman, *The Luminous Darkness: A Personal Interpretation of the Anatomy of Segregation and the Ground of Hope* (New York: Harper and Row, 1965), x.

of Jesus. The crucified Jesus is the fellow sufferer who "never said a mumblin' word."[81] His atoning death expresses God's forgiving and reconciling love, a love that begets love, empowering forgiveness toward one's enemies, even the white oppressor. Slavery was a cross; the struggle for civil rights and social equality has been a cross. Jesus bore these crosses, too. As black abolitionist W. P. Newman put it shortly after the passage of the Fugitive Slave Acts (which gave slaveholders the legal right to claim runaway slaves in the free northern states), "friends of the beloved Jesus, can you and will you stand quietly and see your Savior kidnapped in the person of his poor?"[82] These words echo a widely-held theology of Jesus' real presence with the slaves. William Wells Brown had asked just a few years earlier, "Is not Jesus crucified every day on the plains of the South, in the person of the unprotected slave?"[83]

Sometimes African American suffering in the struggle for justice has been interpreted from the perspective of the cross as suffering servanthood and redemptive suffering. In this conception, peoplehood is linked to vocation in history. Although this may sound like a positive idea, one that valorizes black experience, African American ethicist JoAnne Terrell has pointed out how easily a theology of redemptive suffering becomes an *ideology* of surrogacy and sacrifice, justifying the suffering of African Americans as a divinely-appointed burden.[84] As ideology, this theology of the cross is the rationale by which those with power have justified African American suffering, demanding that African Americans accept their worldly lot as an act of Christian submission. In extreme forms, this way of thinking makes the holocausts of the Middle Passage and slavery somehow, in their deepest meanings, providential goods.

A variation on this interpretation, but one that does not by any means endorse black suffering, is the claim by black sociologist Orlando Patterson that slavery was the precondition for the discovery of freedom as a value and aspiration in the West and in this way led to something good:

81. This expression from an African American spiritual refers to the heroic grace and equanimity of Jesus during his Passion.

82. Ripley, *Black Abolitionist Papers*, 4:64.

83. Ripley, *Black Abolitionist Papers*, 4:3-4.

84. JoAnne Terrell, *Power in the Blood? The Cross in the African American Experience* (Maryknoll: Orbis, 1998).

> Here in brief is what thirty years of historical and sociological scholarship has taught me: without slavery, no genesis of freedom; without the slavery-freedom dialectic, no understanding of Pauline Christianity; without Pauline Christianity, there would have been no Western civilization as we know it.
>
> Is this to exalt slavery? Not at all. Rather, it is to recognize one of the central truths of Christianity, and of the civilization it fashioned: that out of evil and the greatest suffering often comes the greatest good. Isn't that what the Cross is all about?[85]

Patterson does not mean that the evil of slavery is somehow secretly good. The truth that great good can come out of evil does not mean that good justifies evil.

The ideological distortion of the theology of the cross is related to what historians S. P. Fullinwider and Wilson Jeremiah Moses have described as a pervasive and persistent stereotype of "Negro moral character," the view that the African race has a Christlike character exemplified in traits of love, forgiveness, kindness, longsuffering patience, meekness, humility, and so forth.[86] There have been substantial numbers of both black and white adherents to this stereotype since at least the early nineteenth century and continuing well into the twentieth. As a racial myth, it appears in a highly influential form in Harriet Beecher Stowe's *Uncle Tom's Cabin*.[87] In the African American tradition, it has served radical black protest thinkers from abolitionists in the 1850s to advocates of emigration in the late nineteenth century to leaders of the Niagara Movement and the formation of the NAACP in the early twentieth century to voices of the Civil Rights Movement of the 1950s and 60s. It is impossible to rehearse here the rich and varied history of the Christlike myth, which was often associated with a mission theology. In its self-consciously Christian form, it usually involved the claim that African Americans have a special vocation to Christianize, humanize, civilize white America and the world.

85. Patterson, "Paul, Slavery, and Freedom," 266.

86. S. P. Fullinwider, *The Mind and Mood of Black America: 20th Century Thought* (Homewood: Dorsey, 1969); Wilson Jeremiah Moses, *Black Messiahs and Uncle Toms: Social and Literary Manipulations of a Religious Myth* (University Park: University of Pennsylvania Press, 1982), 49-66 and passim. See also Kenneth S. Lynn, *Mark Twain and Southwestern Humor* (Boston: Little Brown, 1959), 105-11.

87. See Moses, *Black Messiahs and Uncle Toms*, 49-66.

Theophilus Gould Steward looked to Afro-Asiatic people as the race that would humanize the world in fulfillment of Paul's prophecy in Rom. 11:25 (see above). Martin Luther King often described African Americans as "God's instrument to save the soul of America."[88]

Sometimes the theology of African American vocation was linked to the idea of redemptive suffering. Of special interest for us is the place of Paul's theology of the cross in the development of nonviolent resistance as a form of redemptive suffering. In a 1924 sermon, Howard University President Mordecai Johnson described Paul as one who "discovered that the way to happiness is the way of the cross. . . . suffering man is the man who takes hold of the realities of life . . . the one who runs from the cross runs from life."[89] Fullinwider notes that Johnson was later deeply impressed by Howard Thurman's theology of redemptive suffering, which Thurman developed after meeting Gandhi and brought to Howard in the 1930s. Johnson himself went to see Gandhi and returned with the teaching of politically redemptive suffering love. Martin Luther King Jr. went to hear Johnson lecture on Gandhi, an event that sparked King's own intensive study of Gandhi's philosophy of nonviolence.[90] One of the challenges for African American leaders in the nineteenth and twentieth centuries was how to integrate the virtues of the "Christ-like Negro" with the righteous rebelliousness of activist black nationalism. King, rejecting both submissive acquiescence and the call for violence by Black Power, worked out a prophetic vision in which an activist quest for justice is pursued through the political strategy of nonviolence, and the practice of that nonviolence as redemptive suffering replaces the Victorian moral rectitude of nineteenth-century romantic racialism. Thus, a Pauline theology of the cross and the paradigmatic suffering love of Jesus are important biblical roots of King's theology of nonviolence and stand in a tradition of African American reflection on redemptive suffering and political activism going back to Thurman's encounter with Gandhi.

An early-twentieth-century reading of black suffering through the Pauline lens of the cross appears in a 1911 poem by African American poet

88. See Frederick L. Downing, "Martin Luther King, Jr. as a Public Theologian," *Theology Today* 44 (1987): 26-29.

89. As quoted by Fullinwider, *Mind and Mood,* 239.

90. Fullinwider, *Mind and Mood,* 239.

Leslie Pinckney Hill. Hill alludes to the election theme of 1 Cor. 1:27-28 in developing the idea that his own people are a chosen nation. To understand Hill's use of Pauline concepts and language, it is important to have some of the words of 1 Cor. 1:18-28 in mind:

> For the message about the cross is foolishness to those who are perishing, but to us who are being saved it is the power of God. . . . For Jews demand signs and Greeks desire wisdom, but we proclaim Christ crucified, a stumbling block to Jews and foolishness to Gentiles. . . . Consider your own call, brothers and sisters: not many of you were wise by human standards, not many were powerful, not many were of noble birth. But God chose what is foolish in the world to shame the wise; God chose what is weak in the world to shame the strong; God chose what is low and despised in the world, things that are not, to reduce to nothing things that are. . . .

In his poem Hill contrasts God's election of the weak with the self-presumption of the powerful nations of the earth, who "spurn the truth of brotherhood" and "trade in life."[91] The poet prays that "all my brothers in distress . . . might know themselves a chosen folk," and he envisions a day when this chosen people, "mingled through/With all the bloods of men," will have the power to enlighten the present world and "make it alive."[92] As we have seen, the idea that the black nation has a special vocation in history to bring about a new America and a new era of justice is found in many different African American thinkers. Hill alludes to 1 Cor 1:27-28 in reflecting on the possibility that "God sends the Negro on a special errand":

> . . . for God hath chosen still
> The weak thing, and the foolish, and the base,
> And that which is despised to work His will;
> And humble men are chartered yet to run
> Upon His errands round the groaning sphere.
> Not many that dispute, Not many wise,
> That so the prophecy may be fulfilled.[93]

91. Benjamin E. Mays, *The Negro's God: As Reflected in His Literature* (New York: Atheneum, 1968), 181.

92. Mays, *The Negro's God,* 181-82.

93. Mays, *The Negro's God,* 180.

"Errand" was a common term for the church's mission in the English-speaking world of the eighteenth and nineteenth centuries. It had associations in many circles with imperialist conceptions of Christian expansion and, in America, with the emerging doctrine of manifest destiny.[94] Hill uses Paul's theology of the cross to challenge American imperialism. According to Paul, God created the church in Christ by choosing the lowly and powerless to shame the wise and the powerful. Hill treats this as a disclosure of how God characteristically works in the world, electing the weak and socially despised to fulfill God's great purposes in history. Hill unites Paul's understanding of election with the idea that African American people have a national vocation (an errand) like Israel's. Applying the language of 1 Cor. 1:26-27 to the concept of black national vocation imparts an anti-imperialist cast to that vocation. The new humanity comes not through violence but by the way of the cross.[95]

In a 1787 evangelistic address, Jupiter Hammon, a slave residing with his master in Long Island, New York, applied 1 Cor. 1:27-28 to African Americans ("Negroes"), characterizing them as the kind of poor, humble people that God calls.[96] Hammon describes the slaves as an oppressed people,[97] but the dominant note of his sermon is not this-worldly liberation but the hope of heaven. Lacking the comforts and happiness of this world, "no people," Hammon says, "ought to attend to the hope of happiness in another world, so much as we."[98]

The theme of 1 Cor. 1:26-27 is also found in African Methodist Episcopal Church founder Richard Allen's famous "Address to Those Who Keep Slaves and Approve the Practice." Commenting on slave insurrections, Allen points out that they are proof that slaves are not content in their state. "God himself hath pleaded their cause; He hath from time to

94. See William R. Hutchison, *Errand to the World: American Protestant Thought and Foreign Missions* (Chicago: University of Chicago Press, 1987); Forrest G. Wood, *The Arrogance of Faith: Christianity and Race in America from the Colonial Era to the Twentieth Century* (New York: Knopf, 1990).

95. A theology of the cross permeates Hill's poem, a subject to which we will return below.

96. Jupiter Hammon, "An Address to the Negroes in the State of New York," in *Early Negro Writing: 1760-1837*, ed. Dorothy Porter (Boston: Beacon, 1971), 313-23. See page 321 for Hammon's application of 1 Cor. 1:27-28 to his slave audience.

97. In his cover letter to the editors who published his address, Hammond refers to their kindness "to those you thought were oppressed" (Porter, *Early Negro Writing*, 313).

98. Porter, *Early Negro Writing*, 321.

time raised up instruments for that purpose, sometimes mean and contemptible in your sight. . . ."[99] Allen does not use Paul's words from 1 Cor. 1:26-27 but seems to have Paul's thought in mind; in any case, Allen's language produces echoes of Paul in my ears.

Another allusion to the way of divine election according to 1 Cor. 1:26-27 appears in an 1865 speech by a black lawyer and activist, John Mercer Langston. Arguing for civil rights, Langston invokes the history of black participation in building the American nation. He mentions the celebrated case of Crispus Attucks, "a mulatto slave, the first American that fell giving his life and blood in defense of his country."[100] John Adams stigmatized Attucks and the other colonial participants in the Boston Massacre as "a motley rabble of saucy boys, Negroes and mulattoes, Irish Teagues and outlandish jack tars."[101] To these slurs, Langston quotes Paul: "Be it so, God takes the weak things of the world to confound the mighty."[102] I cite this example not because I agree with either Adams's prejudice or Langston's assumption that God was on the side of the American colonies, but only to illustrate that Paul's election principle in 1 Cor. 1:26-27 was so well-known among African Americans and its use as an interpretive key to *how God works with people in history* was taken so for granted that one could appeal to it by mere allusion, without explicit quotation or reference.

The theologies of the cross we find in King and his predecessors, as well as in Hill, Langston, and perhaps Allen, might be called "activist" because they cast black people, in their historic suffering, as historical agents, not simply as sacrificial victims of some higher mysterious scheme. Hill's use of 1 Cor. 1:26-27 draws on the link between election and active vocation in Paul's theology of the cross. Analogically speaking, Hill's poem suggests, God has chosen black people, like the Corinthian Christians and Jesus himself, for a work in history. For King and others committed to nonviolent resistance, suffering is not an end in itself but is rather the risk that love takes in seeking justice. If we examine this idea in terms of Paul's theology, it is helpful to distinguish between two sides of the Pauline concept

99. Richard Allen, *The Life Experience and Gospel Labors of the Rt. Rev. Richard Allen* (Nashville: Abingdon, 1960), 71.

100. John Mercer Langston, "Citizenship and the Ballot," in *The Black Abolitionist Papers 1830-1865*, ed. C. Peter Ripley (Chapel Hill: University of North Carolina Press, 1992), 5:389.

101. Ripley, *Black Abolitionist Papers*, 5:389.

102. Ripley, *Black Abolitionist Papers*, 5:389.

of Jesus' death. On one hand there is Jesus' death as a sacrifice, which the black church has long embraced and affirmed as an expression of divine forgiveness that also creates a spirit of forgiveness and reconciliation in those who receive it. That spirit of reconciliation can work social benefits in society. But there is also what might be called the story of Jesus in Paul, which casts Jesus as God's active, obedient servant who lived for others, not himself (Phil. 2:5-11; Rom. 5:18; 15:3; Gal. 2:20; 2 Cor. 8:9). This story, especially when read as part of the larger story of Jesus in the New Testament, is a natural source for the image of Jesus as a nonviolent agent of love in the service of God's will. Lacking worldly power and prestige, he overcomes the wisdom and power of the world through his cruciform life. Here the cross symbolizes Jesus' willingness to give himself for others, his social location with the socially powerless, and the way God works in history through the weakness of suffering love and through people who lack social prestige and worldly power. The nonviolent way of Jesus appears in this light as an indictment of the crucifixion, which is an act of violence that contradicts the way of love revealed in Christ.

As an ideology, "redemptive suffering" is the rationale by which a dominant group justifies imposing a way of pain and deprivation on a less powerful group. By contrast, Paul presents Jesus as one who embraced the way of love, risking and accepting suffering as a freely chosen path, not as an imposition on him by society. His suffering was not culturally conforming but countercultural. In the same way, the nonviolent political action of the Civil Rights Movement was a freely chosen embrace of suffering through socially nonconformist acts (civil disobedience). Martin Luther King and Malcolm X had differing interpretations of the nonviolent strategies of suffering that King advocated. Malcolm and Black Power saw these practices as acquiescence to the nonviolent, passive role in history assigned to blacks by whites. King viewed these acts as a form of redemptive suffering, an activist expression of a theology of the cross, *in protest against* the suffering of African Americans through history, including suffering justified by the *ideology* of redemptive suffering.

In the introduction to one of his studies of messianic black nationalism, African American historian Wilson Moses comments, "I am somewhat embarrassed by the idealism of those who persist in seeing black Americans as 'suffering servants' or as 'God's humanizing agents.' But, at the same time, I dread the loss of black America's special sense of mission, for like Ralph Ellison, I have some misgivings about the future of any society that has been entirely freed from its illusions."[103] Moses closes his book with a counterpoise: "The question confronting black Americans at the end of the twentieth century is whether we can remain separate enough from American culture to assume the role that Martin Luther King, Jr., envisioned — a conscience and a soul for the nation. Alas, I fear this is too heavy a cross for black Americans to be asked to bear."[104]

It is certainly not my place to ask African Americans to bear this cross or any other cross. I should ask instead whether white America is prepared to embrace an activist way of the cross in the struggle for justice in the world. Nevertheless, I affirm the right of African American Christians to interpret their centuries-long quest for racial justice as a vocation that has served and continues to serve not only themselves but all people and that gives the history of their suffering for the sake of justice a double meaning under the cross: as the violence that God opposes and the risk of love that God dignifies.

103. Moses, *Black Messiahs and Uncle Toms,* 16.
104. Moses, *Black Messiahs and Uncle Toms,* 234.

CHAPTER 5

Christ and the Earth in Pauline and Native American Understandings

K. K. (Khiok-khng) Yeo

In attempting a cross-cultural reading between Paul and the Native Americans,[1] I want to acknowledge my limitations as a Chinese and as an academician trained in American institutions. A Native scholar has sincerely admonished me not to write this chapter because, he warns me, Pauline theology is simply too foreign to Native ways of thinking. Native Christian scholars have not tried to develop a Native American interpretation of Paul; therefore, my chance of success is slim. I recognize the wisdom of this Native scholar's advice, yet I have attempted to research and write this chapter anyway, *not* because I want to tell Native Americans what they should think about Paul but because I want to learn from them how I can see Paul with new eyes. I seek a cross-cultural experience, a journey to what is for me a very foreign culture. This chapter attempts to look at Paul through Native American eyes to show the possibilities for a Native American Christian reading of Paul that may help a Chinese Christian (and others with ears to hear) consider fresh possibilities for understanding Paul.

As a non-Native, I depend on those insiders who are willing to share with me their experiences regarding the complex Native American cul-

1. Various designations such as Natives, Indians, American Indians, Native Indians, American Natives, Native American Indians, and American Native Indians are used by scholars. I was informed by a Native friend that use of "Indians" is appropriate by a Native person but generally not appropriate by a non-Native. Hence, I will use "Native" or "Natives," referring to Native American Indians. It should be noted that the words "American," "Indian," and "Native" were not originally self-designations. But since these terms are used pervasively and are widely accepted, it makes sense to use them, but with the historical consciousness that they carry a history. See William A. Young, *Quest for Harmony: Native American Spiritual Traditions* (New York: Seven Bridges, 2002), 12.

tures.[2] Leon Matthews, a Lakota (Sioux) pastor whom I interviewed for this project, encouraged me in my journey to read Paul through Native American understandings. He writes:

> [As Lakota people] we have the idea that Jesus is the whiteman's God and we have our own ways. Paul was educated in the ways of his ancestors and he practiced the ways of his people. Reading Paul's letters we understand that he was a Jew of the Jews and it took a supernatural change of his heart to follow the Christ. Native Americans practice their own religion and walk in the ways of their grandfathers and it is apparent that it will be the work of the Holy Spirit to change the meaning and life of the Lakota person to walk with Jesus.[3]

Should one agree with those who argue that Pauline Christianity and Native American religions have no hope of dialogue? Vine Deloria, for example, describes Christianity and Native religions as incompatible religious systems. Native religions, he points out, refuse to represent deities anthropomorphically in a series of complex relationships and doctrines. Therefore, there is no need to have a personal relationship with the Great Spirit in the Native religions.[4] Further, Christianity's focus on the story of the Fall and the need for redemption, with the implication that the natural world is corrupted, is very different from the affirmation of the goodness of the natural world intrinsic to Native American spirituality.[5] Not only that, Native religions affirm the affinity of the human species with all living creatures; hence, human beings are required to cooperate with the Great Spirit in the task of creating the world. Deloria argues that the biblical understanding of the centrality of humans and human domination over creation is not compatible with Native basic belief.[6]

2. In addition to the many authors I consulted, I want to thank Natives who gave personal assistance. Among them are Justine and Andy Smith, George Tinker, Jace Weaver, and a number of Native pastors, especially Leon Matthews. Matthews is the President and CEO of Oyate Kin Wacekiya Omniciye (The People Gathered to Pray) located in the Pine Ridge (Oglala Sioux) Reservation in South Dakota, one of two indigenous pastors on a reservation of 40,000. He has served the Pine Ridge Gospel Fellowship since 1995. Leon's wife Belva is also an Oglala Sioux tribal member and grew up in the village of Pine Ridge.

3. Personal interview, used with permission.

4. Vine Deloria, Jr., *God Is Red* (New York: Grosset and Dunlap, 1973), 92-93.

5. Deloria, *God Is Red,* 93-94.

6. Deloria, *God Is Red,* 96-98.

Deloria's work is radical. Most Native pastors I interviewed believe there is substantial compatibility between Paul and Native American thought. Most Native pastors are keen to point out the multicultural contexts and communication skills of Paul. Pastor Matthews writes:

> Paul was strictly Jewish in a Gentile environment but he also understood the Greek worldview. . . . Living with Gentiles gave him a unique experience and he was suited for the Great Commission left by our Lord Jesus. Theologically Paul brought a Natural Revelation to our understanding seen in Romans 2:14. Paul has answered the question that many indigenous people are concerned about when they become Christians. Many Native people are concerned about their family and Paul sees that the indigenous people of the world have the Father written on their hearts. Lakota culture was similar as they reached out to the unknown God through sacrifice and community. Their concept of *Tiospaye* (Clans based on Family Ties) was a community where each person had a place in the circle and lived their lives in Respect to the unknown God.[7]

Some Native scholars also take a more positive view of Paul's significance for Native Christian understanding.[8] In what follows, I keep the cautions of scholars like Deloria in mind but also pay special attention to the thinking of Native Americans who look for positive ways to connect Paul and Christian faith with their culture and religion.

In discussing Native American history, life, and teachings in relation to Western traditions, Christianity, and Paul, I cannot avoid running some risks that I want to be clear about at the outset. First, it is very difficult in a study of this length to give a balanced and nuanced picture of Native American cultures and history. There are many Native cultures and many intersecting Native histories, reaching back before recorded memory. William Young sketches the life of Ice Age hunters in the "Paleo-Indian" (Lithic) period (ca. 50,000–4500 BCE) in the North American continent. Evidence of

7. Personal interview, used with permission. Rom. 2:14, to which Pastor Matthews refers, says, "Indeed, when Gentiles, who do not have the law, do by nature things required by the law, they are a law for themselves, even though they do not have the law" (New International Version).

8. I have found examples of this in Bruce David Forbes, ed., *Voices in Exchange: American Natives and Protestant Christianity,* commissioned by Native American Theological Association (not published). Section four of this collection is especially significant. In it Native Christians express their aspiration for a more fully indigenous faith and church.

pottery, heated stones, domesticated corn, and burials of the Archaic period (4500–1000 BCE) has been found in New Mexico. The Anasazi of the Southwest and the Mound Builders had documented cultures by 1500 BCE–1500 CE).[9] Young's research points to at least two to three hundred different languages spoken by indigenous groups in America before 1492. There were some six hundred autonomous societies existing before the arrival of Europeans. In view of this, although one can generalize about Native Americans in the last several hundred years (as I will do), inevitably much detail will be left out; many qualifications that should be made will be left unsaid.

Second, in comparing and contrasting Native American beliefs and practices and those of Europeans and Americans, it is difficult to be fair and evenhanded. Too much brutality and misunderstanding haunt the history of Native and Euro-American relations. To speak positively of Natives in contrast to Europeans may sound like one is creating a hierarchy in which Natives are better than Euro-Americans. To speak positively of Euro-American beliefs and practices runs the reverse risk. Even the effort to give a sympathetic if also critical interpretation of either side at any point or moment in history can give false impressions. Today, some tend to idealize Native Americans. Others tend to rationalize or defend the horrible history of American mistreatment of the Native peoples. I hope to avoid both tendencies. In what follows, I speak of Native cultural ideals. I do not mean that Native Americans have always lived up to these ideals or even that they are shared universally by Natives. For example, when I refer to Native ideals of peace and harmony with all parts of creation, I do not mean to suggest that only non-Natives have engaged in violence or that Native American peoples have always been peace-loving.

I will say very critical things about Euro-American treatment of Native Americans and very positive things about Native American culture and ideals, but I do not want to give a false "Romantic" impression, as if Natives have been ideal human beings who always respected the land and all creatures, living innocent and noble lives in harmony with the pristine state of nature. These are stereotypes. Lewis O. Saum has mentioned that in addition to "the bright side of Indian Life," there is also "the dark side" as well,[10] just as there is with Euro-Americans and the rest of us. For exam-

9. Young, *Quest for Harmony,* 16-19.

10. Lewis O. Saum, *The Fur Trader and the Indian* (Seattle: University of Washington Press, 1965), xi.

ple, Stephen Ambrose has given us a nuanced and complex picture of Crazy Horse, whose life is very similar to that of the warrior personality of George A. Custer. Some Native nations on the great plains cultivated a warrior way of life and treated other Native peoples with violent aggression.[11] Richard Van Der Beets, in *Held Captive by Indians,* says that "American Indians took white or non-Indian captives for four principal reasons: to use as slaves; to ransom (to the English and, later, Americans); to sell (to the French or to other tribes); and to replace, by adoption, those members of the tribe lost or slain in battle."[12] Joel Martin gives a balanced account of how the interaction between Natives and Christians in the past fostered mutual benefits, not just the Christian "colonization" that we often hear about.[13]

With all this in mind, the purpose here is to discuss how Native American cultures can best engage in meaningful dialogue with Pauline theology. The task is to look at the overwhelming oppressions of the past and to trace where Native American biblical interpretation has been and where it may go from here — not just for the sake of Native Americans but also for the global community.

Fundamental Contrasts between Native American and Euro-American Religion: Creation and Redemption

George E. Tinker, a Native American and a professor at Iliff Seminary, sees Vine Deloria's work as foundational. Building on Deloria, Tinker delineates areas in which Native American theology differs from Euro-American theology.[14] For example, the Old Testament narrative and covenant are more compatible with Native traditions than is the New Testament. Tinker is not saying that the New Testament is irrelevant but that Native Americans find in the Old Testament a kind of storytelling that fits

11. Stephen E. Ambrose, *Crazy Horse and Custer: The Parallel Lives of Two American Warriors* (New York: Anchor, 1996).

12. Richard Van Der Beets, *Held Captive by Indians: Selected Narratives, 1642-1836* (Knoxville: University of Tennessee Press, 1973), xi.

13. Joel W. Martin, *Native American Religion* (New York: Oxford University Press, 1999), 67-90.

14. George Tinker, "An American Indian Reading of the Bible," in *New Interpreter's Bible,* ed. Leander E. Keck, et al. (Nashville: Abingdon, 1994), 1:174-80.

their ways of teaching and passing on tradition through oral storytelling. Nevertheless, Tinker challenges those who claim that key narratives of the Old Testament such as the "colonial conquest paradigm" of Pharaoh and his army and the "peasant revolt paradigm" of the Hebrew slaves working for Pharaoh have positive significance for Native Americans because they are challenges to oppressors. Both stories are problematic, Tinker says, because they are based on violence and therefore celebrate the sacrifice of one group for the benefit of the other. These stories are alien to Native American ideals that value harmony over conquest. As a Pauline scholar, I observe that some of Tinker's concerns are addressed by Paul's gospel. More will be said about this below.

Tinker, along with Clara Kidwell and Homer Noley, also contrasts Native American thinking about creation with Christian theology in the Euro-American tradition. They note that Native American stories of creation do not place human beings at the pinnacle of creation.[15] Further, these creation stories are extremely significant in Native American traditions and carry a significance equal to that of redemption stories in the Western tradition. The creation stories are "ontological constructs" used to interpret Native American worldviews. Where traditional Christian theology teaches that the sin of humanity (Adam and Eve) caused a "Fall" of creation, which therefore stands in need of redemption, Native Americans do not see creation as fallen. In their understanding, what human beings need to live good lives and experience blessing is given with creation. Thus, creation, thought of "spatially" (as a world or web of relationships) and not temporally (as a beginning point or act), holds in Native American thinking the place that belongs to redemption in traditional Christian thinking. The title of a recent book on Native religion expresses this idea: *The Land Looks After Us.*[16] The centrality of the earth in Native American life raises a significant question for readers of Paul. Given that he preaches a gospel of redemption that is temporally oriented, what is the relation between creation and redemption in Paul? And is there any possibility of a Pauline theology that can in some ways affirm rather than simply negate the place of the earth in Native American understanding?

15. Clara Sue Kidwell, Homer Noley, and George E. Tinker, *A Native American Theology* (Maryknoll: Orbis, 2001), 35-36.

16. Joel W. Martin, *The Land Looks After Us: A History of Native American Religion* (New York: Oxford University Press, 2001), 67-90. This is a reprint with a new title of *Native American Religion,* cited above.

Recently, Native American theologians have developed the traditional concepts of creation by focusing on environmental ethics, often referred to today as "eco-justice." An example is Jace Weaver's *Defending Mother Earth: Native American Perspectives on Environmental Justice,* which argues that Native American belief systems cannot be articulated without reference to land and creation. To talk theologically one must also talk about environment, the life-giving system.[17] In other words, without eco-justice human survival is threatened because we are all connected within the life-giving system. Kidwell, Noley, and Tinker's *A Native American Theology* also emphasizes eco-justice as intrinsic to Native American worldviews, lifestyles, and theologies.

Euro-American and Native Relations in Political and Missionary Contexts

The Lenape (Delaware) have a traditional epic, the *Wallam Olum* ("Red Record"), which traces the history of the people from creation to the arrival of European explorers at the Delaware River. It ends with a beautiful and unexpected verse: "Friendly people, in great ships: who are they?"[18] Generally speaking, the cultural and religious differences between Native American and Euro-American worldviews are related to their different uses of resources. This difference has often led to tense relations and even warfare.[19] Native Americans accuse Euro-Americans of racism and colonialism resulting in "genocide" and "ecocide."[20] Some argue that the dev-

17. Jace Weaver, ed., *Defending Mother Earth: Native American Perspectives on Environmental Justice* (Maryknoll: Orbis, 1996).

18. Young, *Quest for Harmony,* 65. The Lenape (meaning "real or common people") are an Algonquian-speaking people who before the eighteenth century resided on the east coast of the United States. Today they live in northeastern and southwestern Oklahoma, Wisconsin, and Ontario after at least seven migrations.

19. See Alan Axelrod, *Chronicle of the Indian Wars: From Colonial Times to Wounded Knee* (New York: Macmillan, 1990).

20. Donald A. Grinde, Jr., and Bruce E. Johansen, *Ecocide of Native America: Environmental Destruction of Indian Lands and Peoples* (Sante Fe: Clear Light, 1995); Ward Churchill, *Struggle for the Land: Indigenous Resistance to Genocide, Ecocide and Expropriation in Contemporary North America* (Monroe: Common Courage, 1993) on nuclear waste, toxic dumping, water and other earth resources. On atrocities, domination, and ill treatment of Natives by Euro-Americans, see Bernard W. Sheehan, *Savagism and Civility: Indians and Englishmen*

astations threaten not just the Native American world but also global ecology and human life.[21]

Tinker narrates "the continual and progressive erosion of Native national sovereignty and self-determination over the past five hundred years" in American history.[22] He recounts that the erosion began with Columbus's arrival and making the Native land the property of his Spanish monarchs. Today, he says, the American government and corporate power are draining the resources of the earth.[23] Spain and America sought to "civilize," colonize, and Christianize indigenous populations at not only political, military, and economic levels, but also intellectually, philosophically, and ideologically.

One might imagine that Christian missionaries who came as proclaimers of the good news of freedom and blessing in Christ were different from those Euro-Americans who came as explorers and empire builders. Yet many missionaries further reinforced the ideology of the colonizers: to civilize the Natives was to Christianize and Europeanize them. For example, Moravian missionaries working among the Cherokees (the Ani'-Yun'-wiya) conducted meetings and wrote treaties in German. Later, the Cherokee Council prohibited the missionaries from teaching the Natives German and allowed them to enter the territory only if they advanced the interests of the Natives.[24] George Tinker points to efforts at cultural

---

in Colonial Virginia (New York: Cambridge University Press, 1980); Ward Churchill and Jim Vander Wall, *Agents of Repression: The FBI's Secret Wars against the Black Panther Party and the American Indian Movement* (Boston: South End, 1988); Rex Weyler, *The Blood of the Land: The Government and Corporate War Against the American Indian Movement* (New York: Vintage, 1984). See Young, *Quest for Harmony,* 58-59, on the debate about use of the word "genocide" in Native stories. I prefer to use that word in quotation marks, following Axtell, who differentiates mass killing of a group from the political, economic, religious and social domination of a group. See James Axtell, *Beyond 1492: Encounter in Colonial North America* (New York: Oxford University Press, 1992), 260-93.

21. See Richard Cartwright Austin, *Hope for the Land: Nature in the Bible* (Atlanta: John Knox, 1987), 190-94; "Profile of Environmental Peril" in *After Nature's Revolt: Eco-Justice and Theology,* ed. Dieter T. Hessel (Minneapolis: Fortress, 1992), 3-8; Colin A. Russell, *The Earth, Humanity and God: The Templeton Lectures, Cambridge, 1993* (London: UCL, 1994), 52-93.

22. George Tinker, "An American Indian Theological Response to Ecojustice," in Weaver, ed., *Defending Mother Earth,* 169.

23. Tinker, "American Indian Theological Response," 169-70.

24. George Tinker, *Missionary Conquest: The Gospel and Native American Cultural Genocide* (Minneapolis: Fortress, 1993), 21-111.

genocide in the missionary activities of John Eliot in Puritan New England, Pierre-Jean De Smet in the Northwest, Father Junipero Serra in California, and Henry Benjamin Whipple (1822-1901), Episcopal bishop of Minnesota during the latter half of the nineteenth century.[25]

Euro-American missionaries, just as most missionaries in Christian history, had difficulty distinguishing evangelism and cultural imposition. The civilization campaigns of the kings, corporate companies, and government agencies sought to colonize and civilize Native Americans. The Euro-American ideology of superiority is seen, for example, in John Eliot's answer to the Natives' question as to why English people differ so much from the Natives in their knowledge of God and Jesus Christ, though they all have a common father. John Eliot answers:

> We confessed that it was true that at first wee had all but one father, but after that our first father fell, hee had divers children some were bad and some good, . . . and so the difference arose at first, that some together with their posterity knew God, and others did not; . . . so wee said English men seek God, dwell in his house, heare his word, pray to God, instruct their children out of Gods booke, hence they come to know God; but Indians forefathers were stubborne and rebellious children, and would not heare the word, did not care to pray nor to teach their children, and hence Indians that now are, do not know God at all. . . .[26]

Thinking it was in the best interest of the state, some missionaries cooperated with government policy, supporting the removal of Natives into reservations. Indian reservations eventually became "national sacrifice areas,"[27] a phrase that refers to contemporary environmental policies that use certain lands as repositories of toxic wastes. Col. John Chivington, a Methodist clergyman, led the Colorado militia in the Sand Creek Massacre, in which Black Kettle's band of peaceful Cheyenne were slaughtered. Samuel A. Worcester, a Congregationalist missionary to the Cherokees of Georgia, was one of a few among Christian missionaries who at first went against these practices. His refusal to take an oath of allegiance to the state of Georgia was contested all the way to the Supreme Court. The *Worcester*

25. Tinker, *Missionary Conquest,* 21-111.
26. Forbes, ed., *Voices in Exchange,* 22.
27. Tinker, "American Indian Theological Response," 167.

v. Georgia decision affirmed Native sovereignty and is binding law to this day. But in the 1830s Worcester advocated voluntary removal and lost his credibility among the Cherokees.[28]

With a few exceptions, most missionaries supported the "civilization" programs. For example, Isaac McCoy (1784-1846), originally a Baptist minister and missionary, later, as a member of a federal commission formed to resettle Natives westward, supported the removal and the "civilization" program that accompanied it. He thought implementation of the Indian Removal Act would help the Natives, but he also received good compensation for his work in the resettlement.[29] According to Commissioner of Indian Affairs John Collier, the American government opposed Native American religious practices because "the religions made the tribes strong, and made the individuals of the tribe immune to intimidation or corruption."[30] Missionaries of various denominations pressed the government to promulgate the so-called "Religious Crimes Codes," forbidding the practice of Native religious traditions. In support of these measures, missionaries tried to convince the Natives that their cultures and spiritualities were depraved, offering no hope for the future. The missionaries confused Christianity with their European culture. For them, to be a Christian meant to stop being a Native.

The exploitation of Native Americans in the last five hundred years is difficult, if not impossible, to reverse or correct. Of course, there have been important changes and advances. Young suggests that in many ways the modern era for Natives began in 1933 when President Roosevelt appointed Collier as Commissioner. Collier was committed to Native interests and

28. In December 1829 the state of Georgia declared all territory within the state's boundaries to be under the sovereignty of the people of Georgia, denying Cherokee ownership of their land, and sought to remove them to the west. Worcester and Elizur Butler were imprisoned because of their refusal to acknowledge the sovereignty of Georgia over Indian land. In 1832 Justice John Marshall declared Georgia's law unconstitutional and ordered the release of Worcester and Butler. See Forbes, ed., *Voices in Exchange,* 87-96. On legal and governmental protection of Native lands, see Deward E. Walker, Jr., "Protection of American Indian Sacred Geography," in *Handbook of American Indian Religious Freedom,* ed. Christopher Vecsey (New York: Crossroad, 1991), 100-115.

29. See Forbes, ed., *Voices in Exchange,* 99-107; Isaac McCoy, *History of Baptist Indian Missions: Embracing Remarks on the Former and Present Condition of the Aboriginal Tribes, Their Settlement within the Indian Territory, and Their Future Prospects* (Washington: Morrison/New York: Raynor, 1840), 34-41.

30. Kidwell, Noley, and Tinker, *A Native American Theology,* 176-77.

the principles of Native self-determination, self-government, and self-preservation. Under his leadership, Congress passed the Wheeler-Howard Indian Reorganization Act, which respected Native cultural values and gave Natives the freedom not to attend Christian activities. Young describes the period between 1933 and 1990 as one of coexistence, restoration, and renewal.[31] The 1978 Supreme Court ruling in *U.S. v. Wheeler* finally recognized the full sovereignty of Native nations.

Nevertheless, the legacy of the past has left deep scars and many unrequited injustices. In addition to the "external colonialism" of the past, there is what Tinker calls "internal colonialism" in Native American communities today. He explains:

> The conservative or even fundamentalist posture of many Indian-led congregations in nearly all Protestant denominations is a prime example of what Robert Thomas called "internal colonialism" and Annette Jaimes identifies as "autogenocide." Psychologically . . . American Indian people have so internalized the missionary critique of Indian culture and religious traditions and so internalized our own concession to the superiority of Euroamerican social structures that . . . today, an Indian pastor is more likely than a white missionary to criticize the paganism of traditional spirituality.[32]

The notion of "internal colonialism" raises a critical issue. Is the only authentic Native American Christianity one that has no elements of Euro-American culture? Are Native expressions of Christian faith that do not radically criticize the Bible and Western Christian faith from Native perspectives simply locked blindly into "internal colonialism"? While Tinker's critiques of the missionary conquest are correct, I wonder if conservative or even fundamentalist congregations might find Tinker's critique of them patronizing. I received a wide range of responses from pastors I interviewed regarding this issue. I think that Native congregations and pastors must be allowed to make their own cultural judgments and religious decisions as they contextualize their faith within the dominant American culture and their own Native cultures.

The preceding survey highlights the question of gospel and culture. The motivations of the missionaries were mixed. They worked religiously

31. Young, *Quest for Harmony,* 48-58.

32. Tinker, *Missionary Conquest,* 118.

for the sake of the gospel but culturally for the sake of their own civilization. The government gave them substantial financial incentives for assisting the Natives to assimilate to the government policies. How much of the missionary motivation was *gloria Dei?* It is difficult to tell. Or were the missionaries unable to tell religious from political motivations? In many if not most cases that seems likely.[33] This blind spot reveals the danger of cross-cultural interpretation. Missionaries were concerned with the reign of God's kingdom over all pagan land. This well-meaning motivation supported a colonizing strategy as a way of converting Natives to Christian faith and away from their cultures. Thus, the compassion of the missionaries became a justification for "civilizing" these "ruines of mankind," as one put it.[34]

A minority of Christian leaders disagreed with this understanding of missions. For example, Joseph Brant, Sir William Johnson, and Charles Chauncy, pastor of the Second Church in Boston, "believed that the red man could be a Christian and still remain an Indian."[35] Baptist missionaries in Oklahoma and North Carolina who committed themselves to the Cherokee cultural norms and national priorities, were overwhelmingly successful.[36] Cherokees were quickly able to assume leadership in Baptist churches and to offer their cultural expressions of the Christian faith and liturgical life.[37]

Moreover, just as there have been missionaries who valued Native American cultures, there have also been Natives who valued elements of European culture and sought to remain dynamically Native by creating a new Christian life out of the encounter of European and Native cultures.[38] At the

33. There were exceptions. Roger Williams (1603-1683) and William Penn (1644-1718) stand out (see Young, *Quest for Harmony*, 28-29). Father Louis Hennepin liked to tell stories of Natives that exposed Europeans' false sense of superiority. See Louis Hennepin, *A New Discovery of a Vast Country in America*, vol. 2 (Chicago: McClurg, 1903; reprint of 1698 London edition), 536.

34. R. Pierce Beaver, "The Missions to Native Americans," quoted in Forbes, ed., *Voices in Exchange*, 8.

35. Beaver, "Missions to Native Americans," quoted in Forbes, ed., *Voices in Exchange*, 9.

36. Justin Smith, "Resistance Disguised as Fundamentalism: Challenging the Myth of Assimilation among Oklahoma Cherokees," Unpublished Paper; see William G. McLoughlin, *Cherokees and Missionaries* I, *1789-1839* (New Haven: Yale University Press, 1984), 150-51.

37. Alan Kilpatrick, "A Note on Cherokee Theological Concepts," *American Indian Quarterly* 19 (Summer 1995): 395-96.

38. See Joel Martin, *The Land Looks After Us*, 61-113.

same time, there are voices in the evangelical and conservative branches of Native Christianity — those wings of Native Christianity in which some see only internal colonialism — that champion Native identity and criticize the adoption of Euro-American culture by Natives. For example, Richard Twiss, an evangelical Native Christian writer and President of Wiconi International, advocates evangelization of Native Americans while peeling away Euro-American cultural garments so that the Natives can see Jesus in the light of the Scriptures but contextualized in the Native cultures.[39] One difficulty in interpretation here is that what may look externally like Native assimilation to what the missionaries brought may be a more complex appropriation and reinterpretation. For example, Alan Kilpatrick sees a resemblance between baptism by immersion in Baptist churches and the traditional Cherokee "going to the water" ceremonial ritual.[40]

Differences between Euro-American and Native Cultural and Religious Values

For the sake of comparison, I want to present the *contrasting* worldviews and value systems of Euro-Americans and Natives. Placing worldviews in contrast helps us to see challenges Native Americans have faced in reading Paul in ways attuned to their own culture. The first difference between these worldviews concerns the earth. Mircea Eliade notes that primitive (in the sense of ancient and traditional) cultures emphasize land and cosmos, whereas modern Western culture is preoccupied with history.[41] Native American cultures encourage all to live in community with nature in a relationship that is holistic and cooperative. The peoples of Native cultures value interdependence with Mother Earth and one another.[42] For example,

39. Richard Twiss, *One Church, Many Tribes: Following Jesus the Way God Made You* (Ventura: Regal, 2000). See also Emerson Spider, Sr., "The Native American Church of Jesus Christ" in *Sioux Indian Religion: Tradition and Innovation,* ed. Raymond J. DeMallie and Douglas R. Parks (Norman: University of Oklahoma Press, 1987), 189-209.

40. See Alan Kilpatrick, "Going to the Water: A Structural Analysis of Cherokee Purification Rituals," *American Indian Culture and Research Journal* 15 (1991): 49-58.

41. Mircea Eliade, *The Myth of Eternal Return* (Princeton: Princeton University Press, 1971), xiii-xiv.

42. Richard Erdoes and Alfonso Ortiz, eds., *American Indian Myths and Legends* (New York: Pantheon, 1984).

the Native American community values the "socialization of togetherness." Immediate and extended families and various communities do things together, from work to storytelling. Children are especially cared for by the community as a whole as they also provide the continuity of generations of life. The bonds between grandchildren and grandparents are intimate. Sharing is emphasized because survival of the community is the key. Self-reliance or alienation from the community may mean death.[43]

Donald Fixico's research into Native communities of the Plains, southwestern pueblo peoples, and eastern woodlands groups highlights some important differences between Native American and Euro-American worldviews.[44] Native myths of origin and ancestor stories do not tell about the beginning of time but rather about the order of things, about how the world should be in the panoramic view of reality.[45] Hero and heroine stories tell about the power of all creatures and the sufferings of human beings and thus reveal the extraordinary conditions of all creations and the supernatural world. Stories of origin reveal that human beings are part of the natural world and derive from the earth. Hence, the earth must be respected and cared for by all.[46] Native cultures have long assumed that what we today call the ecological system is an interdependent system, to be valued and cared for as a whole. Therefore, the well-being of *all* in the system is paramount. Fixico points out that "a system of relationship involving mutual respect among flora, fauna, and physical creations of the earth has been regarded as sacred by many Native American groups."[47] The earth is central as "the principal focus of life," and certain sites, especially mountains, are regarded as having a quality of special holiness and spiritual power.[48]

43. Donald Fixico, "The Struggle for Our Homes," in *Defending Mother Earth: Native American Perspectives on Environmental Justice* (Maryknoll: Orbis, 1996), 39.

44. Fixico, "Struggle for Our Homes," 31.

45. See Anna B. Rooth, "The Creation Myths of the North American Indians," *Anthropos* 52 (1957): 497-508. On the creation myths of many Native Americans, see Christopher Vecsey, *Imagine Ourselves Richly: Mythic Narratives of North American Indians* (New York: Crossroad, 1988), 34-63 (Hopi), 64-93 (Ojibwa), 150-205 (peyote).

46. Cultural stories of Indians coming from the earth are told in Erdoes and Ortiz, *American Indian Myths and Legends*. For example, the Jicarilla Apache genesis myth says that people came from the world below (p. 83); the Acoma of the western Pueblos believed the spirit Tsitctinako allowed two girls to live in the world above (pp. 97-98).

47. Fixico, "Struggle for Our Homes," 37.

48. Fixico, "Struggle for Our Homes," 37.

By contrast, modern Euro-American culture in general sees the earth as both an "environment" to be enjoyed and a "commodity" to be tamed, used, and marketed. In this view the human species has exclusive or at least very superior rights to benefit from the earth's resources. Those who create technologies to exploit natural resources are seen as having rights to make use of those resources. The West has emphasized individualism and competition in possessing and using the natural world. The Euro-American colonizers often used violence to take possession of land and resources — violence against Native populations and, from a Native point of view, violence against the land itself.

A second difference between Euro-American and Native American worldviews is their understandings of time and space.[49] Euro-Americans tend to prioritize and subordinate all aspects of existence to temporality, thus emphasizing progress, history, process, and evolution. They tend to understand sacredness in terms of time, such as in the cycle of days, months, and years. The liturgical meaning of events is established by time. For American Natives affinity with the land gives sacredness to space. Tinker explains:

> The land and spatiality are symbolic parameters of a tribe's universe. . . . In my own tribe, for instance, every detail of social structure — even the geographic orientation of the old villages reflected a reciprocal duality of all that is necessary for sustaining life. Thus the *Hunka* or earth moiety situated to the south of the village and the *Tzi Sho* or sky moiety situated to the north represented female and male, matter and spirit, war and peace, but they only functioned fully because they were together and together represented wholeness. Spirit without matter is motion without substance; matter without spirit is motionless and meaningless.[50]

Time is sacred only in relationship to space. The cyclic annual movement of living things is determined by their spatial relationship to each other, to the sun, earth, and moon.[51] The spatial relationships of sun, moon, and

49. Deloria, *God Is Red*, 75-89; Kidwell, Noley, and Tinker, *A Native American Theology*, 44-48.

50. Tinker, "An American Indian Theological Response," 164.

51. On the different views of Western Christianity and Native Americans regarding time and space, see Deloria, *God Is Red*, 111-50.

earth determine the sacredness and meaning of life. On account of this fundamental spatial metaphor, exemplified by the way Natives relate to the land, ecocide is a form of genocide for them.[52]

The spatial worldview explains the spatial dimension of Native religion. The tribal traditions of the Natives that include something like what Western Christians think of as eschatological expectations have a different quality. The "end" is not a fiery destruction of the present world and the dawning of a new heavenly world unlike this one. It is instead a renewal of this world, which happens over and over in a cyclic pattern.[53] An interesting question is whether Paul thinks in terms of cyclic time. As an apocalyptic thinker, he may have. Ancient Jewish apocalyptic includes both cyclic ideas of time (reminiscent of Greek ideas of history) and more linear conceptions of time as irreversible and leading to the end of ordinary history. It is difficult to determine what kind of apocalypticist Paul is because he does not dwell on specifics.

The question of differences between Euro-American and Native American worldviews is not purely academic. It is a question of survival for the Natives. One cannot simply say that each worldview is valid and allow each group to continue its separate cultural interests because the dominant Euro-American worldview has a direct impact on Native cultures. In particular, Euro-American views of "nature" and land have direct consequences for Natives. Native culture and Native ecology are intertwined. For Natives, defending Mother Earth is a way of life and a commitment to transform communities and individuals.

Pauline Theology and Native Hermeneutics

The preceding discussions have been necessary to set the stage for talking about Paul and Native religion, including Native Christianity. We confront now the set of problems I referred to at the beginning. Native scholars, including Native Christian scholars, tend to see Paul's theology as alien to authentic Native ways of thinking.

The following is an attempt to engage Pauline thought with Native worldviews according to traditional theological categories — God and cre-

52. See Tinker, "American Indian Theological Response," 163.

53. Weaver, *Defending Mother Earth*, 14.

ation, creation and anthropology, sin and reconciliation, ethics and community — knowing that neither Paul nor Native Americans would necessarily find these categories intrinsic to their ways of thinking. I do not intend to tell Natives how they should do a cross-cultural reading; this is simply my attempt to do a cross-cultural reading from my Chinese context to Native perspectives and Christianity and Paul. I should also clarify that my choosing the categories below may have been conditioned by my Chinese interests in cosmology, anthropology, and ethics (see chapter 3 above).

God and Gaia/Earth/Land[54]

Christians traditionally emphasize that their faith is strictly monotheistic and interpret the doctrine of the Trinity as an expression of monotheism, not a contradiction of it. Students of Paul agree that he is a Jewish monotheist. Usually interpreters maintain that whatever trinitarian (or binitarian)[55] understandings of God may be present in Paul, they are part of his monotheism, not departures from it.

Whether Native Americans have a clear monotheistic or instead a polytheistic understanding of divinity is difficult to say. Most Christian missionaries told the Native people that by worshiping the sun, the earth, and spirits they committed idolatry. Phillip Deere, however, argues that the missionaries misunderstood Native theology. Natives, he says, did not *worship* the sun. "We merely saw in it the reflection of the sacred, the creator, and used its image to focus our prayers of thanksgiving for the Creator's life-giving power."[56] If Deere is right, there is no inherent contradiction between the basic assumptions of Native theology and those of Paul. But anthropologist Åke Hultkrantz, who has done field research with the Shoshonis, concludes the categories "monotheistic" and "polytheistic" do not really fit Native American thinking about the divine. He argues that the Algonkian *Manitou*, the Siouan *Wakanda/Wakan*, and the Shoshonis'

54. On the history and manifold uses of *Gaia* (a Greek word meaning Mother Earth), see Russell, *The Earth, Humanity and God*, 96-125.

55. On binitarian theology in Paul (language of devotion directed to both God and Christ), see Larry W. Hurtado, *One God, One Lord: Early Christian Devotion and Ancient Jewish Monotheism* (second ed., Philadelphia: Fortress, 1988).

56. Kidwell, Noley, and Tinker, *A Native American Theology*, 52.

Tam Apö represent a theistic belief system in which "different vaguely delimited concepts exist side by side."[57] Hultkrantz maintains that for Native Americans all the spirits are manifestations of the one great Spirit.

The Shoshonis, for example, include in their belief system *Tam Apö* ("Our Father"), the supreme Creator, represented by the sun and the moon; thunder, lightning, and wind spirits; spirits of nature that give supernatural power to medicine men or warriors and appear often as animals and birds; *Tam mbia* (Mother Earth); other spirits; and the spirits of the dead.[58] That of the Dakotas includes Wakan Tanka, the Supreme Being; divinities of the atmosphere including the four winds; rulers of animal species; guardian spirits; Maka (Mother Earth); diverse other spirits; and the spirits of the dead.[59] Native cultures generally believe that divine spirits reside in all things, and such immanent habitation constitutes the sacredness of all. But Native peoples have not traditionally understood or worshipped the Earth as a goddess. They understand Mother Earth as the embodied source of life for humanity.[60]

When I asked Leon Matthews regarding Paul's and Native understandings of God and Spirit, he answered that for Native Americans it is important to establish the Godhead of Jesus because he is the creator of the universe. He writes:

> The increase of the Holy Spirit in our lives will make us pleasing to the Lord, and we can only do this through serving the people. One of the highest values in Lakota culture is the willingness to give up our lives

57. Åke Hultkrantz, *Belief and Worship in Native North America* (Syracuse: Syracuse University Press, 1981), 21.

58. Hultkrantz, *Belief and Worship*, 22. On the cult of the dead among Native Americans, see Hultkrantz, 91-114.

59. Hultkrantz, *Belief and Worship*, 24-25.

60. There is some debate about the origin and use of the terminology of "mother earth" with respect to Native theology. According to Kidwell, Noley, and Tinker, *A Native American Theology*, 53, "The Shawnee leader Tecumseh, in his attempt to promote a pan-Indian alliance to drive whites from Indian lands, adopted the terminology of earth as mother and spread it among tribes that he visited." Sam Gill, *Mother Earth: An American Story* (Chicago: University of Chicago Press, 1987), 156, argues that Mother Earth, a spiritual personification, is a twentieth-century invention of Europeans so as to "define and create themselves as Americans." John Bierhorst argues that political convenience and tactics account for the use of such terms by Europeans. See his *The Way of the Earth: Native America and the Environment* (New York: Morrow, 1994), 91.

> for the people. And this is how Paul sees the Lord Jesus, as the Suffering Servant and the greatest in the kingdom. It is helpful to understand Jesus as God because the power is still in the name of Jesus. The Spirit leads and regenerates human beings. Being Spirit-led is vital to the understanding of the Lakota Native American because the ultimate Spirit is God's Holy Spirit, and being led by the Spirit is the power of a Christian's life.[61]

Matthews told this personal story to show the link between his Christian understanding of the Spirit in Paul and Native beliefs:

> My own mentor once told me what Taku Sku Sku means. It is translated "something sacred that moves." He began with the understanding that this was like a spark, and as the energy grows it becomes bigger and continues to fruition as what we have in our world today. My mentor, who was not a Christian, looked into my eyes and stated that I have the spark in my heart. I felt that he sensed the Holy Spirit in my life and could almost grasp the concept and understanding of what it means to be a Christian. Christians have the Holy Spirit in their lives and this is the power we embrace as our regeneration or new birth begins. Paul was led by the Spirit in powerful ways as we should be today, and Native America will benefit from this obedience. After all, Paul was interested in being obedient no matter the cost.[62]

Some may see here an example of a form of Native Christian faith that is no longer Native in its theology but simply Western. But Matthews's words can also be interpreted within the henotheistic Native American understanding of the divine that we have just examined. The many spirits inhabit the world of nature as the forces of life by which the web of creation holds together in a balanced and ordered way for the benefit of all and are manifestations of the one God.

Some might object that if Native Christians think of God, Jesus Christ, and the Spirit within the framework of a more traditional Native American theology, they have betrayed Paul's monotheism. But the question is more complex than simple distinctions between monotheism and polytheism. In 1 Corinthians 8 Paul affirms the most fundamental Jewish

61. Personal interview, used with permission.
62. Personal interview, used with permission.

belief in the oneness of God: "we know that an idol is nothing in the world and that there is no God except one" (1 Cor. 8:4; cf. Rom. 3:30; Gal. 3:20; Deut. 6:4; Exod. 20:3). A common scholarly interpretation of the situation Paul addresses in 1 Corinthians 8 is that some of the Corinthians may have eaten idol meat in public to prove that idols are nothing and to demonstrate their monotheistic faith and high spiritual state, their superiority to Christians of "weak" conscience who refused to eat idol meat. Does Paul agree with the theology of the strong but challenge their attitudes? He certainly challenges their attitudes, but it is not clear that he simply affirms their theology. In dealing with the question of idol meat, Paul may be avoiding a philosophical statement of monotheism in the sense of how many gods there are and focusing instead on the relationship the believer has to God or to an idol. Paul agrees with the monotheistic confession, "God is one God," but it is not clear that he rejects the idea altogether that there is no spiritual power behind idol worship. The idol may be nothing (agreement with those who eat idol meat), but idol worship does create a relationship with spiritual beings that Paul calls "demons" in 1 Cor. 10:20-21 and "beings that by nature are not gods" in Gal. 4:8. In 1 Corinthians 8, vv. 5-6 are especially important:

> Indeed, even though there may be many so-called gods in heaven or on earth — as in fact there are many gods and many lords — yet for us there is one God, the Father, from whom are all things, and one Lord, Jesus Christ, through whom are all things and through whom we exist.

This statement seems to keep open the philosophical question of whether there are many gods and whether the spiritual beings that exist in the air, the underworld, or the heavens should be called "gods." Instead Paul stresses the loyalty of the church ("for us") to God the Father and the Lord Jesus Christ. I would call this soteriological monotheism. It is like the "monotheism" of the ancient Israelites, who did not hold to the philosophical view that there is only one God but rather embraced Yahweh as the God of Israel, to whom they were to be loyal, rather than go after other gods of other peoples. This way of reading Paul seems compatible with his other assertions of monotheism ("God is one"), which appear to have little to do with philosophical questions about the number of gods in the universe. Instead, Paul affirms God's oneness to make points about redemption. "God is one" means that God the Creator is God of both Jews and gentiles (Rom. 3:29-30). "God is one" also means that the fulfillment of the promise to Abraham is for Jew and gentile apart from the Law (Gal. 3:20).[63]

If Paul's monotheism is not philosophical but soteriological monotheism, it may be closer to traditional Native cosmologies. But Native Americans see many of the multitude of spirits as good. Even if Paul acknowledges that there are many gods, he sees only God in Christ as good. Nevertheless, even here there is reason to qualify. In the Jewish Bible, we find references to divinities described as "angels of God," "the council of YHWH," "the congregation of the holy ones," "the assembly of God," the "sons of God," and the "host of heaven."[64] In Jewish literature of the Second Temple period other figures are described as glorious beyond any ordinary earthly state. Some are glorified human beings; others are god-like or angel-like beings. These include the angel Raphael in Tobit 12, the glorious man in *Joseph and Aseneth* 14, the angel Yahoel in the *Apocalypse of Abraham,* Melchizedek in 11Q13, the angel Israel in the *Prayer of Joseph,* the glorious Jacob in *Joseph and Aseneth* 22, Adam in *2 Enoch* 30, the Son of Man in *1 Enoch* 46, and Moses in the Jewish *Orphica.* These figures are divine or quasi-divine beings, emissaries of God who reflect God's glory or are forms of God's presence.[65] It is difficult to give neat definitions or draw sharp distinctions between different types. Seen in the context of ancient Jewish understandings of the divine, Christ resembles an angel-like or god-like figure similar to some of these others. This may explain why Paul does not worry about whether his ascriptions of divinity to Christ compromise his monotheism. He lives in a Jewish environment where the idea of an angel-like figure being divine or God taking on a human appearance was not regarded as a threat to monotheism. Monotheism meant above all loyalty to God the Creator, who is supreme over all other beings, good and evil, and is the source of salvation and blessing. In other words, this soteriological monotheism of Paul does not exclude belief in a plurality of

63. Paul's appeal to the oneness of God in Gal. 3:20 is part of an obscure argument that in his mind somehow supports the idea that the promise comes not through the Law but through faith.

64. See Exod. 23:20-23; 1 Kgs. 22:19-22; 2 Chron. 18:18-22; Ezek. 1:26-28; 8:2-4; Dan. 7:9-14; 10:2-9.

65. I would like to acknowledge my debt here to Lawrence Mattera, "Angelology and Angelomorphism: Conceptual Matrix of Early Christology" (M.A. thesis, Northern Baptist Theological Seminary, 1999).

divine beings. It is in this respect closer to Native American ways of understanding the divine than it is to post-Enlightenment theology, which is philosophically monotheistic.

So Paul may take it for granted that the universe contains many spirits, many supernatural beings besides the God of Jesus Christ. He might have seen some of these beings as good (in the sense of angels that are good divine beings subordinate to the Most High God). He may have seen Christ as the supreme angel-like divine being who is above all others but subordinate to God the Father. And Paul's "God is one" is not a numerical philosophical statement but a soteriological confession. All this together creates possibilities for common ground between traditional Native American ways of thinking and Pauline theology. Native Christians can work out their own ways of appropriating this Paul; it is not for me to decide.

Nevertheless, there is a fundamental difference between the fluid theology of the ancient Paul and the henotheism of traditional Native theology. For Paul, there is no source of life or benefit outside God in Christ. None of the angels are appropriate benefactors to whom Christians should turn in prayer. No service or respect is owed to them so that they will do their jobs in the universe and thus keep the cosmos in good order for human well-being. But in Native understanding, the spirits that animate the world are benefactors of humanity and the cosmos as a whole. Carl Sweezy writes of his Native understanding of God:

> We believed in a power that was higher than all people and all the created world, and we called this power the Man-Above. We believed in some power in the world that governed everything that grew, and we called this power Mother-Earth. We believed in the power of the Sun, of the Night-Sun or Moon, of the Morning Star, and of the Four Old Men who direct the winds and the rains and the seasons and give us the breath of life. We believed that everything created is holy and has some part in the power that is over all.[66]

Leon Matthews points out that the first American missionaries misunderstood the Native's "witchcraft." He writes:

66. Carl Sweezy (Arapaho), ca. 1881-1953, as quoted in Weaver, ed., *Defending Mother Earth,* vi.

> In a Lakota understanding of the witches that were burned in Salem in early American history the Lakota see them as healers and not demon possessed women. Animism is valued as a means to manipulating the spirits in the cosmology of the Lakota people. Christians are warned to stay away from such people. We can see that Lakota people have a different understanding of the manipulation of spirits.

Paul can celebrate the earth as God's creation (1 Cor. 10:26) and therefore as God's gift for humanity. He may assume that there are many good angels who do God's bidding. But he does not present the earth or any of the angels as human benefactors whom people are to pray to or honor or trust. Instead he stresses that God in Christ is the sole benefactor of humanity and that the earth is in the same predicament as human beings: it is weak, suffering, subject to futility and death, and waiting for redemption from God (Rom. 8:18-25). This is an apocalyptic perspective on the earth.

It is also an urban perspective. Paul's mission is city-oriented. Outside the city he speaks of the "sea" and the "wilderness" but not of the countryside.[67] Wilderness and sea in his writings appear as places in the natural world where human beings are in danger. He does not have (or at least does not express) any experience of the natural world as spiritually healing, a place of encounter with the divine. However, there may be deeper analogies between Paul's urban theology and Native American Christian earth-connected spirituality. Cities for Paul are places of community where he establishes Christian communities. The popular philosophies of the city, the various clubs and associations, the existing urban networks all shape his conception of the church as community, even as they provide models and settings for the Christian community. A careful reading of Paul in his urban social context shows how he uses and modifies existing forms and ideas of community in the light of the gospel.[68] Perhaps one can look at non-urban community, Native community in close contact with nature, and ask what Pauline community would look like if it is not the city but the land that supplies the setting and preconditions of community.

One possible avenue of analogy is Paul's adoption of a traditional idea from his urban culture, the "body" as a way of thinking about a social

67. On this point, see Wayne A. Meeks, *The First Urban Christians: The Social World of the Apostle Paul* (New Haven: Yale University Press, 1983), 9.

68. Meeks, *First Urban Christians* demonstrates this in many ways.

group, and his reshaping it in accord with his understanding of the gospel (1 Corinthians 12). This involves a challenge to typical ancient Mediterranean ways of defining status and ordering life hierarchically.[69] Native Americans believe that all living things have spirits that interconnect all in the circle of life. And all have special gifts, strengths, and roles in the larger web of life. Therefore, "[f]or Natives, bonding with the earth is part of their life, culture, and history."[70] So they respect and care for plants and trees and know that plants and trees have their own spirits in the created order of things. The Lakota people use the phrase *mitakuye oysain,* meaning "for all my relations," or "for all the above me and below me and around me things," to speak of the goodness and interconnectedness of all relations.[71] What might a Pauline understanding of this conception of interconnectedness look like, one that follows Paul's teaching on the inversion of hierarchies and status? I pose this as a question to suggest that much fruitful cross-cultural thinking could be done between modern scholarship on Paul and Native American thought and Christian traditions. Although modern scholarship on Paul is predominantly Western, use of if for thinking about Paul in Native terms need not be controlled by Western assumptions.

Anthropology and Creation

Eco-justice affirms the value and interrelatedness of all forms of life. Native worldviews share commonality with various Christian traditions regarding not only the interrelatedness of human beings but also the sacred worth of all forms of life. According to Fixico, the Native attitude is that all plants and animals have a "philosophically equal role in life."[72] Creation and the order of things show humanity the way to be human. Plants and animals are vital parts of life's system, just as humans are also essential parts of the same system. As Fixico explains, "Nature provided everything needed by Natives, causing them to realize their inferiority and to ac-

69. A recent discussion of Paul's adoption and reshaping of the common "body" metaphor for community and society is Dale B. Martin, *The Corinthian Body* (New Haven: Yale University Press, 1995).

70. Fixico, "Struggle for Our Homes," 39.

71. Kidwell, Noley, and Tinker, *A Native American Theology,* 48.

72. Fixico, "Struggle for Our Homes," 36.

knowledge that power greater than themselves . . . a Creator . . . who provided an environment for them in which to live."[73] As a result, Natives did not see themselves as the center or pinnacle of creatures but as "a small part of the larger circular order of life ordained by the Creator." They traditionally teach that human beings are part of a whole, not lords over that whole but ethically responsible to it. Nevertheless, Kidwell, Noley, and Tinker point out, "many elders in Indian communities are quick to add that of all the createds, of all our relations, we Two-Leggeds alone seem to be confused as to our responsibility towards the whole."[74]

Paul does not treat human beings as lords of creation. The "dominion" model of humanity's relation to nature seems more modern and Western than ancient. Many Christian theologians have recently criticized this theology and have argued that the Scriptures long associated with it do not support it. In Romans 8 Paul uses subjugation language of creation, but does not name human beings as the subjugators or lords of creation. Instead, he says that creation was subjugated to futility, the power of death, to which human beings are also subject (Rom. 8:18-25).

Romans 8 describes God's love for creation by viewing creation and humanity in solidarity. The redemption of the one is the redemption of the other. Their destinies are interlocked. Both creation and humanity face the same enemy — death or futility. Death is the destructive force that makes creation fall short of God's intention and glory. Futility, likewise, is the destruction of creation's purpose, the frustration of creation's effort to be itself. The solidarity between humanity and creation is seen in their groaning and suffering together (8:19-22). The Spirit (God's presence) also "groans" with the church and, by implication, with the "groaning" creation. In other words, God is immanently present in creation, experiencing what creation experiences and working to liberate creation from bondage, death, and futility. This theology of creation has similarities with the Native American understanding of God's immanence in creation. But one difference is that Natives do not traditionally think of humanity and creation as two different subjects the way Paul does.

In Romans 8, the cosmic salvation of Christ brings about the transformation of the suffering world, the redemption of the *whole* creation. The ultimate purpose of God is to restore *all creation, not just human be-*

73. Fixico, "Struggle for Our Homes," 34.

74. Kidwell, Noley, and Tinker, *A Native American Theology*, 38-39.

ings, to wholeness.[75] Salvation in Paul's understanding is "displayed in the cosmic universality, not just in terms of anthropocentric particularity."[76]

It follows from Paul's discussion of God's concern for creation that human beings should regard creation the way God does. In Paul's day this regard did not have eco-justice implications because humanity was not a significant threat to creation. In our time the Western post-industrial nations, with the United States as the leading environmental polluter, do threaten nature. Therefore, an eco-justice practice is warranted by Paul's theology of the suffering creation. This ethic is compatible with the special Native concern for creation. "The Indian way," says Jeanne Rollins, "is to live with nature, not against it."[77] This calls for "a compatible and working relationship with all living things . . . [assuming the responsibility] to provide for the good of all the community and to have respect and reverence for all of creation."[78] Or, in the words of Salvador Palomino,

> For us, it seems unthinkable that man — who as the "beloved offspring," the "son of God," is also divine — should be superior to other living beings and do as he pleases with the Earth, regarding Mother Nature as an object of consumption, to be conquered, suppressed, transformed, violated, poisoned to the point of destruction just to satisfy whims and not needs.[79]

Before leaving Romans 8 I want to call attention to an insight from Paul to help us work toward a common or shared vision of the cosmic salvation in Christ. Rom. 8:28-30 expresses a hope of cosmic salvation. Paul

75. See the excellent discussion by Ernst Käsemann, *New Testament Questions of Today,* trans A. J. Montague (Philadelphia: Fortress, 1969), 168-82. "[T]hat faithfulness with which the Creator persists in his work of creation in spite of, and beyond, the falling away of his creatures and with which he preserves his creation and gives it a new foundation. . . . Thus [the righteousness of God] is for Paul God's sovereignty over the world revealing itself eschatologically in Jesus" (p. 180).

76. Paul Santmire, "Healing the Protestant Mind: Beyond the Theology of Human Dominion," in *After Nature's Revolt: Eco-Justice and Theology,* ed. Dieter T. Hessel (Minneapolis: Fortress, 1992), 69.

77. Jeanne Rollins, "Liberation and the Native American," in *Theology in the Americas,* ed. Sergio Torres and John Eagleson (Maryknoll: Orbis, 1976), 204.

78. Rollins, "Liberation and the Native American," 204.

79. Salvador Palomino, "Three Times, Three Spaces in Cosmos Quechua," in Weaver, ed., *Defending Mother Earth,* 15.

presents a grand narrative of Christ as the unifying force to bring reconciliation between people and applies it directly to "the weak" and "the strong" at Rome (14:1). Paul tells each group to welcome the other as God welcomed them in Christ. This conflict between the weak and the strong may rest on differences between gentile Christian views of life in Christ and conservative Jewish Christian views. Perhaps elements of ethnic animosity underlie the tensions as well. Paul's grand narrative envisions the unity of Jews and gentiles according to God's impartiality.

Some may assume that if Paul has a grand narrative, he is thinking imperialistically, wishing to impose his own vision where there are multiple conflicting "narratives." But Paul does not advocate or practice a promotion of the grand narrative in an imperialistic way. He does not sanction or practice coercion or violence in promoting his gospel. In fact, he sees such practices as antithetical to the gospel, which is to be offered in persuasive words and demonstrations of love.

It is up to God to create the conditions of the grand narrative. Paul believes that the Creator sent a last Adam, Christ, to bring salvation to all. That "all" includes creation. The fulfillment of that salvation will be a cosmic reunification — God all in all (1 Cor. 15:28). This includes a reunification of all peoples divided by ethnicity and culture, both Jew and Greek, both Native and Euro-American. Unfortunately, the manner and form of the European gospel brought to Natives made the gospel a servant of political and cultural imperialism. The effect was to make all talk of reconciliation, unity, and harmony between Natives and Europeans a hierarchical unity in which Europeans dictated the terms of unity. This kind of unity is not genuine and does not fit with Paul's grand narrative. But Christians cannot accept as an alternative a path to segregation without possibility for integration or an embrace of unqualified pluralism with no hope of common ground and shared life. That would betray the grand narrative of God's revelation in Christ. I believe that Paul offers a third possibility: a coexistence of those who (1) affirm the equality of all in sin and grace; (2) accept that many differences are not only unavoidable but good, rather than insisting that unity must be achieved through the obliteration of all differences (which usually means that those who are politically weaker must give up their identities and assimilate to the strong); and (3) live by faith so that greater good is achieved for all as each complements and builds up others and gives special protection to the weak. This vision is communal, not individualistic. Not only does it imply a new community across ethnic, economic, and gender differences (see Gal. 3:28), it also implies a new community with nature because creation is included in the ultimate "all in all" of God's embrace. A Native Christian theology may find points of resonance with Paul on these points.

Hamartiology, Soteriology, and Christology

Kidwell, Noley, and Tinker argue that "[t]he Christian concepts of original sin and salvation through Christ are antithetical to Indian concepts of personal power based on dreams, visions, and initiation into esoteric knowledge of deity."[80] Individualistic Western concepts of "sin" and "salvation" are foreign to Native thinking. Sin in Native societies means not living up to one's responsibility. Consequently, sin has ill effects on the well-being of the community. The Native words that missionaries used to translate the biblical understanding of sin generally mean making a mistake or being lost. The Muscogee (Creek) word for sin means "to bother someone." The Choctaw words for sin are *aiashachi* and *aiyoshoba; aiashachi* means "to err at; to make a mistake at"; *aiyoshoba* means "error, wandering, sin, place of sin." The root *yoshoba* means "lost or gone astray."[81] Kidwell, Noley, and Tinker comment that these meanings "convey some aspects of sin in Christianity but certainly do not connote either the depths of human depravity that sin represented in the strongly Calvinist tradition of Protestantism or the stain of original sin in Catholicism."[82]

For Native Americans "salvation" means a return to a state of "community."[83] Kidwell, Noley, and Tinker observe that the Cherokee designated "certain towns" as "sacred sites where people could seek sanctuary when they had transgressed social norms."[84] There are important parallels here to medieval Christian social practices and to ancient Israelite practices. That is, one finds forms of communal understanding in the West and in biblical faith before the rise of individualism that have strong affinities with Native forms of community. It is important to keep in mind here that

80. Kidwell, Noley, and Tinker, *A Native American Theology,* 18-19.
81. Kidwell, Noley, and Tinker, *A Native American Theology,* 101.
82. Kidwell, Noley, and Tinker, *A Native American Theology,* 18-19.
83. Kidwell, Noley, and Tinker, *A Native American Theology,* 18-19.
84. Kidwell, Noley, and Tinker, *A Native American Theology,* 18-19.

Paul belonged to a world in which community was valued above individuality. He is not an individualist.

Natives also kept communal times of restoration. For example, "The Green Corn Ceremony was a time of forgiveness that restored all people to proper relationships."[85] Kidwell, Noley, and Tinker compare the Corn Mother of the Native tradition with Christ. The stories of the Corn Mother are pervasive in Native cultures. They tell of the origin of corn and the sacredness of life and food. Kidwell, Noley, and Tinker see in the willing self-sacrifice of the first mother, the Corn Mother, for her children an idea that resembles in important ways the story of Christ. In the Penobscot version of the story, the mother requests her own death against the will of her husband. Some versions of the story have it that her children murder her, though again she requests her death. The corn is regarded as sacred and eating it as a sacramental meal like the Lord's Supper because it is a consumption of the flesh of the First Mother. She gives her life for her children so that they, "the people," might live. She provides food for her children in the absence of game as she shakes the corn off her body. Two of her children discover the source of food and accuse her of tricking them. The Corn Mother's death is the death of the first human, and her burial continues to provide food for later generations. She returns to the earth. Through her, the ancestors continue to live in their descendants through the eating of the corn and through memory. Although the story is violent, it is also opposed to violence. Some versions (in which a son kills the Corn Mother) stand as a warning about the potential for male violence in society.[86]

Similar images of redemptive self-giving are found in the New Testament and especially in Paul. The sacrificial love of God for the creation in Paul's theology centers in Christ's suffering. In the cross, Paul sees not only an atonement *for* human sin (Rom. 3:25; 5:6-8; 8:32; 2 Cor. 5:14-15; Gal. 2:20; 3:13; 1 Thess. 5:9-10), but also God's suffering solidarity *with* humanity and participation in the life and trials of creation to bring about the reconciliation of all with God. This divine suffering with and for humanity aims at reconciliation, a distinctly Pauline idea in the New Testament (Rom. 5:10-11; 11:15; 1 Cor. 7:11; 2 Cor. 5:18-20). "God was in Christ," Paul says, "reconciling the world to himself" (2 Cor. 5:19). Here the focus is on the human world. But in Romans 8 and 1 Corinthians 15, as we have seen, the redemp-

85. Kidwell, Noley, and Tinker, *A Native American Theology*, 18-19.
86. Kidwell, Noley, and Tinker, *A Native American Theology*, 81-82.

tion and unification of the whole creation is the final goal of God's suffering and reconciling love. This vision is also continued in the deutero-Pauline letters Colossians and Ephesians, which put special emphasis on the cosmic scope of redemption (Col. 1:18-20; Eph. 1:22-23).

The cosmic Christ in whom God suffers with and for the world to bring all things into reconciliation is not the Corn Mother. The Corn Mother stories express a theology that is consistent with the fundamental Native conviction that "the land looks after us." Agricultural and fertility stories of redemption and sustenance do not fit Paul's vision of a suffering and weak creation subject to futility. Hence, while the Christ story and the Corn Mother story share similarities, they are not the same story in different words. But the Corn Mother story does provide categories of thought and experience that connect with Paul's gospel. And Paul's gospel, especially when understood in its cosmic scope, connects with the Corn Mother story. There are elements of common ground and common concern here.

Ceremonies and Ethics: Reciprocity and Wholeness

Native Americans do not call their ceremonial life "worship." They use the word "ceremonies" instead. In these ceremonies, which include dancing and singing (often on feast days), Natives pray and offer praise to the Mysterious Other, the spirit world, the Creator.[87] Religious experiences of transcendence are common through dreams, visions, and initiations. Natives see these as communications with the spirit world. Medicine men often use pipes in healing ceremonies and for "vision quest," seeking a vision from the spirits that will guide one's life or the life of one's people. Ceremonies, dances, and feast days are significant parts of life, expressing the power of life in beauty, harmony, order, and wholeness. The Navajo use the term *hozho* to speak of "the ideal environment of beauty, harmony, and happiness."[88] *Hozho* and the Chippewa term *pimidaziwin* also mean "long life, good health, and happiness."[89] In this sense "beauty" is not an aesthetic concept but a quality of the world accessible through everyday expe-

87. Kidwell, Noley, and Tinker, *A Native American Theology*, 56.
88. Kidwell, Noley, and Tinker, *A Native American Theology*, 18, 109.
89. Kidwell, Noley, and Tinker, *A Native American Theology*, 109.

rience and calling for a moral-religious response. The beauty of life is found in ways of life that seek longevity, quality of life, happiness, and harmonious relationships with all, using the power of life for the good of the community.

"Maintaining harmony and balance requires that even necessary acts of violence be done 'in a sacred way,'" explain Kidwell, Noley, and Tinker.[90] Hence, Natives have traditionally practiced ceremonies before hunting, before war, and after war. For example, the Osage War ceremony and the buffalo hunt ceremony entail eleven-day rituals to consecrate the lives that will be lost. In these ceremonies, the participants speak words of apology and thanksgiving. The purpose of post-hunting and post-war ceremonies is to cleanse the hunters and warriors before they reenter the village.[91] Kidwell, Noley, and Tinker interpret these ceremonies as an expression of the conviction that all relations must be governed by reciprocity. If life is taken, this calls for a reciprocal spiritual act, which the ceremonies fulfill. There are also ceremonies of reciprocity for other activities involving the use of the land and animals. Ceremonies of self-sacrifice also express the principle of reciprocity. In the same manner, ceremonies involving self-sacrifice also come under this general category of reciprocity. In painful ordeals such as "the Rite of Vigil" (the "vision quest") and the Sun Dance, "the suffering the supplicant takes upon himself or herself is usually thought of as vicarious and as some sort of reciprocation."[92]

The Green Corn ceremony, the Snake Dance, the Sun Dance, purification ceremonies (sweat-lodge ceremonies), the sacred pipe, are all aspects of the social construct, performed periodically for the well-being of the community.[93] One can find themes in these ceremonies that are also found in Paul's teaching on the Lord's Supper as an experience of the unity of Christ's body and a proclamation of Christ's sacrificial death.

Leon Matthews sees Paul using elements from his culture "to capture the meaning of life, which is God reconciling the world with Himself."[94] Matthews refers to the Lakota people's Sun Dance ceremony of sacrificing on a tree. The people begin with a *hanbleca* (seeking a vision) where the person fasts for four days and goes on top of a hill to seek his or

90. Kidwell, Noley, and Tinker, *A Native American Theology,* 43-44.

91. Kidwell, Noley, and Tinker, *A Native American Theology,* 43.

92. Kidwell, Noley, and Tinker, *A Native American Theology,* 42.

93. Kidwell, Noley, and Tinker, *A Native American Theology,* 42-43.

94. Private correspondence, used by permission.

her vision. Sometimes there are visions and sometimes there are not. Matthews explains:

> After being on the hill for these days the person makes a commitment to the people to dance for illness or other meaningful things within his or her family. When they dance they pierce their flesh on the chest and sometimes on the back. They will dance and suffer for the people. In the end they will give flesh to signify their sacrifice to the people. The tree in the middle, which they refer to as the tree of life, can be seen in Jesus' life as well.[95]

Matthews further observes:

> Retracing some of the things we have talked about we can see many windows of opportunity in which we can share Jesus. In the *hanbleca* we know that Jesus went away to be alone with his Father. Seeking a greater understanding is what the Lakota do when they search for the Creator's vision to them. Flesh sacrifice was required, and what better offering than the sacrifice of God Himself in the incarnate God-man? The tree the Lakota hang from is a tree that gives life. Jesus, as painful as it seems, and disastrous, brought life and redemption to the world. These are some of the things that I believe Paul would have used to reach Native people. The church has done a disservice to the Native American people in condemning the ways of the people and calling them pagan without understanding the deep meaning of the life-ways of the Lakota people.[96]

For Matthews, Native traditions contain common ground with Paul's gospel. Where Kidwell, Noley, and Tinker see parallels between Native traditions and Christian faith but do not regard Native traditions as a path to Christianity (a kind of "propaedeutic"), Matthews takes a more "evangelical" view. What he sees as resonances between Native religion and Christian faith, he regards as ways of reaching Native people for the gospel. This path to Christianity involves a transformation of the former beliefs, not a negation.

95. Personal interview, used by permission.
96. Personal interview, used by permission.

End-Time Myths and Eschatology

Jace Weaver divides Native American end-time myths into two types, showing that most of the myths are concerned with ecology. The first group consists of moral cautionary myths, similar to the biblical stories of Noah or Sodom and Gomorrah. For example, in a Cheyenne story the world rests on a pole in the far north that sits on a giant, snow-white beaver. If humanity makes the beaver angry, it will gnaw at the pole and the world will come to an end when the pole is chewed up. The second type of myth has a cyclical or natural understanding of the cosmos. This type is represented by stories of re-creation after great cataclysmic events. Stories of cataclysmic prevention are also told. A Lakota story tells how a woman weaves the world. Once her weaving is done, the world will come to an end. In the story, her dog pulls the threads from her weaving every time she goes away to tend the fire. In this way the dog prevents the world from coming to an end.[97] Both the story of the Great White Grandfather Beaver of the North and the Lakota weaver story point to an end-time doom if exploitation of the earth's resources continues.

Most popular end-time myths have a millenarian ecological hope. For example, in 1762 a Delaware prophet named Neolin proclaimed a message of freedom and prosperity promised by the Master of Life after the defeat of the Euro-Americans. He called a confederation of Natives under the Ottawa war-leader Pontiac to fight the Euro-Americans in the Great Lakes region.[98] In 1805 Tecumseh, a Shawnee prophet, promoted a similar revolt against Euro-Americans from Florida to Saskatchewan. Tecumseh's spokesman, his brother Tenskwatawa, a charismatic speaker, claimed to be the incarnation of Manabohzo, the Algonkian cultural hero.[99] Yet another example are the Ghost Dance movements of 1870 and 1889 that promised the resurrection of dead friends and relatives.

Paul's eschatology focuses very little on specific details about the future and concentrates on generalized statements of judgment and hope revealed in the gospel of Christ. For example, the end-time teaching of 1 Thessalonians does not provide a detailed schedule of the world's end.

97. Jace Weaver, "The End of the World," in *American Journey: The Native American Experience* (cd-rom; Woodbridge: Research Publications, 1999).

98. Kidwell, Noley, and Tinker, *A Native American Theology*, 156.

99. Kidwell, Noley, and Tinker, *A Native American Theology*, 156. They also give accounts of end-time myths among the Cherokee and Apache peoples.

Instead, it offers comfort and hope of resurrection to those who are suffering or fearful that they or their loved ones may be excluded from the coming salvation. And 2 Thessalonians warns against thinking that the end has already arrived (in some mysterious way?). Other eschatological statements in Paul's letters also provide comfort, warning, encouragement, and ethical urging. In these respects, Paul's eschatology is like the future hopes expressed in story, vision, or prophecy among Native Americans. Hope is not speculative or esoteric; neither is it fixed precisely to detailed timetables but remains fluid. Eschatology serves to encourage and urge to responsible action.

Paul looks forward to the defeat of all God's enemies, including Satan and the power of death (Rom 16:20 and 1 Cor. 15:26). The whole creation will be released from its bondage to futility (Rom. 8:21) and God will be *all in all* (1 Cor. 15:28). The Native concern for the whole web of life has helped me to appreciate the cosmic dimension of Pauline theology and its ecological implications.

Syncretistic Native Christian Movements and the Meaning of Jesus' Death

Syncretistic myths drawing on both Native and Euro-American traditions were popular in the Ghost Dance movement of the late nineteenth century. For example, Wovoka saw a mystical vision of Jesus Christ coming to wipe Euro-Americans off the North American continent. This judgment would be followed by the resurrection of the dead and the flourishing of the buffalo. According to Kidwell, Noley, and Tinker, "Amer-European misunderstanding and fear of the Ghost Dance as a locus of political resistance led to the Wounded Knee massacre," after which the Ghost Dance was banned. But in the 1970s Henry Crow Dog and Leonard Crow Dog brought back the Ghost Dance.[100]

The largest syncretistic messianic movement among Native Americans is the peyote religion, with adherents of up to a quarter of the Native population in the United States.[101] Peyote is a turnip-shaped cactus that grows in northern Mexico and southern Texas. The debate continues

100. Kidwell, Noley, and Tinker, *A Native American Theology,* 156.
101. Kidwell, Noley, and Tinker, *A Native American Theology,* 160.

among Christian leaders (Native and non-Native), among scholars (Christian and non-Christian), and among government authorities over the validity of the use of this plant in medicine or as a sacrament in church rituals. It is traditionally used by Native Americans as "a sacred medicine that protects, allows one to see the future or find lost objects, and instructs users in how to live."[102] Is peyote a harmful drug or "the voice of God," as Reuben Snake, a leader of the Native American Church (NAC), the principal peyote group, claims? In the mid 1990s the NAC had eighty chapters across the United States and Canada, with a membership of 250,000.[103] Since its inception, it has strongly advocated the use of peyote in churches. But the NAC's position on the use of peyote does not always gain the sympathy of Native traditionalists or non-Native Christians, who think the NAC compromises Christian faith.

The two main rites of the NAC are the Half Moon way and the Cross Fire way.[104] Those who practice the Cross Fire way use the Bible, practice water baptism, and acknowledge Jesus as Lord and Savior in whom they find words of eternal life and healing. They also stress his future coming. Those who follow the Half Moon way do not use the Bible at meetings. Jesus is not as central as in the Cross Fire way, but prayers are offered in Jesus' name. While the Cross Fire way and Half Moon way may sound like different branches of the NAC, each with its own adherents, "[i]n practice, there is much interchange between the two rites, with persons often attending both."[105]

Kidwell, Noley, and Tinker challenge what they see as superficial ways of thinking about Native Christian faith, as if a Christianity can be Native on the basis of "pipes on altars, or church decorations, or fulfillment theology," without touching the deeper questions of "thought worlds and systems."[106] The importance of this point is evident when we consider the place of Jesus' death in Native perspective. Among many Natives who embrace Christian traditions, the triumphant, eschatological Christ seen in the Ghost Dance movement of Wovoka and Christ's future coming emphasized in the use of peyote are more valued than the suffering Christ.

102. Kidwell, Noley, and Tinker, *A Native American Theology*, 304.

103. Kidwell, Noley, and Tinker, *A Native American Theology*, 324.

104. In describing these two rites I am following Kidwell, Noley, and Tinker, *A Native American Theology*, 160-61.

105. Kidwell, Noley, and Tinker, *A Native American Theology*, 161.

106. Kidwell, Noley, and Tinker, *A Native American Theology*, 165.

And here we meet an important challenge to any attempt at a Native theology of Paul, for whom the death of Jesus is central. For Paul, fulfillment hopes, like those of the Corinthians, are a false gospel if they are not qualified by the cross. New Testament scholars and Christian theologians often speak of this in the language of Luther as Paul asserting a "theology of the cross" against the Corinthians' "theology of glory." But in Native experience and history these matters look very different. Jace Weaver writes: "I do not believe that Native communities, assaulted and deeply damaged by more than 500 years of colonialism, can believe that God in any way wanted or needed the death of Jesus on the cross to be 'reconciled' with humanity."[107] According to Weaver, "many Natives aver that the crucifixion was the work of humanity and that when it occurred God wept."[108]

This Native perspective on the cross deserves a response from Christians who insist on interpreting the cross only in sacrificial terms, especially if sacrifice means the appeasement or propitiation of God, a largely discredited interpretation.[109] Paul also sees the crucifixion as a human act of opposition to Jesus and his way (1 Cor. 2:8) and as the work of Death, the last enemy. The sacrificial nature of Christ's death in Paul can be rightly understood only if one begins with Paul's assumption that the powerful of the world put Jesus to death, thus bringing about his full taste of the fate of the world under the power of Death. God and Christ are agents in this drama. God "gives" the Son and Christ "gives himself"; this giving expresses for Paul the sacrificial love of God in Christ for the world (see Rom. 5:6-11; 8:32; Gal. 2:20). Sacrifice here is not propitiation. To borrow Native categories of thought, it is God's way of working the logic of reciprocity to restore humanity and all creation. A Native Christianity that incorporates Native practices and ways of thinking but as a matter simply of "pipes on altars, or church decorations, or fulfillment theology" faces the challenge of coming to grips with Paul's theology of the cross. At the same time, reading the cross of Christ through Native eyes and history is a challenge to non-Natives. We, too, have something important to learn

107. Jace Weaver, *That the People Might Live: Native American Literatures and Native American Community* (New York: Oxford University Press, 1997), 182.

108. Weaver, *That the People Might Live,* 182.

109. On the debate over the words *hilastērion* (expiation or propitiation) and *paresin* (passing over or overlooking) in Paul's discussion of Christ's sacrificial death in Romans 3, see James D. G. Dunn, *The Theology of Paul the Apostle* (Grand Rapids: Eerdmans, 1998), 212-18.

from Native Americans about the interpretive decisions we make in working out our own theologies of the cross. And that is of great value, even if it is not in the end possible to develop a theology that is both truly Native and truly Pauline.

Conclusion

This journey *to* Paul from Native American life and thought has also been a journey *with* Paul to Native life and thought. At many points I have seen opportunities for positive connection between Paul and Native traditions, as well as possibilities for new ways of seeing Paul through Native traditions. I have included some but not all, since my aim is not to present a definitive guide to Native Christians on how they should read Paul but simply to make suggestions. Even that may be too bold.

My journey has raised more questions than it has answered. While there are many ways of developing a Native reading of Paul that illumines Paul's thought and enriches Native Christian life and theology, one must not overlook some of the very basic problems that place limits on Native appropriation of Paul. The most significant problem has to do with the understanding of creation in relation to redemption. For Paul, creation is the subject of divine redemption. In Native teaching, creation is the agent of divine redemption. In Paul, only God in Christ is savior and giver of gifts; in Native thinking the whole of creation in all its animate parts brings blessing to humanity. A basis for eco-justice in Paul is that God loves creation, which is fallen, weak, suffering. For Natives, eco-justice flows from the conviction that the earth is our Mother. Creation — even if it suffers and is vulnerable to human activity — holds the power of life and blessing. God in creation redeems a humanity that errs and sins, but neither humanity nor creation as a whole is "fallen." "The land looks after us," as the Native saying goes. It may be impossible to honor traditional Native teaching about creation within a Native interpretation of Paul. In that case (and reinforced by the other tensions we have seen), a Native scholar is right when he warns that a Native appropriation of Paul cannot be done. One way to read this chapter is as a demonstration of that Native scholar's judgment.

On the other hand, more conservative Native Christians take a different view. I have tried to honor their attitudes toward Paul as well. One of the difficulties here, however, is that there has not yet been a Native American engagement of Paul that interacts with the historical Paul reconstructed by modern scholarship. Nor has there been interest in describing Paul's theology as a distinctive New Testament voice. In more conservative Native Christianity, Paul is interpreted not on his own terms but as part of a pattern of Christian faith based in the Bible and influenced to varying degrees by Western missionary traditions. Generally, Paul is not a central figure in Native Christianity. Speaking as a Pauline scholar and with sensitivity to the perspectives of Native Christians such as Leon Matthews (and others I have spoken with), I have tried to suggest sympathetic Native Christian approaches to Paul. But these are for the most part my suggestions. It is not clear that a Native scholar who engaged the historical Paul would follow the same paths I have followed.

Of course, conservative Native Christians can use Paul in bits, the way the church has often treated the Bible as a kind of wisdom tradition from which one pulls this or that teaching or idea without doing justice to specific patterns of thought in any given part of the Bible. Perhaps the result is another form of the failure to deal with the deeper questions of "thought and world systems," as Kidwell, Noley, and Tinker warn. Nevertheless, the Western church has not read Paul in a historical-critical way but treated him as part of a more or less seamless biblical revelation. So I want to be careful not to insist that unless Native Christians appropriate the historical Paul, informed by biblical scholarship, they have not really appropriated Paul but only a superficial version of him.

A further consideration is "how much" or "what kind of" Native tradition is necessary for a Native Christian reading of Paul to be authentically Native and not simply a repetition of European missionary theology. How much "contextualization" to the Native tradition do Natives need in order not to be "internally colonized," as Tinker put it? While the critiques of Tinker and others about internal colonization as an effect of missionary conquest have great merit, we should also respect Native congregations and pastors when they make their own cultural judgments and religious decisions about contextualization. And here we find a wide range — from syncretistic forms of Native Christianity to forms that are more assimilating in the direction of Euro-American patterns of church life and teaching.

Western scholars — and those with Western educations in Paul such as I myself — should be especially careful not to require a form of contextualization of Paul for Native Christians (or any other non-Western

Christian communities) that counts as genuine only those expressions that somehow mirror the whole integrated pattern of the historical Paul's thought. Westerners themselves do not embrace Paul on these terms. For example, we do not embrace Paul's ancient cosmology but re-read Paul on the assumptions of a modern cosmology. We do not embrace Paul's historical assumptions or his eschatological expectations without some hermeneutical mediation based on our own knowledge of history and our awareness that his expectation of a near end of the world did not come to pass. It is therefore fair to look for ways in which hermeneutical mediations might be made between Paul's cosmology and Native cosmologies. Paul's cosmology cannot be simply imposed on Natives — by Natives or non-Natives — as if being a Christian required assent to ancient Mediterranean worldviews. Moreover, Native Christians with American educations face the special challenge of working out hermeneutical mediations not only between Paul (or any part of the Bible) and Native cosmologies but simultaneously between Native cosmologies and modern science.

Finally, there is the question of how the gospel, in this case the gospel as preached by Paul, poses challenges to any culture. Paul entered Greek culture and encountered non-eschatological ways of thinking and told people to believe that the only solution to this world is a new world and that the human situation is much more dire than they thought! I myself as a boy first encountering Christian faith felt that much of this Pauline teaching was a cultural imposition on me as a Chinese person. I felt free to reject it and focus on the ethical aspects of Paul's teaching. I assumed that the eschatology was simply part of Paul's ancient Mediterranean way of thinking and did not carry universal significance. Today I am much more aware of how everything in Paul is somehow connected with his eschatology. At the same time I recognize that one cannot simply appropriate Paul's eschatology for life today without some hermeneutical adjustment. One can imagine Paul challenging Natives by telling them to reject their views that God works blessing through creation, to embrace his teaching that the only solution to the problems of this world is a new world that is just appearing and about to arrive fully any time now, and to accept with him that all human beings are in bondage to sin and death. To what extent would that be cultural imposition and to what extent a prophetic word on target?

I have been clear that my role in reading Native traditions from a

Pauline perspective and vice versa is not that of the prophet to Natives. So I am very hesitant to draw the line on this or that issue between cultural imposition and the proper cultural challenges that the gospel presents to any of our cultures. My hope is that a reciprocal process of dialogue will allow Paul's theology and the Native teachings to shed light on each other. In the process, I have learned how to be a fuller Christian as I discover how Native teaching and perspectives expand my horizon. I become a more *ecumenical Christian* beyond the *limits of a particular* culture, nationality, community, and experience.

CHAPTER 6

Paul's Journey to Russia

Herold Weiss

Attempting a journey to a foreign culture in order to learn from its dialogue with Paul, one is confronted with a problem. Cultures are not static artifacts. In terms of this chapter, one must decide with which Russia, or with which aspects of Russian culture, Paul is to dialogue. Russia went through a traumatic revolution in 1917 and has been going through another traumatic upheaval since the collapse of the Soviet Union. Some would argue that the communist struggle against capitalism has given way now to "bandit capitalism," and that this chapter should deal with that. Others may think that communism has left an indelible imprint on Russia, and that due notice should be given to it. For better or worse, I have chosen to deal with traditional Russia, pre-1917 Russia. While admitting that secularist forces have made deep inroads into the culture, the traditional values of Eastern Orthodoxy are still powerful in Russian society and therefore my attention is focused here on the Russia of Eastern Orthodoxy.

The Role of the Scriptures

Eastern Christianity has been closely tied to its biblical roots. The sacredness of the Scriptures is manifest at every liturgy, when a copy of the Gospels kept in a special place behind the iconostasis is taken in a procession around the nave as an icon. It may be said that the text occupies the place reserved for the host in Western Catholicism. Like the Latin Vulgate, the Slavonic Bible was the most important influence in the language of the Slavic peoples who converted to Christianity in 988. Of course, the text and the icons that became so prominent had come from Byzantium in

Greek dress. Thus Russian Orthodoxy has always looked to Constantinople and to the Greek Fathers for the roots of its culture.

The need for doctrinal refinements brought into Christian discourse the philosophical vocabulary of Platonism, Stoicism, and Neoplatonism. But the biblical text was still considered primary. All theological positions needed to have a scriptural foundation. The authority of the biblical text as Scripture has never been tested or disputed, even if conciliar and dogmatic declarations are also the basis of Orthodoxy and beyond dispute.[1] Still, it is instructive to realize that the faithful are quite free to pursue theological and historical questions as long as they also affirm the Church's dogmas. Timothy Ware (Bishop Kallistos of Diokleia) declares: "Orthodoxy, while regarding the Church as the authoritative interpreter of Scripture, does not forbid the critical and historical study of the Bible."[2] The role of Scripture in the Orthodox doctrinal statements is to provide the skeletal support. Orthodoxy did not develop a tradition of scriptural commentaries that attempt to establish the peculiarities of biblical authors. All of them are at the service of the church.

One of the exceptions to the Orthodox tendency to proof-text rather than comment on Scripture is the body of commentaries on Paul by Feofan the Recluse, written at the Vysha monastery between 1875 and 1882. His commentaries proved a great success and were reprinted three times before his death in 1894. They are still available and in demand today. Even though he read German, French, and especially English exegetes, Feofan relied primarily on the works of John Chrysostom and Theodoret.[3] As Margaret Mitchell has amply demonstrated,[4] Chrysostom set up Paul for his audiences as the exemplar of virtue who was to be imitated by those who were to be citizens in the Christian empire of the late fourth century. Chrysostom's own intimacy with the thought of Paul became legendary. In later centuries

1. For a list of them, see Timothy Ware, *The Orthodox Church* (London: Penguin, 1963), 207-12.

2. Ware, *The Orthodox Church,* 209.

3. For the life and work of Saint Feofan the Recluse I am indebted to the excellent dissertation of Mikhail Kulakov, "'The Infinite Diversity of Persons': Individual Personality in the Ascetic Theology of St. Feofan the Recluse (1815-1894)" (unpublished, Christ Church, Oxford, 2000), 39.

4. Margaret M. Mitchell, *The Heavenly Trumpet: John Chrysostom and the Art of Pauline Interpretation* (Hermeneutische Untersuchungen zur Theologie 40; Tübingen: Mohr, 2000/Louisville: Westminster/John Knox, 2002).

it was believed that Paul had directly inspired Chrysostom's homilies on the Pauline letters. Chrysostom, who was a hermit for two years but then returned to urban life and rose to high ecclesiastical office, saw in Paul his model and pictured him as the ascetic who participated fully in the life of the world. This vision of Paul became dominant in the Orthodox East. Following this tradition, Feofan also gives his readers a Paul who teaches them how to live in the world, purging themselves of the passions and cares that prevent the life of the soul from fully manifesting the image of God.

The Constitution of the Person and Freedom

As a student at the Kiev Academy, Feofan was greatly influenced by Petr S. Avsenev, known by his students as "the meek philosopher." Avsenev had accommodated the ideas of the Spirit coming from the German Romantics with the spirituality of Eastern mysticism. Eastern Christianity had been the cradle of the Desert Fathers and the anchorites who sought solitude and communion with God at the most basic levels of human experience. For Feofan, Paul provides guidance for the warfare of the Spirit against the desires and the inclinations of the flesh. Salvation is attained after a struggle taking place in the soul. It is necessary for the soul to be "inspirited"[5] in a way that leads to life in a "spiritual body" (1 Cor. 15:44). While enslaved by the passions, persons are incapable of attaining knowledge of the world around them, or of themselves. Enslavement to sin destroys the ability to distinguish oneself from the external world, so that everything around is part of oneself. In such a condition, self-knowledge and personhood are impossible. It is only when the Spirit, whose attributes are consciousness and freedom, "inspirits" the soul that personhood becomes possible. The attainment of self-consciousness brings freedom with it. The human vocation, therefore, is an ascetic struggle for the freedom of the soul.

Feofan's understanding of the person as created by the Spirit into self-consciousness was influenced by the romantic notion of the need to penetrate the depths of one's being in nature at the subconscious level. Schleiermacher located religion at the root of being, where the soul is not influenced by external stimuli but is at its truest self. Once stimuli affect the soul and the person consciously intellectualizes experiences, the rela-

5. Kulakov, "Infinite Diversity," 14.

tionship to the world is no longer immediate but mediated by the mind. Schleiermacher insisted that religion was unmediated.[6] In this, he was following the romantic rediscovery of nature as supportive of the human good and as the foundation for any human achievement. Eastern Orthodox Christianity had never lost touch with the goodness of human nature. In its view, the fall of humanity had not rendered human beings depraved, much less "totally depraved." Even if the image of God in human beings is in need of restoration, just as some painted canvas after some years may need some restoration to fully recover the original artistic impression placed on it,[7] this does not mean that fallen humans are bad. Salvation entails the restoration of the image of God in human beings. For Feofan, this means the recuperation of a person as a person and of the ability for self-expression.

Orthodox Christianity insists that only persons in the exercise of their will are able to sin. Nature cannot sin, nor can human beings "by nature." There is no such thing as a sinful nature. This fundamental understanding of the human condition is based on the words of Paul in Rom. 5:12: "As sin came into the world through one human being's trespass and through sin death, also in this way death came into all human beings because all have sinned."[8] Latin translations of the Greek text had "in whom all have sinned" for the last phrase.[9] This allowed Augustine to teach that sin, and especially the guilt attached to it, reside in fallen human nature. In the West this came to be known as "original sin," the notion that after Adam and Eve all human beings are born in sin. This teaching was reinforced by the words of the Psalmist: "In sin did my mother conceive me" (Ps. 51:5). Thus sexuality became intimately attached to sinfulness, and in-

6. Friedrich Schleiermacher, *On Religion: Speeches to Its Cultured Despisers*, ed. and trans. Richard Crouter (Cambridge: Cambridge University Press, 1988), 18-54.

7. The metaphor was first used by Athanasius, *The Incarnation of the Word of God*, trans. by a religious of C.S.M.V. (New York: Macmillan, 1946), 14.

8. At issue is what causes all human beings to sin. Did Adam's sin introduce mortality or sin and guilt?

9. The Greek phrase *eph' hǭ pantes hēmarton* became in Latin *in quo omnes peccaverunt*. The Greek expression *eph' hǭ* understood literally means "upon whom" or "upon it" (if the pronoun is understood as neuter rather than masculine). As an idiom the phrase may also be understood as "because," which is how the Greek Fathers always understood it and as modern translations of the text do. For a discussion of the different understandings of the pronoun (as either neuter or masculine) in the West, see Gerald Bray, *Biblical Interpretation: Past and Present* (Downers Grove: InterVarsity, 1996), 216-18.

fants are held to be born in need of baptism to wash away the guilt attached to their sinful nature.

Reading Paul's words in Greek, the Eastern Fathers saw mortality, not original sin and its guilt, as the consequence of Adam's sin. The words of Paul, "For as in Adam all die, so also in Christ shall all be made alive" (1 Cor. 15:22), were considered determinative. For a person to sin, the person must will or act. No sin can be assigned to a person on account of his or her nature. To return to Rom. 5:12, as a consequence of the entrance of mortality into the human horizon, appetites, passions, and survival instincts also entered the human environment and, on account of these, "all human beings have sinned." Death is what causes the descendents of Adam to sin. Just as it cannot be said that the life of Christ is applied to every human being automatically, it cannot be said that the sin of Adam is applied to every human being automatically. Sin is not transmitted trans-generationally by nature or sex. In the East the Fall is viewed primarily as the entrance of death, the last enemy to communion with God. It is not a question of guilt and its elimination. The West has viewed the Fall primarily as a legal problem, while the East sees it as a personal problem.[10]

Eastern Christianity has a very strong mystical bent. The mystical impulse is to drown oneself in the ocean of being. This means that autonomous self-expression, the satisfaction of the passions, is precisely what one seeks to conquer in the struggle for the soul. The consequence of sin is mortality and the splitting of the unity that binds all human beings. As sinners, individuals see themselves as discrete persons alienated from all other human beings and God. Mystics seek to reestablish their being in the unity that existed in nature before the Fall. The Pauline image of the church as the body of Christ is understood in Eastern Orthodoxy as that which calls attention to the unity in nature of all the members of the body (Rom. 12:4-5). This union allows for the development of the person by the Holy Spirit and the will.[11] The nature in question is the human nature assumed by Christ at the incarnation.

Another Pauline metaphor has also been interpreted in this context within the mystical Eastern tradition. In 1 Cor 3:11, Paul insists that Chris-

10. On the reading of Rom. 5:12 by the Eastern Fathers, see John Meyendorff, *Byzantine Theology: Historical Trends and Doctrinal Themes* (New York: Fordham University Press, 1974), 143-46.

11. Vladimir Lossky, *The Mystical Theology of the Eastern Church,* trans. by members of the Fellowship of St. Alban and St. Sergius (Cambridge: Clarke, 1957), 121-22.

tians can be built only on Christ as the foundation. This means that the foundation is the human nature of Christ. Christ did not take any one particular way of being human; he took what is common to all humans. In other words, his incarnation is the demonstration of the unity of human nature. When human beings are "founded upon Christ, who contains our nature in His divine Person, we may attain to union with God in our created persons; we may become, after the image of Christ, persons having two natures."[12] The goal of the Christian life is for persons to have two natures and thus be full expressions of the image of God. For persons to have two natures, however, it is necessary first for them to be fully in touch with human nature.

For Feofan freedom is "the ability to make a conscious and independent decision regarding an external or internal impulse, demand or circumstance."[13] By inspiring the soul and making it free, the Spirit allows the person to become master of the self, capable of surrendering to God's will. Even though this freedom is only internal, within the soul, it makes possible "the whole burnt-offering of freedom," that is, the subjection of the will, which is the precondition for God's power to bring about the divine-human interpenetration that is salvation. There is no tension between the human effort in the exercise of the will and the divine grace that is at work in the salvation of humanity. Grace and human freedom are not seen as separate or at odds with each other. As expressed by Gregory of Nyssa, "The righteousness of works and the grace of the Spirit, having come together in one place, fill the soul in which they are united with the life of the blessed."[14] The two are not analyzed in order to establish causal connections. Thus grace is not conceived as the reward for the right exercise of the will, nor is it seen as the support for a "righteousness of works." A synergy of the divine and the human wills is inherent to the restoration of the image of God in human beings.

Feofan insisted that outside of God's will no one is free.[15] Human beings who exercise the freedom to sin demonstrate that they are not totally outside God's reach. Their spiritual freedom is real. As for external freedom, following the tradition of the Eastern Fathers, Feofan considers it a

12. Lossky, *Mystical Theology*, 185.

13. Kulakov, "Infinite Diversity," 175.

14. Gregory of Nyssa, "De Instituto Christiano," *Patrologia Graeca* 46.269C, quoted in Lossky, *Mystical Theology*, 197.

15. Kulakov, "Infinite Diversity," 176.

phantom. The primary evidence is found in 1 Cor. 7:21-22. The Slavonic Version renders v. 21 as "even if you can gain your freedom, make use of your present condition now more than ever." Feofan then elaborates with a reference to the "divinely ordained limits of slavery."[16] External circumstances do not and should not determine the condition of the soul. Freedom of the will has to do with matters of the soul, and the multiform slavery of the material world is part and parcel of a hierarchically constituted universe.

Before his reclusion at Vysha, Feofan saw the momentous reforms accomplished by Tsar Alexander II such as the emancipation of the serfs, the restructuring of local governments, the institution of judicial review (including attempts to extend it to the ecclesiastical judiciary), and some liberalization of censorship.[17] This, however, did not make Feofan, the student of Paul, less of an authoritarian traditionalist who, like the ancient Greeks and Romans, understood that external freedoms and rights were related to rank.[18]

In his analysis of Feofan's writings, Mikhail Kulakov sees at their center a contradiction in the concept of freedom. On the one hand, Feofan follows Paul's understanding of the Spirit as the supreme power in the life of Christians that transforms them into spiritual women and men. On the other, he negates the existence of freedom in the external world. Socially and politically he is a strict traditionalist who understands society hierarchically and allows for the existence of freedoms and rights only in reference to social class. Politically he explicitly supports the autocracy of the Tsar and grants legitimacy to the empire on condition that the Orthodox Church exercises absolute religious and moral control.[19] In this he is not being forgetful of Paul. Some readers of Paul are troubled by the realization that Paul was not explicitly concerned with the liberation of the slaves

16. Kulakov, "Infinite Diversity," 178.

17. Kulakov, "Infinite Diversity," 31.

18. Kulakov, "Infinite Diversity," 178.

19. It must be recognized that many of the most rational minds in the West denied freedom to some and linked freedom to social class. John Stuart Mill, for example, wrote, "The reciprocal sacred duty to respect the independence and nationality that binds civilized peoples does not apply to those peoples for which independence and nationality are known evils or at least dubious goods," *Disquisitions and Discourses* (London: Longmans, Green, Reader and Dyer, 1875), 3.167-68, quoted in Edward Said, *Culture and Imperialism* (New York: Knopf, 1993), 80.

in the Roman Empire or with the elimination of slave ownership among Christians. In his letter to Philemon, for example, he asks Philemon to welcome Onesimus back into the household as a brother in Christ, but not to grant him freedom from the slavery he had tried to escape.[20]

The Eastern concern with the constitution of the person is also at the center of Nicholas Berdyaev's[21] thought. He also belongs among those Eastern intellectuals who do their theologizing in dialogue with the West, having lived much of his life in Paris while in exile from Stalin's Soviet Union. He represents the Russian philosophical tradition that is concerned with matters of the Spirit and struggles against both Orthodox ecclesiastical dogmatism and the secularizing impact of either communism or Western philosophy. His book *The Destiny of Man*[22] takes for its motto an epigram from Gogol's notebook for 1846: "It is sad not to see any good in goodness." Its main concern is to explore the tensions that exist within the good in the fallen world of good and evil. In agreement with the Orthodox tradition, Berdyaev considers the anthropology of *divine-humanity* to be the central idea in Christianity. Thus, while he understands that all theology speaks the language of myths and symbols and that only apophatic mystical theology comes closer to God as the infinite mystery that underlies existence,[23] he affirms that the divinity in man is absolutely real.[24] The nature of human beings springs from two sources: from the image and likeness of God and from non-being, the abyss of freedom. The "nothing" *(nihilo)* out of which God created a being in the divine image and likeness was meonic freedom.[25]

Unlike Feofan, who understood freedom to be an attribute of the Spirit, Berdyaev sees freedom as an ontological element in human existence. From this platform, Berdyaev launches an argument against the scholastic

20. It is most telling that Dale Martin, *Slavery as Salvation: The Metaphor of Slavery in Pauline Christianity* (New Haven: Yale University Press, 1990), does not refer to Onesimus or to the Pauline attitude toward the actual practice of slavery at all.

21. This name has been commonly rendered in English as Berdyaev but also appears as Berdiaev.

22. Nicolai Berdyaev, *The Destiny of Man*, trans. Natalie Duddington (New York: Harper and Row, 1960).

23. Berdyaev, *Destiny*, 24. "Mystical negative theology brings us closer to the final depths. The limit to rational thought is set by a mystery and not a taboo" (p. 25).

24. Berdyaev, *Destiny*, 82.

25. Orthodox theology has maintained a distinction between *mē on* (non-being), and *ouk on* (absolute nothingness). The classic text for *creatio ex nihilo*, 2 Macc. 7:28, reads *ouk on*. This allows Berdyaev to remain within the bounds of Orthodoxy.

tradition that centers the discussion of good and evil on the freedom of the will. This development, he contends, was necessitated by the juridical understanding of sin and salvation developed in the West.[26] Freedom of the will was brought into theological discourse by "utilitarian pedagogical considerations," as a way of making human beings responsible for choosing wrongly between good and evil.[27] Its basic problem is that it requires the enslavement of human beings to God's will. It works on the assumption that the end justifies the means. Salvation is attained by submission.[28] It forever confronts human beings with the need to choose between alternatives imposed from above, thus keeping them in fear and indecision. Ultimately, it is not liberating. The measure by which a life is evaluated is whether it has reached to a higher good. Against this, Berdyaev argues that "man's moral dignity and freedom are determined not by the purpose to which he subordinates his life but by the source from which his moral life and activity spring."[29] The source shapes personality, which is constituted by a free act of God that transforms non-being (meonic freedom) into being. Here Berdyaev is building on the words of Paul. The one who raised Christ from the dead is "the one who calls the things that are not as things that are" (Rom. 4:17).

God's creation of human beings must be understood not purely in terms of the Old Testament but also christologically, involving two acts. In the first act God appears as the Maker who transforms non-being into being. The myth of the Fall makes clear, however, that God cannot prevent the evil resulting from meonic freedom. In the second act God appears as the suffering God who takes upon himself the sins of the world. God descends "into the depths of freedom out of which springs evil as well as every kind of good."[30] Berdyaev interprets the incarnation in a dogmatic rather than a juridical way. This means that for him Christ's death is necessitated not by the need to meet the Law's requirements but by the divine intention to be one with humanity. The Christian understanding of hu-

26. Most prominent in this Western tradition is Anselm's insistence that God cannot forgive sins without proper satisfaction for the offense by those liable. See Anselm, *Why God Became Man,* 11, 15, 19, in *Saint Anselm: Basic Writings*, trans. S. N. Deane (La Salle: Open Court, 1964).

27. Berdyaev, *Destiny,* 79.

28. Here Berdyaev is critical of traditional Orthodoxy, which, as noted above in the case of Feofan, considers the submission of the will as essential to salvation.

29. Berdyaev, *Destiny,* 80.

30. Berdyaev, *Destiny,* 25.

man beings must start here. Even if the manifestation of the God-man took place "when the time had fully come" (Gal. 4:4), his sacrifice had been established before the foundation of the world (Rom. 16:25-26; 1 Cor. 2:7; 1 Pet. 1:20). On this basis, Berdyaev argues,

> The most important thing for ethics is man's nature, the spirit in which he acts, the presence or absence in him of inner light, of beneficent creative energy. Ethics must be based upon the conception of energy and not of the final end. . . . Ethics must be based upon the conception of creative freedom as the source of life, and of the spirit as the light which illumines life.[31]

While concerned with the same problem that preoccupied Feofan, Berdyaev radicalizes the mystical understanding of human nature for the benefit of *all human beings at creation.* The power of the Spirit is the power of freedom present from eternity in that which is not created. The redemption of freedom by the divine descent to the abyss of non-being took place before the foundation of the world and is at the core of human nature. This understanding of human beings is basic to solving the tragedy that is human life. In the human world evil is touched by good and vice-versa. At its core is a basic Pauline concept: the recognition that even that which is "good" and "spiritual" within the world may bring about death (Rom. 7:12-14). Any conception of the human predicament that does not take this into account is bound to be deceptive. The Law is powerless in the face of sin. The problem with the doctrine of the freedom of the will is that it idealizes good and evil.[32] Rather than conceiving the human vocation to be the attainment of a higher good, Berdyaev argues that human beings were created to be creative. Thus he pushes the Orthodox conception of the person, central to the thought of Feofan, to a higher plane. The tragedy of human existence is not bound to fate, as in the classical Greek conception, but to the freedom that is at the core of human existence.[33] Human beings are free ontologically, and not just as servants of the moral law. They may exercise their freedom not only to rebel against God but also to create, with good and bad results. They are capable of conceiving new values. "The world of values is not a changeless ideal realm rising above man and free-

31. Berdyaev, *Destiny,* 80-81.
32. Berdyaev, *Destiny,* 43.
33. Berdyaev, *Destiny,* 30.

dom; it is constantly undergoing change and being created afresh." In their relationship with God, human beings are free not just in the sense that they can turn toward or against him, but also as "being able to co-operate with God, to create the good and produce new values."[34]

On this account, "The only way to God is through man." The only way for God to express himself in the world is through interaction with humans, "through the refraction of the divine principle in human freedom."[35] Human beings answer the divine call not by obedience to an external authority but by exercising the freedom inherent in their very being. The life they live as an answer to God is bound to be a creative cooperation of the divine and the human, not a denial of the vital forces in human life. "This presupposes a new ethic based . . . upon gracious spiritual power,"[36] rather than on external norms or a teleological "good." For Berdyaev, Paul is the one who "wages a passionate struggle against the power of the law and reveals the religion of grace. Law comes from sin and makes sin manifest. Law denounces sin, limits it, but cannot conquer it."[37] Like Paul he also recognizes that, on account of the incapacity of the law to conquer evil, human beings must be understood differently, as having in the source of their being gracious spiritual power as an ontological element of the personality. As already noted, for Berdyaev the sacrifice of Christ is the second divine act in the creation of humanity. Those who are crucified and alive with Christ live energized by the Spirit (Rom. 6:1-6). It would seem that for Paul the power of God that brings about life is working on earth in the gospel. The gospel is not a new teaching, a doctrinal system, a theology. It is "the power of God unto salvation" (life, Rom. 1:16). And salvation is first and foremost liberation by the Spirit that created the ultimate reality: the Risen Lord. In the Eastern tradition this is taken seriously to mean that the object of Christianity is communion with God in the person of Christ, the crucial element of Paul's gospel. Only the power of the Spirit can triumph over sins, which the Law can only judge and condemn (Rom. 5:16). Only the power of the gospel actualizes the divine life among human beings.

As the image and likeness of God, persons have unconditional value, and no abstract idea of the good can be placed above them.[38] Paul gave him-

34. Berdyaev, *Destiny,* 44.
35. Berdyaev, *Destiny,* 54.
36. Berdyaev, *Destiny,* 78.
37. Berdyaev, *Destiny,* 85.
38. Berdyaev, *Destiny,* 106-7.

self and his coworkers much value by considering them and himself coworkers with God in bringing life to humanity (1 Cor. 3:9; 2 Cor. 6:1-2). Berdyaev sees human beings as coworkers with God in the creation of values. In this Berdyaev radicalizes the Pauline view of the Law against the more conservative stance taken by ecclesiastical Orthodoxy. There has always been tension among the readers of Paul on how to reconcile Paul's view of the power of the Spirit with the authority of the church as a channel of the Spirit. This tension is quite evident when ecclesiastical Orthodoxy and Berdyaev are compared. While Berdyaev fully embraces the creative power of the Spirit as the ontological principle of an anthropology fully dependent on christology, ecclesiastical Orthodoxy, like ecclesiastical Catholicism, emphasizes the language of the letter to the Ephesians to the effect that, as the "body of Christ," the church is built on the foundation of the apostles, with Christ as the chief cornerstone (Eph. 1:22-23; 2:20). It is within the church and not in humanity that the mystery of the union of the human and the divine is found. Therefore, it is only in the church that the restoration of the image of God in women and men may be accomplished by the Holy Spirit.

While Berdyaev did not become a recluse or a monk, he also understood that the Christian must develop the power present in the personality in order to creatively live in the world as a challenge to the norms and mores of society. Both Berdyaev and Feofan saw consequences for the present in the Pauline promise of a spiritual body, but not the consequences usually seen by Western interpreters. Western modernity has been intrigued by history, at times even conceiving of history as a kind of salvation train taking humanity along to God's desired terminal. This has meant that interpreters of Paul have emphasized the temporal tension between what is already accomplished by Christ in a historical past and what will be accomplished by him in the future. Western culture is concerned with teleology, with progress toward a goal. Feofan and Berdyaev, as good Eastern Christians, are more concerned with the beginning.[39] Salvation is based on the way God made things. The essence of things is what determines their outcome. Thus both Feofan and Berdyaev point out that Christians must live in the body into which Christ himself was incarnated. This has significant consequences for the way in which Christians live in society.

39. Concern with the beginning as the determining factor in human existence within Christianity may be traced to the *Gospel of Thomas,* an early Christian document that evolved to the form discovered at Nag Hammadi from oral traditions of the first century.

Life in Society

Most students of Paul agree that in his view the person renewed from above does not live according to the norms and values of society at large but by the understanding of the good provided by the Spirit (Rom. 12:1-2). Berdyaev also denies the authority of all social constraints upon the person. Thus, even if there are other contradictions in his thought, he does not exhibit Feofan's contradiction of the person who is free and yet bound to the Tsar and the Orthodox Church. For Berdyaev the paradox of freedom in history is that aristocratic, free minorities use the law to repress the majority. The masses, who are the bearers of tradition, custom, and public opinion, at times find the strength to rise against the aristocracy. On such occasions, however, they do not struggle to gain freedom. Lamentably, they seek to impose anew old customs and traditions.[40] The inability of revolutions with popular support to bring about social improvements necessitates the leadership of a spiritual elite who can create new values and transform the human condition.[41]

This is consistent with Berdyaev's universalizing conception of the incarnation as the revelation of the human person and with his understanding of the human vocation as creative. The kingdom of God is where the value of persons stands above the value of all the kingdoms of the world. The Orthodox disdain for capitalism is due in large measure to its understanding that capitalism places money and the accumulation of wealth above and in opposition to human beings and the kingdom of God.

It is not difficult to see that Paul was deeply concerned with the freedom of new creatures for life, for God, in Berdyaev's terms, for creativity. This freedom is being thwarted by the power of sin which has entered the world and now reigns in it (Rom. 5:12, 14). For Paul, sin is an agent in the human soul that through the passions, taking advantage of the weakness of the flesh, brings about death (7:5, 13). Sin is also a cosmic power that has "entered" the world and now "rules" it. As such it holds humanity captive. Everyone sins, and as a result everyone dies (5:12). The hegemony of sin and its "wages," death, is ensured by the Law, which, even though it is "spiritual" and "good" (7:12, 14), has become within the fallen creation the

40. Berdyaev, *Destiny,* 96.

41. Nicolas Berdyaev, *The Beginning and the End* (History of Thought 14; New York: Harper and Row, 1952), 201-8.

instrument of enslavement (Gal. 3:23; Rom. 7:6). To bring about freedom from the power of the Law, sin, and death, a greater power is needed. That can only be the power of life in God, that is, the power of the Spirit, the power of the gospel (Rom. 1:16; 15:16; 1 Cor. 1:17-18, 24; 2:5; 4:20; 2 Cor. 13:4). Berdyaev's theology emphasizes this aspect of Paul's thought. Life is not determined by norms but by the power that energizes it. The human predicament is not due to the Law that demands the death of the sinner, but to the human misuse of freedom, which results in the creation of evil conditions for life. Paul's understanding of sin can also be seen as coming from meonic freedom, a human act out of the depths of non-being. In Romans 5 he contrasts the act of Adam with the act of God in Christ. This opposition places Adam in an exalted position. Adam's freedom made it possible for him to open the door to sin and death. Even if Paul describes Adam's act as disobedience (Rom. 5:19), he makes clear that this disobedience was not determined by the Law, which came into the world much later by the hand of Moses. For Paul, therefore, sin is not defined as "the transgression of the Law" since there was sin when there was no Law.[42] Paul defines sin as what is done independently of God, without faith (Rom. 14:23). The Pauline definition of sin fully allows for the understanding of sin as an expression of non-being, the abuse of meonic freedom.

The Centrality of the Incarnation

Eastern thinkers do not see the Fall primarily in juridical terms as the result of the transgression of the Law. Rather they see it mystically as a crack in the human-divine person — in Berdyaev's terms, as the working of meonic freedom in opposition to the power of the Word that created all things. This flaw is in need of restructuring. The divine and the human in the person are still there. The divine and the human, however, are not to be understood primarily in an abstract, sharp contrast between the natural and the supernatural. They must be understood in terms of a holistic, mystical communion.

Athanasius, the defender of what became Orthodoxy after the Council of Nicaea (325 CE), already recognized the centrality of the incarnation and the formation of the person in the image of God. In *The Incarnation of*

42. Paul uses this definition of sin only when adopting the Jewish point of view in order to make a rhetorical argument.

the Word of God, he insisted that the Word (Logos) who prepared for himself a special body in the body of the Virgin Mary was *none other than* God.[43] Salvation, then, entered the world through the incarnation. The human predicament, according to Athanasius, was twofold. On the one hand, God had originally created human beings in the image of God. This meant that they were capable of communication with God and knowledge of God. Sin, however, had damaged this image, distorting the imprint of the Logos, leaving humans incapable of knowing God. As a result humanity is in a process of degradation that is making it like animals without reason, since the fading of the image results in the loss of Logos. Besides, since the creation accomplished by God in the beginning was out of nothing *(ex nihilo),* on account of sin and its concomitant brutalizing of the soul, humanity would ultimately become nothing, having regressed back to its source. Were this to happen and God's creative action come to naught, God would lose face. God's Word (the Logos) incarnated himself in order to counter the two effects of the Fall. First, by dying on the cross *in place of humans* he triumphed over the power of death and satisfied the demands of the Law. Second, by living and teaching among humans he restored in them the vanishing image of God, enabling them to regain knowledge of God and aspire for higher things. Thus he destroyed the power of death and reversed the regression toward nothingness. For Athanasius it is important to emphasize that what died on the cross was the body that had lived untouched by sin. The Logos incarnated himself in a specially prepared sinless body and is immortal, incapable of dying. In fact, while on earth in his human body, the Logos continued to create and maintain the universe, which totally depends on him for its continuous existence. In this vision of salvation, the resurrection serves to prove the sinlessness of the body that died on the cross in order to establish the power of life over death.

Within this tradition, salvation is accomplished by the incarnation of the Logos. This indwelling stamped the image of God in the body that lived in Palestine, showing to women and men what the image of God really looks like, providing the model to be imitated. After Athanasius, Orthodox theologians explained the blending of the human and the divine as an internal communication of properties. Thus the process of salvation is understood as the process of deification *(theosis),* a restoration of the fallen human to the divine original intention when created in the image of

43. Athanasius, *The Incarnation of the Word of God,* 10.

God. This is a process that takes place mysteriously in the soul, is energized by the Holy Spirit, and is fostered by the communion of the saints, what Berdyaev distinguishes as "communality or *sobornost*."[44]

Deification

Central to Orthodoxy is the human vocation to deification. What this means is not always well understood or represented fairly by Western Christians. The idea is, at its roots, Pauline: "Just as we have borne the image of the man of dust, we shall also bear the image of the man of heaven" (1 Cor. 15:49). More often, Paul writes about glorification. He affirms that the work of the Spirit is to change humans "into his image from one glory to another" while they are "beholding the glory of the Lord" (2 Cor. 3:18). It is not difficult to see how the language of glorification soon came to be understood in terms of "participation in the divine nature" (2 Pet. 3:18) and deification. This language of the New Testament received dogmatic clarification in terms of the definitions arrived at in the christological controversy and the distinction, central to Orthodoxy, between God's essence and God's energies (on this, more later). Thus, to be glorified, to be deified, to partake of the divine nature, to be in union with God is not to be changed from a natural to a supernatural person. It is union with God's energies, which permeate the natural world as God's grace. It does not involve the human or the divine essences. Human creatures become divine by grace, by participating in the divine energies. In the same way that Christ remains God while becoming human by the incarnation, women and men remain human while "partaking of the divine nature" by deification.[45]

This concern for the presence of the divine and its creative power in the lives of human beings is fully shared by Paul. He became a very controversial figure in apostolic Christianity because he found divine power not in the expression of God's will, in the Law, but in the creative Spirit who raised Christ from the dead. For him life and freedom have their source only in the creative power of the Spirit. Both can only be found living in Christ, in the Spirit. Life in the Spirit may include moments of ecstasy (1 Cor. 14:18), or trips to the third heaven (2 Cor. 12:2), experiences which

44. Berdyaev, *Destiny,* 58. (Berdyaev's translator has "communalty.")

45. Lossky, *Mystical Theology,* 87.

make believers unaware of their material surroundings. Paul would feel quite at home among those who emphasize the power of the Spirit in the life of Christians as the energy of the personality. He also understands the Spirit as the creator of the person (2 Cor. 5:17; Gal. 6:15). Orthodox spirituality effectively echoes the Pauline sentiment "I bow my knees before the Father, from whom every family in heaven and on earth is named, that according to the riches of his glory he may grant you to be strengthened with might in the inner self by the Spirit" (Eph. 3:14-16).

The Ascetic Life

The contrast between a basically juridical reading of Paul, so characteristic of the West, and a mystical conception is illumined by Berdyaev when he deals with asceticism. Asceticism may be a renunciation of life according to monastic "rules," another instance of a legalistic morality. In that case "it is powerless to raise life to a higher level."[46] As such, asceticism tends to become an end in itself. In the process, it "warps life and creates a revolt in the subconscious and contradictions in the conscious mind. Finally such asceticism becomes pharisaic and purely formal."[47] This asceticism is inimical to a religion of self-improvement and personal salvation. It is a form of "religious utilitarianism."

True asceticism, Berdyaev argues, conceives itself not as an attempt to reach the highest level of individual spiritual life, but as a way of reaching total immersion in what is common to all human beings: human nature. Rather than an attempt to escape, sublimate, or control human nature, it is a way of embracing human nature. It seeks to establish life on its essential foundation. The Fall split humans into clans, nations, and races; thus the original unity of nature was disestablished. It is only in discovering the nature common to all that individuals achieve true freedom. Only then do they gain for themselves their own person as a manifestation *(hypostasis)* of human nature. This definition of human beings as constituted by human nature in a *hypostasis*, which was carved out by the fourth- and fifth-century theologians involved in the christological controversy, has remained basic to Orthodoxy. Nature does not exist by itself. It can be

46. Berdyaev, *Destiny*, 95.
47. Berdyaev, *Destiny*, 122.

found only in a *hypostasis.* The human predicament is that individuals live as isolated persons and thereby lose their freedom, since freedom is sustained by the power of their common essence. Asceticism, then, is the way to freedom. It is the way for individuals to discover the nature common to all and thereby to realize their own person. Feofan would say that it is the way for individuals to distinguish themselves from the world around them by coming to terms with human nature as such.

Individuals who on account of sin do not have possession of their own persons cannot be asked to submit to God's will. For such a demand not to be tyrannical, it must be made to a subject who has freedom, as Berdyaev insists. Only in self-realization, in freedom, may persons truly give themselves over and become agents of God's grace. The goal of mystical asceticism is to make it possible for "the inspirited soul" to be perfectly united both to the divine nature in the Trinity and to the human nature that is common to all. It is based on the understanding that the rift created by the Fall is not only between heaven and earth but also within the earth. As a consequence, human beings live in alienated isolation. It has become difficult for them to share with each other. The humanism of the Enlightenment established the individual as the measure of things and is widely rejected in the East: when a society structures its laws on the rights of single individuals, it is institutionalizing the Fall.

God and the World

In the West, under the influence of Thomas Aquinas, theology developed along the lines of the distinction of natural and supernatural. Divine activity in the world is explained as an incursion of the supernatural into the natural, as a divine hand causing an effect within the world. In Western theology, divine grace is also understood as a divine cause within the cause-and-effect continuum. In the Eastern tradition, there is no such thing as pure nature untouched by the divine.[48] Divine grace is constantly present in the world naturally impregnating that which is not God with divine energy. This means that God is not understood as Wholly Other, absconded in a realm totally out of reach to humans. The Western kind of theology leads to the idea that divine activity in the world is a tampering with nature. In Aris-

48. Lossky, *Mystical Theology,* 101.

totelian terms, God is the First Cause in a universe where everything is comprehended as a link in the chain of causes and effects.

The East conceives the relationship of God to the world differently. God's uncreated energies are constantly emanating to sustain and guide the world. The world itself is best understood when comprehended in an integrative, holistic way rather than in a dismantled, analytical way. This is true also in science. It is very unfortunate that, due to ideological, political tensions, Western and Russian approaches to biology during the twentieth century, for example, were not complementary, as they surely could and should have been. While Western biologists studied life from a reductionistic approach, seeking to learn about it by reducing it to genes and molecules, in Russia biologists sought to understand life by integrating it into ecological environments and interplanetary relationships. As a result, the work of Vladimir Vernadsky, who at the turn of the century worked as a student with Pierre Curie in Paris and in 1926 published *The Biosphere* in Leningrad,[49] has been ignored until recently in the West. Vernadsky was the first to integrate the study of life to the study of the earth. For the Russian intellectual it is normal to seek to understand the particular within the whole, to integrate things. Vernadsky was an embodiment of the Russian intellectuals who populate the stage in famous plays by Chekhov. He offered a scientifically erudite view of biological life on earth in literary terms that breathe the holistic spirituality of the culture. Take, for example, this short quotation:

> A new character is imparted to the planet by this powerful cosmic force. The radiations that pour upon the Earth cause the biosphere to take on properties unknown to lifeless planetary surfaces, and thus transform the face of the Earth.[50]

This language may sound stilted to Western scientific ears today, but it reflects the Russian attitude toward the world as a mystery in which unknown energies have much to do with the way things are. The Western sec-

49. Vladimir I. Vernadsky, *The Biosphere*, trans. D. B. Langmuir (New York: Copernicus, 1998). It is rather telling that it took until the collapse of the Soviet Union and the end of the Cold War for this landmark work, a standard text in Russian universities, to be made available in the West.

50. Quoted by Vaclav Smil, *The Earth's Biosphere: Evolution, Dynamics, and Change* (Boston: MIT Press, 2002), epigraph for chapter 1.

ularization of the natural world has not penetrated very deeply into Russian culture, and the Western concern for the single individual seems wrong-headed to the Russian mind.

Within a theological vision, God's image in human beings is understood to reside not in their nature but in their person *(hypostasis)*. Persons, therefore, using the resources of their freedom and the divine energies of the power of the Spirit, are transformed into the image of God, which it is their vocation to be. In this effort, as the Eastern tradition understands it, there is no tension between grace and works because in a mystical understanding of the cosmos the causal nexus need not be determined. Grace permeates human beings in all their activities. Nothing done by humans is done outside the reach of divine energies. The cosmos is understood to be divided not between the natural and the supernatural but between the created and the uncreated. God's grace is constantly bringing forth that which is not. God's grace in human beings is constantly enabling them to restore the image of God in them. The determination of direct agency and legally recognized credit is not a consideration. In this context, the Pauline preoccupation with works of the Law, dependent as it is on the prominence of Torah, is bypassed.[51] Rather than being concerned with the legal demands of the Law, asceticism addresses the necessity of becoming a full person in Christ, in the image of God. This gives to ascetic life a totally different orientation.

The Question of Suffering

As Berdyaev explains it, "asceticism is a dangerous thing and cuts both ways."[52] Asceticism may dry up the soul of pity for sinners, heaping condemnation on them, viewing their suffering as fully deserved. This is a perverted notion of the redeeming power of suffering. On the other hand, asceticism may give rise to Christian love. An asceticism that is mystical understands suffering as participation in the human condition of living in the face of death. The cross of Christ is the cross that all humanity bears in

51. It is estimated that not one in ten Russian peasants, who are extremely religious, knows the Lord's Prayer or the Ten Commandments. See Orlando Figes, *Natasha's Dance: A Cultural History of Russia* (New York: Holt, 2002), 320.

52. Berdyaev, *Destiny*, 121.

the fallen creation. Just as the incarnation shows basic human nature, the cross shows basic human life. As Paul says, Christians live crucified with Christ (Gal. 2:20). They have Christ's death in their bodies (2 Cor. 4:10). They bear on their bodies "the marks of Jesus" (Gal. 6:17). But Christian love recognizes that bearing the cross of Christ must always be a free act, as Paul insists. No one should want to nail another human being to her or his cross for their salvation. Rather, Christian love wishes for neighbors the cross of Christ because it brings light to their suffering. Recognizing that my neighbor bears a cross sparks compassion, makes me wish to take it upon myself, to share his burden. As Paul advises, "Bear one another's burdens, and so fulfill the law of Christ" (Gal. 6:2).

Dostoyevsky was tortured by the problem of the suffering of innocent children. As originally conceived, *The Brothers Karamazov* was to deal with this theme. It was this problem that made him struggle with his religious upbringing and his faith. Out of pity, "the most certain and indisputable of man's feelings,"[53] one may find nonsensical the notion that God is lovingly involved with suffering humanity, as Ivan Karamazov, the university-educated, more intellectually oriented of the three brothers, forcefully expresses. On the other hand, as the strongest of human experiences, pity "is the strongest proof of man's belonging to a higher world."[54]

The universality of suffering in the world and the human response to suffering are central concerns of Eastern asceticism. As Berdyaev states it, "Man and his suffering are the central conception in the religion of the God-Man. This is the fundamental *motif* of Russian religious thought which is more humane than any other."[55] As this quotation makes clear, Russians have identified themselves as a people who suffer in a redeeming way. This has fanned their aspirations to be a messianic nation, destined to save humankind and the Christian West from their individualistic pursuit of happiness. Embracing the cross of Christ, as Paul advises Christians, has consistently been interpreted in Russian Orthodoxy as a call to enter fully into human nature and participate in the life of Christ, which inevitably includes the cross.

Eastern asceticism is not primarily oriented toward the personal at-

53. Berdyaev, *Destiny,* 120.

54. Berdyaev, *Destiny,* 120.

55. Berdyaev, *Destiny,* 122. By "humane" he does not mean kind or virtuous, but seriously and positively concerned with the human reality. Figes writes of the Russian "cult of passive suffering" in *Natasha's Dance,* 296.

tainment of a beatific vision, but toward embracing the human race, toward that which is common to all human beings, human nature and the pervading suffering in it. In the initial description of Alexey, or Alyosha, the youngest of the Karamazov brothers, Dostoyevsky tells the reader that he is "a lover of humanity."

> He seemed throughout his life to put implicit trust in people; yet no one ever looked on him as a simple or naive person. There was something about him which made one feel at once (and it was so all his life afterwards) that he did not care to be a judge of others — that he would never take it upon himself to criticize and would never condemn anyone for anything. . . . And this was so much so that no one could surprise or frighten him even in his earliest youth.[56]

This characterization is a condensation of the traditional Russian ideal of the spiritual soul. Dostoyevsky's narrator has previously said that young Alyosha was neither a fanatic nor, in his opinion, a mystic. Of course, Dostoyevsky is drawing distinctions important to him. In this case it means that Alyosha fully identifies with suffering humanity.

For Berdyaev, mystical asceticism recognizes in suffering both good and evil. It accepts suffering for the neighbor by the power of love. It affirms life and is creative. True love, however, is not inspired by the illusion that it is possible to free women and men from suffering altogether and give them happiness. A mystical asceticism is not a way of escaping the life of the world with all its problems, but a way of embracing it in order to redeem suffering by love. The message of the cross is that God also suffers. The power of suffering reveals the mystery at the core of the divine nature. The mystery of suffering can elicit from humans pity, compassion, and love. It can draw them to God, as much as it can make them rise against God, as Berdyaev points out. The suffering of ascetics is not a means to purge their sins, neither in this life nor in the next. Orthodoxy rejects strongly the idea of purgatory. Sin is not a juridical problem that can be solved by means of penance or satisfaction. To suffer is human. It should be used to integrate humanity even more closely and thus undo the effects of the Fall. The exercise of pity, as Berdyaev says, is the strongest proof of human participation in the divine nature.

56. Fyodor Dostoyevsky, *The Brothers Karamazov,* trans. Constance Garnett (New York: New American Library, 1957), 28.

Unlike the tradition that developed in the West, where sin came to be understood as an offense for which the sinner had to give satisfaction and salvation became a legal transaction in which the Law plays a central role, in Orthodoxy salvation is a mystical, communally-based perfecting of the personality. As argued by Maximus the Confessor (ca. 580-662), the proper understanding of the process of deification does not mean the displacement of the human but the restoration of the whole person to its original integrity, to the very essence of the human.

The Mystical Struggle

Paul saw the struggle of Christians in the rift between the will and the hand. Unlike Plato, who thought that knowledge of the good necessarily leads to doing the good, Paul understood that knowing and willing do not necessarily result in good actions. Finding himself doing what he did not will (Rom. 7:19), Paul identified a different power in his life directing his conduct. To combat this "other law" (7:23) ruling over his life Paul could find only one option, the superior power (law) of the Spirit who raised Christ from the dead (8:2). Mystical asceticism is concerned with this struggle and its resolution. Asceticism is submission to the power of the Spirit for victory over "the other law in my members."

This struggle is against life in the flesh, which is now ruled by sin. Feofan found in seclusion the answer to Paul's problem. Thus he came to be considered a master of the spiritual life that triumphs over the flesh. While in seclusion he had extensive correspondence with hundreds of laypersons who considered him their spiritual director. In this role Feofan appealed to Paul to give direction to those who, unlike himself, were living outside the walls of a monastery, facing more directly the social and political challenges of life in the world. In this he also had a mentor in John Chrysostom, who like Feofan also entered a monastery, but who, unlike Feofan, rather than going into deeper isolation as a recluse chose instead to go back to life in society, and from the pulpit, as a mouthpiece of Paul, he advised the faithful on the Christian way of life in the world. As a recluse, Feofan found comfort in the example of Paul's intensive life of prayer, particularly described in 1 Cor. 14:15, 18. Certainly Paul affirms the importance of private prayer to God in the closet, an aspect of his teaching that a more rationalistic West has tended to bypass.

As a recluse Feofan became a *starets,* an "elder," or spiritual director to whom people write or make pilgrimages to in order to receive guidance for the deification of life. Probably the best known among the elders in the West is the fictional Father Zossima,[57] the hermit to whom Alyosha Karamazov eagerly attached himself. Dostoyevsky describes an elder as a monk to whom novices attach themselves voluntarily in an indissoluble bond that requires a special obedience sustained by confessions. Dostoyevsky says that novices desire "to escape the lot of those who have lived their whole life without finding their true self in themselves." He then elaborates, "This institution of elders is not founded on theory, but was established in the East from the practice of a thousand years."[58] The elder provides a very concrete personal model. About Father Zossima, Alyosha thinks:

> He is holy. He carries in his heart the secret of renewal for all: that power which will, at last, establish truth on the earth. All men will then be holy and love one another. And there will be no more rich nor poor, no exalted nor humbled, but all will be as the children of God, and the true Kingdom of Christ will come.[59]

Pilgrims from far and near come to the monastery to be healed and receive a blessing or instructions from elder Zossima. His fame and the love the people have for him are very great, so that when the crowds come to him "they fell down before him and wept merely at seeing his face." Seeing this Alyosha understands what is taking place.

> Oh! he understood that for the humble soul of the Russian peasant, worn out by grief and toil, and still more by everlasting injustice and everlasting sin, his own and the world's, it was of the greatest need and comfort to find someone or something holy to fall down before and worship.[60]

Two things are important here: One is the theme of the Russian as a suffering soul, burdened with sin. The other is the Russian need to be tangibly in

57. Most interpreters of Dostoyevsky see in Father Zossima a spokesperson for the author.

58. Dostoyevsky, *Brothers Karamazov,* 35-36.

59. Dostoyevsky, *Brothers Karamazov,* 38.

60. Dostoyevsky, *Brothers Karamazov,* 38.

touch with someone or something holy in order to find redemption. Messianic, talismanic objects or persons are highly revered. Sacred models to be imitated are indispensable. The popularity and the power of the elders were feared both by the church hierarchy and the Tsar. The elders were seen as possible leaders of popular uprisings since the gospel they proclaimed spoke against the poverty suffered by the common people. On that basis, Leo Tolstoy, who was not even an elder, was excommunicated.[61]

The ascetic way of life is not just for monks. Monasteries fulfill an important function also for the laity. They are centers to which the laity may come for periods of intensive spiritual warfare to strengthen the personality. The most popular monastery in the nineteenth century was Optina Pustyn in Kaluga province, about 125 miles south of Moscow. Gogol, Dostoevsky, Tolstoy, as well as most of the great writers of the time made pilgrimages to receive guidance from the famous elders who resided there. From this perspective, monasteries have been described as "clinics for the soul."[62]

The Importance of Sacred Objects

In Orthodoxy, as we have seen, there is great concern with the relation of the divine with the human, the sacred and the profane. One is to be in touch with the sacred in order to become deified. This expresses itself in attitudes toward the written Word now concretely among humans in the book of the Gospels. Its procession among the faithful from behind the iconostasis is one of the high points in the liturgy. The most powerful presence of the sacred among us, though, is the Word made flesh. The most revered religious icon in Orthodoxy is that of the Virgin and Child. While in the Catholic West the emphasis has been on Mary's sexual purity, her status as a virgin throughout her life, in the Orthodox East the emphasis has been on her motherhood, *bogoroditsa.* In the religious consciousness of the people her divine motherhood practically plays the role of the trinity as the central mystery of the faith. The motherhood motif is often visualized by showing the Virgin's face pressed against the head of her Child.[63] Icons

61. Figes, *Natasha's Dance,* 294.

62. Figes, *Natasha's Dance,* 294.

63. Byzantine art developed two types of icons of Mary. One represents her as the

of Mary usually include either the word *Theotokos* (Bearer of God), or *Mētēr Theou* (Mother of God). Both designations intend to make clear that Mary is not the mother of a human being. By her most intimate communion with the divine while bearing her son, she is the prototype of the divine-human. She is the exemplar of salvation.[64]

The East sees Mary as the one who gave human nature to the God who became human and as the one who at Pentecost received such a full portion of the Spirit that she became fully deified. In the words of Lossky, "So the most pure nature which itself contained the Word, entered into perfect union with the deity in the person of the Mother of God."[65] As such, she is the model and the precursor of human deification.

A vivid picture of the popular appreciation of Mary is given by Chekhov in his famous short story "Peasants." In it, life in Zhukovo, a forgotten village in the Russian countryside, is centered around the tavern. The church is next to the manor house and it is necessary to cross the bridgeless river in order to get to it. Chekhov writes:

> Even in Zhukovo, in this "slaveytown," there was once an outburst of genuine religious enthusiasm. It was in August, when throughout the district they carried from village to village the Holy Mother, the giver of life. It was still and overcast on the day when they expected *Her* at Zhukovo. The girls set off in the morning to meet the icon, in their bright holiday dresses, and brought Her towards the evening, in procession with the cross and with singing, while the bells pealed in the church across the river. An immense crowd of villagers and strangers flooded the street; there was noise, dust, a great crush. . . . And the old father and Granny and Kiryak — all stretched out their hands to the icon, looked eagerly at it, and said weeping:
>
> "Defender! Mother! Defender!"

---

queen of heaven. Here both Mary and the Christ child face forward as distinct individuals. The other emphasizes motherly tenderness by having Mary's head bent toward her son. Few examples of the second type are now found in Greek Byzantium, but they are the more common type in Russia. See Georgi P. Fedotov, *The Russian Religious Mind* 1: *Kievan Christianity, The Tenth to the Thirteenth Centuries* (New York: Harper, 1960; English original: Cambridge: Harvard University Press, 1946), 375-76.

64. This may be contrasted with the West's veneration of Mary on account of her willingness to submit to God's will, her obedience.

65. Lossky, *Mystical Theology*, 193-94.

> All seemed suddenly to realize that there was not an empty void between earth and heaven, that the rich and the powerful had not taken possession of everything, that there was still a refuge from injury, from slavish bondage, from crushing, unendurable poverty, from the terrible vodka.
>
> "Defender! Mother!" sobbed Marya. "Mother!"
>
> But the thanksgiving service ended and the icon was carried away and everything went on as before, and again there was a sound of coarse drunken oaths from the tavern.[66]

It has been said that Orthodox theology is not to be found in words but in colors.[67] Its icons are its theological texts. Among the icons, the one depicting the Mother of God is the most prominent.

Most Orthodox icons are characterized by the lack of backgrounds or foregrounds. Nothing shares space with the Virgin and Child or saint. There are no shadows, no external sources of light. The icon is illumined by an inner light that emanates from the inner life of the Virgin and the Child or saint. This inner light is the very image of God in humans that makes possible the deification of the entire person by communion with the divine and the communication of its properties or attributes to the human being. In the words of Paul, it is "the light of the gospel of the glory of Christ" (2 Cor. 4:4). In Berdyaev's terms, the inner light is the spark of freedom and creativity that guides the person. Icons are sacred objects. Their function is not decorative or didactic. It is to a large degree talismanic.[68] The faithful confess their sins not to a priest but to an icon, with a priest sometimes in attendance as a guide. Icons are "a gateway to a holy sphere."[69]

To actualize the communion of the saints the Orthodox church building has an iconostasis, a wall separating the place where the congregation stands from the place where the sacred objects, particularly a copy

66. Anton Chekhov, *Peasants and Other Stories,* ed. and trans. Edmund Wilson (New York: New York Review, 1999; original 1956), 346.

67. Fedotov, *Russian Religious Mind,* 1.374.

68. See Tatiana Vladyshevskaia, "The Role of the Devotional Image in the Religious Life of Pre-Mongol Rus," in *Christianity and the Arts in Russia,* ed. William C. Brumfield and Milos M. Velimirovic (Cambridge: Cambridge University Press, 1991), 30-45.

69. Figes, *Natasha's Dance,* 299.

of the Gospels, are kept. It is covered with images of the saints with whom the congregation particularly wishes to have communion.[70] The role of these images (icons) is not to instruct the illiterate masses in the accounts of the Gospels, as it is in the West. They serve as models, facilitators of the human struggle for deification. They are witnesses to the effectiveness of the Spirit to deify human beings.

Life in Christ is understood communally and sacramentally as the saints share in the bread and the wine.[71] In fact, in most village churches the bread is brought by the women who baked it early that morning, and pieces of all the breads brought to the meal are eaten by everyone. This concretely represents the one common nature of the many. The bread is leavened, since in Orthodoxy leaven is viewed not as symbolizing the presence of sin but as a sign of the effectiveness of the resurrection even now. In the culture of Orthodoxy, the warfare against the demons of the soul and the restoration of the image of God in each person are sustained by the community. This is *sobornost,* to be distinguished from a community made up of individuals. It is a "communality" characterized by the freedom with which spiritual persons come together on account of what they have in common.[72] The fact that as individuals they have different gifts does not in any way break the bond of their common origin. This emphasis of the Eastern tradition is quite Pauline, and one which Westerners obsessed with identifying themselves individually could learn from. Most students of Paul agree that he envisioned life in Christ not as a private affair, but as the life of members of one body. Personal gifts, as Berdyaev insists, are not what constitute the person; they make it possible for persons to give form to their creativity and give to their "communality" the values of the kingdom of heaven.

70. For a description of the organization of the iconostasis, see Fedotov, *The Russian Religious Mind* 2: *The Middle Ages, The Thirteenth to the Fifteenth Centuries,* ed. John Meyendorff (Cambridge: Harvard University Press, 1966), 358-60.

71. Unlike developments in the West, where Aristotelian influences made the doctrine of the real presence necessary, in the East the sacredness of the bread and wine is accepted intuitively as brought about by the mysterious divine energy that creates what was not.

72. *Sobornost* derives from *sobor,* "cathedral," "assembly." Berdyaev takes the word from Aleksei Khomiakov, who in the 1830s and 1840s developed the notion of the true community of free sisters and brothers bound by their common faith rather than the laws and dogmas of the church.

The Mystic's Goal

While the culture of Orthodoxy is mystical and ascetic, its goal is not denial of the body as something inherently evil that must be escaped. The legacy of Augustine's negative attitude toward sex is not part of Eastern Christianity and its culture. Orthodoxy has a positive attitude toward the body on account of its holistic understanding of the person and its positive view of human nature. The body is an integral part of the person, sharing with the holy by the mutual interpenetration of the divine and the human that culminates in a perfect union of the two.[73] Western mysticism is more intellectualized and is based on a struggle with self. Eastern mysticism is more intuitive, based on incarnation and the human condition. It values experience.

For Western mysticism in general the goal is to gain a vision of the divine essence. Mystics in the West and in the East practice contemplation, but with different goals. In the West the goal is spiritual ecstasy. John of the Cross and Teresa of Avila speak the language of marriage and its consummation in the bridal chamber. In the East the goal is natural communion with humanity.[74] Ecstasy consists in the loss of all sense perception, an out-of-body experience. In the East, as Lossky says, ecstasy is valued only by novices in the spiritual life.[75] In this, I would also think, Paul would be in agreement. He does not make much of his tantalizing reference to a trip to the third heaven during which he lost awareness of his body (2 Cor. 12:2), and he mentions it rather reluctantly. It appears that his crucifixion with Christ is more important to him than his ecstatic journey through the spheres. An ascetic spirituality seeks immersion into the human that participates in the divine on account of the incarnation. Divinity can be experienced only by a full humanity.

The West begins its contemplation of the Trinity by looking for the divine nature, which is conceived as primordial to the Trinity. In the East, the Trinity is approached christologically, that is, by means of a person, in order to establish one's participation in the divine life. Thus the language of Paul about being dead to the world and living in the light of the glory that shines in the face of Christ is very prominent in Eastern spirituality. As Gregory of Nazianzus says in one of his poems:

73. See Lossky, *Mystical Theology,* 224-25.

74. Berdyaev, *Destiny,* 151-53.

75. Lossky, *Mystical Theology,* 208-9. Lossky seems to be engaging in a polemic with Russian sectarians such as "Wailers" and the "Jumpers," who valued trance-like states.

> From the day whereon I renounced the things of the world to consecrate my soul to luminous and heavenly contemplation, when the supreme intelligence carried me hence to set me down far from all that pertains to the flesh, to hide me in the secret places of the heavenly tabernacle; from that day my eyes have been blinded by the light of the Trinity, whose brightness surpasses all that the mind can conceive; for from a throne high exalted the Trinity pours upon all, the ineffable radiance common to the Three. This is the source of all that is here below, separated by time from the things on high. . . . From that day forth I was dead to the world and the world was dead to me.[76]

The asceticism of the Russian culture, which wishes to embrace humanity with love, is so pervasive that it is not uncommon for students of Russia to refer to the inhabitants of this land as a cloistered society fully regulated by the observance of the religious festivals and eager to identify itself by its Orthodoxy even more than by its Russianness.[77] Russians live their religion at the religious festivals, during which, Chekhov writes, churches look like marketplaces as the people wander around taking in all that is offered.[78] The culture of Orthodoxy has been tightly bound to the celebration of the festivals of the Christian year.[79] As is to be expected, however, the festivals represent amalgams with the indigenous religious traditions of the Russian steppes.[80]

76. Gregory of Nazianzus, "Poemata de seipso I," *Patrologia Graeca* 37.984-85; quoted in Lossky, *Mystical Theology*, 44.

77. Figes, *Natasha's Dance*, 301.

78. Anton P. Chekhov, "Easter Night," in *The Early Stories*, trans. Patrick Miles and Harvey Pitcher (New York: Macmillan, 1982), 92-101.

79. In Chekhov's stories the most common chronological markers are to the religious rather than the secular calendar. Life is lived in reference to the religious feasts.

> Next day was Easter Sunday. There were forty-two churches and six monasteries in the town; the sonorous, joyful clang of the bells hung over the town from morning till night unceasingly, setting the spring air aquiver; the birds were singing, the sun was shining brightly. The big market square was noisy, swings were going, barrel organs were playing, accordions were squeaking, drunken voices were shouting.

"The Bishop," in *Peasants and Other Stories*, 453.

80. Figes, *Natasha's Dance*, 301.

The Russian Way of Knowing God

In the Eastern tradition, *theology* has to do with the mystery of the Trinity that has been revealed to the church. Penetrating the mystery does not bring about more knowledge. The object of theology is communion, an experience. God's revelation in Christ is intended to give life,[81] to make possible communion with the divine by the restoration of the image of God among human beings. This communion brings about deification, participation in the divine nature without the loss of the human. In other words, to know the mystery of the Trinity in its fullness is to enter into perfect union with God, to attain to the deification of the human. This mystical theology seeks the experience, in the words of 2 Peter, of being "partakers of the divine nature" (1:4). As Irenaeus, Athanasius, and the Eastern Fathers repeated over and over, God became a human being so that humanity might become God. The process by means of which human beings attain to participation in the divine nature is also described as a process guided by the divine light, which finally arrives at the blinding light of the Trinity. This is the language of Paul: "And we all, with unveiled face, beholding the glory of the Lord, are being changed into his image from one degree of glory to another. For this comes from the Lord who is the Spirit" (2 Cor. 3:18). This affirmation of Paul is the foundation for the Eastern understanding of the Christian life and salvation as the deification of the Christian community by the operation of the Spirit, the uncreated energy of God.

Orthodoxy views salvation as the deification of human beings when the Logos dwells in the flesh.[82] In other words, as already noted, the incarnation is central. Therefore, John, the Evangelist of the Word made flesh and the more abundant life, is the most important New Testament witness to theological truth in the Eastern tradition. But the individualistic ten-

81. In a mostly neglected essay Rudolf Bultmann argued that the New Testament presented the object of divine revelation as life rather than knowledge: "The Concept of Revelation in the New Testament," in *Existence and Faith: Shorter Writings of Rudolf Bultmann,* ed. and trans. Schubert M. Ogden (New York: Meridian, 1960). His argument never gained acceptance in the rationalistic West.

82. John Meyendorff, "Christ as Savior in the East," in *Christian Spirituality: Origins to the Twelfth Century,* ed. Bernard McGinn and John Meyendorff (New York: Crossroads, 1986), 231-51. Specifically on Feofan, see J. J. Allen, "An Orthodox Perspective on 'Liberation,'" *Greek Orthodox Theological Review* 26 (1981): 71-80.

dencies of John are softened by appeals to Paul, the mystic of life in Christ. Paul is the one who describes Christians as persons who form a body that concretizes the presence of Christ in the world even now. It is only as members of Christ's body that they can fulfill this role.

According to Paul, human beings must see "the light of the gospel of the glory of Christ, who is the image of God." "The god of this world," however, spares no effort to prevent women and men from seeing what would bring about their salvation (2 Cor. 4:4). Accordingly, salvation is realized by seeing the image of God that is enshrined in the gospel of the glory of Christ. Participation in this vision of the glory of Christ, who as a person of the Trinity is the image of God, brings about the mutual indwelling of the divine and the human that makes possible the deification of the person *(hypostasis)* even while the human nature remains perfectly human. This was the case with the Christ, who became human without in any way changing his divine nature.

The mystery of the essence of God manifested in the Trinity, which in itself is a rationally incomprehensible manifestation of divinity, demands that theology be apophatic. Before the mystery, believers may experience communion and receive life, but they cannot put into language what they are experiencing. About God silence is golden. In terms of knowledge, the better part of wisdom is to claim ignorance. In this, the East builds its case on Paul's report of his mystical experience. Telling of his trip to the third heaven, when it comes to details he insists "I do not know" (2 Cor. 12:2). Thus theology, which strictly speaking is concerned only with God,[83] can only affirm God and keep silent. Paul's reticence is often appealed to as the best advice for the theologian.

Orthodoxy has emphasized the mystery of God's essence, but has also insisted that the energies of God are continually at work so that there is no such thing as "pure nature." A natural procession of the divine energy emanates from the divine essence, making God known within the world. Thus, while God is essentially unknown, the energies of God are within the grasp of human knowledge. This understanding of God is based on words of Paul: "For what can be known about God is manifest in them ['those who unrighteously suppress the truth']. . . . The unseen power and deity of

83. Within Orthodoxy, discourse about God's attributes, qualities, activities, etc., does not belong to theology but to "economy," the maintenance of God's household and the norms for its operation.

God, since the creation of the world, are seen by the mind in the things that have been made" (Rom. 1:19-20). The divine energies, "the power and deity" of God, are to be understood as really God, not as parts or attributes of God. In this way God is known, even if the essence of God remains hidden in mystery. The Pauline words, "what can be known about God," clearly suggest that there is that which cannot be known about God, requiring an apophatic theology that keeps silent about God's essence. The permeating presence of God's energies within the world, however, is not to be understood as a supernatural causal addition to the natural world. God's grace is very real in nature, most of all in human nature. Divine grace is not the injection of a supernatural cause that brings about a scientifically unexplainable effect in a closed natural world. Rather the divine energies, God's grace, are continually at work within nature, always bringing into being things that are not. God's grace energizes the human ascetic life so that it may bring about the perfect liberation of the soul. In this, there can be no analytic differentiation between the human and the divine causes at work.

The call for an apophatic theology within Orthodoxy is not necessitated by the complexities of the Trinity, rendering any effort to explicate it incapable of doing justice to its many nuances and fine distinctions. In fact, God is simple, and theology should be an effort at simplification. Only in the fallen world things got complicated. Silence is required by the human inability to penetrate the mystery, by the incomprehensible nature of God. The experience of communion with the divine is both sublime and simple. Thus theology should remain simple even as it is profound.

The virtue of the simple is highly esteemed in Russia. In *Virgin Soil,* Turgenev refers to the desire on the part of those planning a revolution for equalization of the highly fractured Russian society as an effort at simplification. At the end of the novel, its tragicomic hero Alexey Nezhdanov gets drunk, and half embarrassed, half jokingly, he stammers to Marianna: "You always talked of sim-sim-plification; see now, I'm really simplified. For the people's always drunk, so — ."[84] Unable to bridge the gap between the intellectuals and the people, recognizing his failure as a revolutionary, Alexey commits suicide. In his note to Marianna he writes: "I could find no way out of it. I could not *simplify myself;* the only thing left was to blot myself

84. Ivan Turgenev, *Virgin Soil,* trans. Constance Garnett (New York: New York Review, 2000), 287.

out altogether" (italics original).[85] The desire for simplification in life, which in this novel is a desire for identification with humanity, is a characteristic of Orthodox culture. The wisdom of this world may be complicated, but the foolishness (simplicity) of God is not part of it. Thus in Russia, there has developed a great deal of admiration for the fool of Christ, the one who lives according to the foolishness of God: "The word of the cross is foolishness to those who perish" (1 Cor. 1:18); "It is God's pleasure to save those who believe through the foolishness of preaching" (1:21); "Let those among you who think themselves wise in the world become fools in order to become wise" (3:18); "We are fools for Christ's sake" (4:10). In Russia, these words of Paul are read not as rhetorical exaggerations, but as open invitations. In the words of Fedotov, "the radical irreconcilability of the two orders — that of the world and that of God" is considered essential to the message of Paul.[86] Paul's words are taken as a critique of worldly success. Between the fourteenth and the seventeenth centuries, several "fools for Christ's sake" were canonized by the Orthodox Church in Russia. Ecclesiastical canonizations have ceased primarily on account of the difficulties encountered in distinguishing between real and feigned religious foolishness. For the laity, however, "a madman with religious charisma . . . is always a saint, perhaps the most beloved saint in Russia."[87]

The Holy Fool, the *yurodivyi,* appears often in Russian works of art. These wandering prophets and healers were simple men who lived off the alms of the people who revered them and sought their help both for healing and divination. Often they are represented as the quintessential Russian. Even though their clothing and the wearing of a harness on the head and chains under the shirt may have their origin in Asian shamanism, their presence in society is considered to be following the words of Paul. They were often the guests of provincial nobles. At Yasnaya Polyana, the country estate of the Tolstoy family, an elderly *yurodivyi* became a permanent member of the family.[88] The Holy Fool is the folkloric embodiment of the Russian paradox of the human-divine commingling for life in this world.

Eastern Orthodoxy has consciously defended its more mystical, intuitive, subjective way of being a Christian in opposition to Western Chris-

85. Turgenev, *Virgin Soil,* 287. It should be noted that Marianna is the embodiment of the Russian eagerness to suffer for a cause.

86. Fedotov, *Religious Mind,* 2.322.

87. Fedotov, *Religious Mind,* 2.324.

88. Figes, *Natasha's Dance,* 372.

tendom. It is said that when Peter the Great founded his new capital on the shores of a European sea, on land recently captured from Sweden, a European nation, he was trying to open up his cloistered country. Ever since Russia has been divided between Westernizers and Slavophiles. From the perspective of the Slavophiles, the problem with the Westernizers is that they do not think with their hearts. Having become analytical, they have become "soulless robots."[89] No greater tragedy can be imagined. The Russian soul is inherently spiritual. In the conception of Russian Orthodox faith, the soul is empowered by grace to be a person who, like Christ, participates in two natures.

89. Christian Caryl, "Window on Russia," *The New York Review of Books* 50/8 (May 29, 2003): 28.

CONCLUSION

At the Crossroads

In bringing our cross-cultural journey with Paul to a close, we make no attempt to produce a comprehensive synthesis that presents some kind of global cross-cultural Paul. Instead, we offer some observations and raise some questions about the identity and coherence of Pauline theology in relation to the cultures we have surveyed and the themes we have discussed.

Cross-Cultural Themes in Pauline Perspective

Cultural Models of Human Success and Aspiration

According to Justin Martyr, in his *First Apology*, the Christians at Rome would listen to extended readings from the sacred writings and then the president would offer an exhortation, encouraging the community to imitate the examples set before them in the reading. The view that classical and sacred texts are a fund of good examples to be emulated (along with bad examples to be avoided) was quite common in antiquity. Paul speaks the language of emulation when he calls believers to imitate God or Paul himself. He also holds up Jesus as a model to be followed and as a living presence to whom Christians are being conformed by the transforming power of God.

Every culture offers its models of what a good and successful human life looks like. Often these models are conceived as cultural types, and they may be embodied in historical or fictional persons. They may be cultural icons, revered as bearers of cultural values and identity, emulated in modest ways by those who are in no position to be larger-than-life heroes or saints themselves. In the preceding chapters we have met a variety of such cultural models: the rugged individualist of North American imagination — self-reliant, detached, sometimes a violent savior figure (the John Wayne, Dirty Harry, Rambo type); the charismatic *caudillo* and the artful *el vivo* of South American imagination — living above the law, fatalistic, death-enamored, devoted to friendship, psychically disconnected from work as an identity or ethic; the proper Confucian of Chinese ideals — "kingly outside and sagely inside," devoted to family, community, tradition, and a discipline of self-cultivation that serves these institutions. We have subjected each of these cultural types to a Pauline critique and found that they offer ways of being human that are at points in tension with the image of Christ. At the same time, we have explored elements of each that resonate in some ways with Paul's language and his conception of being a human being in Christ. Articulating these resonances typically requires important qualifications: there are grounds for a special dignity of the individual in Paul but not for detachment from community or rugged self-reliance; there is a place for human beings to participate in works of redemption but not as savior figures; Christians are in some sense beyond law, but they are not lawless or justified in using freedom from the law to serve themselves; crucifixion with Christ makes "death," properly understood, a way and focus of the Christian journey but not an end in itself or an aesthetic value; moral propriety is an important part of the church's witness to the world, but at the same time Christians are not to be conformed to the world; self-discipline is an important dimension of the moral quest, but neither the mind nor the will can conquer the power of sin.

The preceding summary of contacts and contrasts is overly simplified, and we refer readers to the more detailed and nuanced discussions in the preceding chapters. Here we wish only to reinforce that this kind of comparison is a revealing way of doing cross-cultural Pauline interpretation and that it ought to entail at least three critical dimensions.

First, it is important both to read the cultural type or trait in its own cultural setting and also to read Paul's language about being in Christ, being conformed to the image Christ, etc., in *its* cultural context. Otherwise, any comparisons will be superficial. Those who are able students of a given contemporary culture but have little knowledge of Pauline scholarship may tend to be erudite in their contemporary cultural readings but superficial in how they read Paul. On the other hand, Pauline scholars who do not engage in cultural analysis with the same care and rigor they bring to their study of Paul are liable to bring a simplistic interpretation of contemporary culture under a profound Pauline gaze that can only overwhelm but not fairly criticize and illumine. The challenge is to be equally sophisticated in listening to both Paul (in his ancient cultural context) and to contemporary culture.

Second, unless we imagine that the Pauline ideal of a human being in Christ is so unique that it transcends human culture altogether, any critique of a given cultural type must be attentive not only to points of contrast with Paul but also to points of similarity. These points of resonance can be identified and interpreted analogically, so as to allow for the mix of differences and similarities involved in all cross-cultural comparisons of the "same" or "similar" things in two cultures. For example, the dissolution of social hierarchies announced in Gal. 3:28 — no more Jew and Greek, male and female, slave and free — creates a kind of equality, and the evangelistic way that the grace of God calls and embraces the specific human being — Paul, Priscilla, Timothy and not simply groups as superior to particular persons — does create a kind of individualism. This equality and this individualism are analogous to equality and individual identity in the American tradition. But this is not to say that they are identical or that there is no place for a Pauline critique of American notions of equality and individual identity. Hence, using analogical reasoning to identify and explore resonances between Paul and the American tradition is properly both assimilating and contrasting. Likewise, we have applied analogical reasoning in comparing the Confucian communal ethic of *ren* with Paul's ethic of love and the Native concern for Mother Earth with Paul's teaching about the redemption of creation.

Third, our comparison is never between Paul and this or that culture as fixed objects graspable in their unchanging identity by any well-equipped and reasonable mind. Paul in his culture and Paul in any culture in which we consider him is always known to us only as a product of interpretation. Moreover, there is always more than one reasonable way to interpret any complex thing. For this reason, it is important that we be self-aware about the choices we make in interpretation as we go about the process of comparing and contrasting Paul's image of the human being in Christ with any contemporary cultural type. Consider, for example, the following argument from the chapter on Paul in Chinese perspective. *Li* in the Confucian sense of order and propriety correlates to the Law in Paul in a way that leads to the insight that *ren* as the animating soul of *li* is very similar to Paul's idea of love as the animating principle and fulfillment of the Law. This view depends on certain judgments about how to interpret *li, ren,* and their relationship in the Confucian tradition, as well as on certain judgments about how to interpret Paul's view of the Law and how he relates love to the Law. These judgments are, in our view, eminently defensible, but they are not the only reasonable ways to interpret Paul or Confucius. An argument in their favor is that they help build a bridge between Christian faith and Chinese self-understanding.

The Human Situation

Theological categories provide another basis for comparison. One of these categories is "the Fall" or what is sometimes termed today the "human situation" or "human predicament." It is fascinating to ask whether Paul is morally optimistic or pessimistic about humanity. His indictment of humanity in Rom. 1:18–3:20 (together with 5:12-21) has long been regarded as proof of his moral pessimism about humankind as a whole. Twentieth-century Pauline scholarship came to the general conclusion that for Paul human beings are under "sin" as a cosmic power, from whose grasp they are powerless to free themselves. There have been a few dissenters who have questioned whether Paul understands "sin" as a power in this way. A contemporary "cultural" consideration in this interpretive debate is that the dominant interpretation assumed that Jews are slaves of sin, incapable of leading any kind of authentic moral life. Hence, many if not most of those committed to some version of the so-called "special way" *(Sonderweg)* for Israel as part of a Christian theological rapprochement with Jews and Judaism have tended to downplay or reject the idea that Jews, apart from faith in Jesus as the Christ, lack the spiritual resources for a moral life pleasing to God. According to the "special way" interpretation, God continues in covenant with Israel through the Law; the gospel of Christ is for gentiles.

What about Confucians? The Confucian understanding of moral self-cultivation seems much more optimistic than Paul's view (traditionally understood) of human moral possibilities. Is Confucius overly sanguine, or is Paul overly pessimistic? There is a moral fatalism among

Argentineans and a moral optimism among Americans. Is the Argentine anthropology for that reason more Pauline than the American? And does moral pessimism — individually and nationally — protect the Argentine spirit from being collectively seduced into forms of self-righteous manifest destiny that have, arguably, long been part of the American psyche? In both Confucian and Native American myths, there is nothing comparable to the Christian idea of a Fall or the Pauline view that sin is a cosmic power that takes humanity in thrall. On the other hand, there have been some recent notes of dissent to this way of interpreting Paul. Some see sin in Paul not as an overpowering external influence but as wrongful human action and its personal and social results.[1] This moves the interpretation of Paul closer to both Confucian and Native understandings of the human situation.

Another angle on this question is to ask whether Paul holds to a view of Christ as the way of salvation that rules out the possibility of others — individuals and communities, including non-Christian religious communities — living lives that are morally pleasing to God. This is one of the most important questions in inter-religious dialogue. The answer to this question reveals the goal and the process of reading Paul cross-culturally. In his chapter on Paul in Native American perspective, Yeo has argued from Romans 8 that Paul appeals to the grand narrative of Christ as the unifying force for all peoples and cultures, along with the natural world. This grand narrative is gracious and inclusive, not sectarian or confessionally exclusive. Similarly, Krister Stendahl has found in Paul's view of Israel a model for an analogous Pauline view of other religious traditions. According to Stendahl, the revelation of Christ opens up a way for gentiles, who are also joined by a small number of Jews like Jesus' disciples and Paul, but the Law (Torah) remains God's way of salvation for Israel as a whole. Hence, Paul's view of the integrity and authenticity of Israel's life with God under the Law is a caution against all forms of religious imperialism and, by implication, Israel becomes a model in Christian theology for Christian thinking about other religions.[2] Is it theologically possible to think of Israel as both object of

1. See Stanley K. Stowers, *A Rereading of Romans: Justice, Jews and Gentiles* (New Haven: Yale University Press, 1994).

2. Krister Stendahl, *Paul among Jews and Gentiles and Other Essays* (Philadelphia: Fortress, 1976), 132; cf. Stendahl, *Meanings: The Bible as Document and Guide* (Philadelphia: Fortress, 1984), 215.

evangelism (Paul did, after all, affirm the mission of Peter to the circumcised) and as an elder sibling in faith, whose way has its own legitimacy and its own relation to the Messiah apart from Christianity? If so, this Christian way of thinking about Israel may provide a model or analogue for Christian relations with other religious traditions — such as Chinese and Native American religious traditions. Can other religions be friends of the church, on Pauline terms, not simply as dialogue partners in a politically correct relativistic sense but as conversation partners to whom the church also bears Christian witness and seeks to persuade and from whom the church also seeks to learn? It may be that Paul's view of Israel, even when conceived in terms of the "special way" theory, does not stretch this far. But it is fair to ask whether, in the light of two thousand years of experience and an expanded knowledge of the peoples and history of the world, Paul's own doctrine of divine impartiality and universality ("Is God the God of the Jews only? Is he not also the God of the nations?" Rom. 3:29) calls for a more open and dialogical approach to the world's religions and non-Christian peoples, even when the missionary impulse is maintained.

Eschatology

Until the late nineteenth century, Paul's eschatological outlook — and that of early Christianity as a whole — was treated as a point of doctrine to be affirmed, sometimes as an especially relevant teaching (in periods of apocalyptic expectation), but not as the all-pervading category of his thought that late-nineteenth-century scholarship discovered it to be. This discovery proved initially to be an embarrassment for faith in the modern world since it involved the realization that Paul (and the rest of the earliest Christian movement) expected an imminent end of the world that never took place, a non-occurrence that seemed to disconfirm Christian claims. The problem was especially acute because the expectation of a near end of the world and a transformation of the created order could no longer be disregarded as a minor point compared with what mainstream Christian faith understood as the central moral and spiritual tenets of the faith. As Albert Schweitzer showed in synthesizing the scholarship of his day, the expectation that the world was already in the process of coming to an imminent end and being cosmically transformed stamped the whole fabric of early

Christian thinking, giving a distinctive cast to Christian understanding of salvation, the moral life, the church and its place in the world, and so forth.[3] Hence, Pauline apocalyptic eschatology, which could not be relegated to a minor position in his thought, could not be embraced either, inasmuch as the world did not come to an end in the first century. Consequently, the whole edifice of Pauline Christianity was put in question.

There have been two basic theological responses to this quandary. One approach sees the non-occurrence of the apocalyptic end of the world, against Paul's expectations and the logic of his theology, as a reason for rejecting the literal apocalyptic cast of his thought and treating it symbolically instead. Rudolf Bultmann's "demythologizing" program[4] belongs here but so do other approaches that differ in important ways from Bultmann's. A second view is that apocalyptic eschatology remains meaningful for moderns (and postmoderns) and can be appropriated realistically and quasi-literally without being taken in a strictly literal way. In Pauline scholarship, J. Christiaan Beker has been the champion of this approach.[5]

Generally speaking, Chinese and Native American conceptions of history and cosmology have little room for apocalypticism, which means that it is easier to develop an indigenous Chinese or Native American appropriation of Paul by treating apocalyptic in Paul symbolically rather than literally or realistically. For example, the concern for the whole of creation in Romans 8 has symbolic value in a Native American context, even if the temporal cast of Paul's views there and his apocalyptic notions of the bondage of the earth make less sense to most Native Americans. This is not to say that Native American Christians should avoid challenging their own cultural traditions in the name of Paul. Nevertheless, given the choice between two plausible hermeneutical approaches to Paul, one that insists on accepting apocalyptic realism because it addresses fundamental questions

3. Albert Schweitzer, *The Mysticism of the Apostle Paul,* trans. W. Montgomery (New York: Holt, 1931); *The Quest of the Historical Jesus: A Critical Study of Its Progress from Reimarus to Wrede,* trans. W. Montgomery (New York: Macmillan, 1948).

4. One of the best presentations of Bultmann's demythologizing program is found in Walter Schmithals, *An Introduction to the Theology of Rudolf Bultmann* (Minneapolis: Augsburg, 1968).

5. J. Christiaan Beker, *Paul the Apostle: The Triumph of God in Life and Thought* (Philadelphia: Fortress, 1980); *Paul's Apocalyptic Gospel: The Coming Triumph of God* (Philadelphia: Fortress, 1982).

of suffering and theodicy that trouble the West (as Beker argues)[6] and another that rejects apocalyptic realism but embraces elements of apocalyptic as symbols of God's love for the whole of creation and of the inextricable connection between humanity and the created order (as Ernst Käsemann argues, developing the Bultmannian tradition),[7] it is understandable if some Native Americans would prefer the second of these hermeneutical possibilities. Moreover, when Christians of European background listen to Native American voices and discover the inner logic of Native American experience and thought, they may be persuaded to adjust their own ways of appropriating Pauline eschatology.

The Confucian retrieval of a golden age in the past Chou dynasty does not share the kind of eschatological hope of Pauline theology. Paul's eschatological hope is more than a fulfillment of paradise in the Garden of Eden. It is a new creation that transcends everything that has gone before and therefore eludes ordinary description in this-worldly terms (see 1 Corinthians 15). But precisely at this point of difference between the Confucian and Pauline worldviews and hopes for the future, both have something to learn from each other. Chinese Christians, such as Yeo, find in the Confucian tradition a wisdom for living in this world and its institutions. Paul, who expected the present world to pass away in his time, offers only limited help to communities that must make everyday, practical sense of the present world, which is still around after twenty centuries. At the same time, Paul offers a source of critique of the present world from the standpoint of God's new creation. He also preaches a hope that sustains faithful living when even the best wisdom of this world fails and love's labors seem futile.

Freedom

Freedom has figured importantly as a theme in our study. Plantation catechesis used Paul to indoctrinate American slaves in unfreedom and contentment with their lot. *Rioplatenses* applaud freedom from the law, but see themselves as bound to fate, as doom or destiny. The Chinese follower of

6. See Beker, *Paul's Apocalyptic Gospel.*

7. Ernst Käsemann, "The Righteousness of God in Paul," in *New Testament Questions of Today,* trans. W. J. Montague (Philadelphia: Fortress, 1969). See also Robin Scroggs, "Ernst Käsemann, "The Divine *Agent Provocateur,*" *Religious Studies Review* 11 (1985): 260-63.

Confucius seeks self-mastery, a kind of freedom from unwanted influences within, but also honors the binding obligations of family, community, and tradition, which look like a kind of servitude in the eyes of postmodern Americans, for whom freedom typically means the individual's right to non-interference from others and non-encumbrance from social duties in the quest for personal self-fulfillment. By contrast, freedom and unfreedom for many Native Americans is symbolized in the boundaries, literal and symbolic, of the reservation and the memory of past forms of freedom that resemble and also contributed to the American frontier notion of freedom — of unbounded open spaces and the individuality of the warrior. Traditional Native American worldviews do not operate with the Western notion of human freedom from nature, which has served as a basis for Western technology and the use of the natural world for good and ill. For Natives, the human being is part of the natural order and should seek harmony with it.

Americans of European heritage are exceptional in imagining that there is such a thing as freedom in the absolute. Other cultures recognize that freedom is always relative, always freedom "from" and freedom "for." For Paul, freedom through Christ is liberation from past servitudes for slavery to Christ. Because believers are part of a new creation guided by love, the service in which their liberty expresses itself is to be freely embraced and affirmed in each situation or moment of moral testing. It is not a grudging obedience to authority or an unhappy compliance out of fear but service to God in joy.

Paul's command to the Corinthians, "Do not be slaves of human beings" (1 Cor. 7:23), probably meant that believers ought not to sell themselves into slavery, whether to make good on a debt, redeem an enslaved loved one, acquire the security of membership in a household, or for some other reason. We take Paul as being opposed in principle, if not always in his instructions to his churches, to the socioeconomic institution of slavery in the Roman world. As we understand it, the reason for this opposition is that slavery to human beings threatens the freedom Christians are to have for service toward God. The same goes for other worldly obligations, including marriage. Although Paul does not enjoin Christians from marrying, he thinks the freedom of singleness is generally a better state in which to serve God "in this present time of difficulty" (1 Cor. 7:27-29). In every worldly set of obligations there are limits, constraints, and loyalties that may compete with one's obligations to God. Worldly freedom as freedom for God is therefore a good thing in Paul's estimation.

The cautious, non-admonitory tone and rhetoric of Paul's discussion of freedom in 1 Corinthians 7 suggests that he thinks about the practical meaning of freedom in terms of the different situations in which Christians find themselves, that is, that his thinking about freedom is "contingent" on circumstances, as Pauline scholars sometimes like to say. There are no hard and fast rules to govern Christian attitudes toward specific forms of freedom and obligation in society. The freedom principles of the gospel are to be worked out in terms of the dynamics of particular times and places. This is very significant in cross-cultural settings and says a great deal about Paul's understanding of the gospel. For Paul, the gospel cannot be identified with what society considers at a given time to be obedience to God. Freedom in obedience must be measured against the gospel message and discerned concretely in specific circumstances.

Dominant American notions of freedom entail the ideal of individual freedom of thought, speech, conscience, and way of living from the control of the state (or of state religion). This cultural tradition, which has profoundly shaped American law, owes much to doctrines of freedom of conscience and soul liberty developed and established in colonial times, doctrines that are in turn indebted as much or more to Paul as to any other biblical witness. But the American notion of freedom has also evolved into the right and obligation to pursue one's own interests, so that freedom "for" in American culture usually means freedom for self — self-development, self-actualization, personal happiness. Any analysis of American freedom from a Pauline standpoint must take account of the ways in which Paul's theology warrants certain aspects of American freedom and strongly opposes others.

But the picture changes when we look at American freedom through African American eyes. One can argue that slavery and its legacies have so significantly impeded the African American pursuit of basic social and cultural freedom, the kinds of freedom that people in any society should be able to take for granted, that "freedom for self-realization" is not susceptible to the same critique that appropriately applies when these concepts are operative in "white" culture. Freedom for self-realization has a different orientation in the black context. Self-realization typically carries a collective sense of group freedom from the limits imposed by discrimination, from the devaluing of black cultural expression by the dominant culture, and from the white ideology that encourages African Americans to assimilate to the dominant culture in self-negating ways. Of course, the picture is much more complicated than these broad brush strokes suggest, given the class stratification of African American society and the many other divergences of experience, opinion, and perspective among black Americans. Nevertheless, it is crucial to take account of distinctively African American history and experience in working out a Pauline analysis of freedom in African American culture. We think that the principle of divine impartiality in Paul warrants nonviolent projects of group or "national" self-realization as a proper African American communal and cultural expression and working out of the principle, "Do not become the slaves of human beings." At the same time, to the extent that blacks in the United States have imbibed the culture of individualistic self-realization, which makes one's own personal quest for happiness the highest value, Paul's judgment on this kind of living for (and enslavement to) oneself falls with equal severity on them as it does on white folk who live only for themselves. And the principle of divine impartiality in Paul also extends to both white and black forms of familial and ethnic self-absorption — pursuing the interests of my family or my group without thought for others or any sense of obligation to them.

Russian Orthodox culture has a strong sense of the freedom of the soul to develop a personality in the image of God, as God originally created it. The human project is not a pursuit of happiness but perfect communion with God. This is possible only for those who have found their place in nature and produces a distinctive orientation to the interior life. For the politically conservative Feofan, this kind of freedom is spiritual, not social and political. By contrast, in Berdyaev the freedom of the soul extends to both the internal and the external, social realm. Yet for both, it is the incarnation of Christ that transforms nature so that the process of freedom becomes possible.

Nationalism

Nationalism is a conspicuous feature of our time and, depending on how one defines it, plays a role in most if not all modern cultures. Many Americans tend to use the term "nationalism" of ethnic groups and countries outside the United States. Most people think of "nationalism" as something bad and dangerous that one finds in the Third World and among minority ethnic groups in the Second World. Groups seeking independence, sovereignty over disputed territory, or an increase of their borders in the name of ancient rights, religion, or some other creed are labeled "nationalistic" — especially if they use any kind of violence in pursuit of their political goals. Americans who take this view often do not see the United States as itself nationalistic, an opinion that many others in the world dispute, charging that America pursues goals internationally that are dictated by a powerful nationalistic ideology. Historians have traditionally linked American nationalism to the concept of "manifest destiny," which provided a warrant in the nineteenth century for expansion from "sea to shining sea," subjugating indigenous peoples in the process. That destiny was understood as a divine right or mission, part of the onward march of Christian "civilization" with America in the lead. The continued expression of American nationalism (and manifest destiny) in the twentieth and twenty-first centuries is an ongoing topic of debate.

Russian nationalism, like nationalism in the United States, has a prominent religious component. Many Russians have thought that their nation has been assigned a divine mission, and this view has often had a strong millennial component. Russia is where the kingdom of God will be established, bringing to fruition God's eternal purpose for creation. By and large, utopianism in Russia did not produce break-away movements seeking salvation for the elect few. Whether utopian or millenarian, Russians have tended to focus on the nation as a whole as bearer of a messianic mission. Dostoevsky's "Russian idea," presented in his *Diary of a Writer,* compares Russia with Europe, which he characterizes as riddled by class conflicts. By contrast, he says, the Russian people have been endowed by God with spiritual qualities that can bring about justice and harmony on earth. A similar kind of nationalism was also promoted by the ecclesiastical understanding of Russia as a Third Rome, the true heir of Christian Rome and Byzantium.

But nationalism is not always about territorial sovereignty or the aspirations of a state (or a people's interest in achieving statehood). It sometimes expresses itself in ethno-cultural interests and values unconnected with statehood.[8] African Americans have long seen themselves as a "nation within a nation" (Martin Delany). Peter Paris has characterized the nationalistic aspirations springing from this self-understanding as "soft" nation-

8. On non-state nationalism, see Donald L. Horowitz, *Ethnic Groups in Conflict* (Berkeley: University of California Press, 1985); Milton J. Esman, *Ethnic Politics* (Ithaca: Cornell University Press, 1994).

alism when they have to do with cultural preservation and pride, group solidarity for the sake of "uplift," as an older term expressed the idea of social, economic, and cultural progress for blacks in America.[9] We also find this type of nationalism among Native Americans. According to Gerald Alfred, Native nationalism is not pan-Indian but rather takes many local community forms, each with its own histories and nationalistic traditions.[10] It is not static, fixed, or primordial but fluid, adaptive, and creative. Thus, we find, for example, Mohawk Christian nationalism expressed in both an embrace of Jesuit-influenced Christianity and the continuation of traditional Native beliefs.[11]

We do not find a place in Paul's theology for self-assertive, imperialistic nationalism pursued through violence. Moreover, there is a strong principle of universal human equality and kinship in Paul, expressed in the theme of divine impartiality and the baptismal formula of Gal. 3:28. It is possible to interpret Paul as advocating a Christian transcendence of ethnic identity that leaves all such distinctions behind or renders them altogether unimportant. Perhaps being a Jew or a gentile (or male or female or slave or free person) is what Greeks called an *adiaphoron,* a matter of indifference. We note that Paul calls circumcision and uncircumcision "nothing" (1 Cor. 7:19), which suggests that they are a matter of indifference. But we also note that he does not treat these categories as matters of indifference in the Greek sense, that is, as mere matters of preference about which there is no need to argue. He tells Jews *not* to undo the marks of circumcision and insists that gentiles *not* receive circumcision (see 1 Cor. 7:18; Gal. 5:2). It matters that Jews remain Jews and gentiles gentiles. Brad Braxton has interpreted this seeming paradox by arguing that it is the way Jew and gentile often functioned in Judaism as a hierarchy (Jew as superior to gentile) that Paul rejects.[12] Paul brands these identities "nothing" when they

9. Peter J. Paris, *The Social Teaching of the Black Churches* (Philadelphia: Fortress, 1985), 10. See the longer discussion of nationalism in the chapter above on Paul in African American perspective.

10. Gerald R. Alfred, *Heeding the Voices of Our Ancestors: Kahnawake Mohawk Politics and the Rise of Native Nationalism* (Oxford: Oxford University Press, 1995), 12-14, 191.

11. Alfred, *Heeding the Voices,* 33-47, 68-69. Alfred argues that Christian identity was one of two powerful motivations in the Mohawk migration from the Mohawk Valley to a new northern settlement in Canada.

12. Brad Ronnell Braxton, *No Longer Slaves: Galatians and African American Experience* (Collegeville: Liturgical, 2002), 94.

are understood as forms of social *status* in a religious or political pecking order. But this does not mean that the identity of being a Jew or gentile, male or female, does not count in other respects. In fact, if we follow the interpretation of many scholars today, who see Paul affirming in Romans 11 an irrevocable divine election of (ethnic) Israel, then it matters theologically in Paul that Jews remain Jews (that Israel remains Israel). It also matters that gentiles remain gentiles. Does impartiality also demand that the various ethnic identities within the broad category of "gentiles" also carry value, at least by implication in our thinking through of the meaning of Paul for today?

Paul never considers this question. But we can specify some Pauline principles or criteria that would have to be satisfied by any affirmation of ethnic identity or "nationalism." First, it would have to be egalitarian both internally and externally, harboring no chauvinism, xenophobia, or ethnocentrism. Second, it would have to be non-aggressive and non-imperialistic. Third, it would have to express the other-centeredness of the crucified Christ. No actual nationalism has ever come near satisfying these criteria. Nevertheless, if Herder[13] was right that nationalism (or, if we prefer, "ethno-cultural" identity) is a basic element of human identity, satisfying a fundamental human need, then we cannot hope to eradicate it but must find ways to interpret and evaluate its various expressions. There is a close parallel here with a Christian approach to ego formation and self-affirmation as a human need of the *individual*. We recognize this need and at the same time preach the virtues of reciprocity and altruism that are, arguably, utopian goals for any individual but remain nonetheless crucial Christian ideals as aspirations and bases for self-criticism.

Suffering and Blessing

All cultures have traditions about how prosperity and blessing are acquired, however these are defined. A pervasive South American tradition holds that success is a matter of wits, shrewdness in circumventing the law, adeptness in cultivating, enjoying, and exploiting personal connections, and good fortune at the hands of fate. The theory of many if not most

13. On Herder, see the discussion of nationalism in the chapter above on Paul in African American perspective.

middle-class North Americans is that success comes from hard work, the fairness of the American way (social and legal), and God's blessing on that way and on the good people who belong to it. As a sub-group of those who hold this view, many middle-class African Americans also have traditional ways of qualifying it. They see race as an important factor in American success, charge that the American way (social and legal) is not reliably fair, and see God not as a champion of the American way but more often as a "way-maker" who overcomes American injustice. For many Chinese, success comes through self-cultivation in loyalty and conformity to family expectations and traditional culture, seeking balance, avoiding any appearance of projecting oneself beyond one's proper place, fitting in rather than "sticking out," pursuing the goals set by one's family — all of which puts one in harmony with the universe and thus brings happiness.

Russians have a great deal of respect for the person who exemplifies the power of the soul to make sense of the world and achieve wisdom. The Orthodox live in a culture of social restraints and respect for authority; nevertheless, they expect the individual to develop his or her personality according to God's will. One is to cultivate the spiritual life, which includes the arts and the life of the intellect. In Russia there is great admiration for the uniqueness of the creative spirit in each human being, a spirit to be nurtured in the inner life and expressed in communal life. But this view of a life well-lived faces challenges today in the rise of what has been called "bandit capitalism," which brings what many see as a crasser view of the purpose of a human life in the form of material happiness too much like what Russians dislike about the popular American pursuit of happiness exported in American advertising, movies, and other media.

Traditional Native American conceptions of blessing include material well-being, but not on a Euro-American scale. Blessing is to be sought in harmony with the natural order and with the community. Sacred rituals help to preserve the balance of an eternal order of life from which each person or animal or tree or spirit derives its share.

Of course, the preceding characterizations are somewhat simplistic and do not tell the whole story of how people think about the logic of their own lives. Optimistic North Americans committed to the Protestant work ethic may well blame bad luck or unfairness when things do not work out for them. Latin Americans haunted by the shadow of inexorable fate do pray for God's help and intervention against fate. Chinese do not always see fitting in as a guarantee of success and sometimes seek to turn or avoid family expectations as a way of achieving their desires. Native Americans are not always harmonious in their relations with one another or the natural world. Just about everyone hedges their bets, tries alternatives when conventional wisdom fails, and looks for shortcuts that contradict what they otherwise believe is the tried and true road to success. Nevertheless, a culture's way of projecting the good life and how to achieve it — reinforced in parental admonitions, cultural clichés, public and private education, and popular culture — has a powerful shaping effect on expectation and practice. When we dissent from the conventional wisdom about success, it is often only by adjusting or qualifying our more basic agreement with what our culture or subculture tells us.

Paul grew up in a culture that taught him two things about success. First, the Torah (and devotion to it) is the way to success (see the following extremely influential Scriptures: Psalm 1; Josh. 1:8-9; and Deut. 30:15-20). Second, God loves Israel and answers the prayers of his people. Israelite tradition also qualified these two axioms in important ways. The Scriptures contain many stories of the suffering and non-prosperity of the righteous, and God's way of providing help and blessing in answer to prayer was seen as often mysterious, lodged in God's freedom and timing according to a wisdom that may elude human beings. Nevertheless, the pious operated on the assumption that devotion to God's Law and trusting reliance on God in prayer were the ways to blessing. In Galatians 1 and Philippians 3 Paul describes his own zeal for the Law when he was a Pharisee bent on advancing himself. Paul's gospel transforms the traditional conception of the way to blessing just sketched. According to the arguments of Galatians and Romans, the way to blessing is not the Law but Christ. The Law is incapable of bringing blessing or producing the righteousness that belongs with blessing. The patriarchal promises, Paul says, do not depend on the Law but are fulfilled apart from the Law in Christ, who inherits them and distributes them to his followers (Gal. 3:16, 19, 26–4:7). One implication of this, it appears, is that not only the Law of Moses but all law, "works" as such, are rejected as ways to blessing. Blessing comes by grace apart from works.

Christ as heir of the promises and source of blessing is the crucified and risen Christ. In Galatians, Philippians, and especially the Corinthian correspondence, Paul puts the accent on the power of Jesus' death and participation in that death as the way to blessing (justification, sonship, the Spirit, the life of Jesus, exaltation, and glory). One way to interpret this in terms of Paul's Jewish heritage is to say that for Paul the Jewish tradition of the suffering righteous, which in some of its expressions poses a problem for the theory of blessing through Torah faithfulness, becomes focused in the death of Jesus, who is the suffering righteous one par excellence: the crucified Messiah. Moreover, whereas the tradition of the suffering righteous typically casts the righteous as Torah-faithful, who for that reason will ultimately be vindicated, so that the connection between Torah and blessing is also vindicated, Paul opposes Torah and righteous suffering in his interpretation of the death of Jesus. Hence, the resurrection as God's vindication of Jesus is not a vindication of the Law as a way to blessing but is the overcoming of the Law as a curse on Jesus and on Law-keepers (Gal. 3:10-14). Not only that, it is not only the righteous who suffer: the whole creation, human and non-human, is dominated by the power of death (Romans 8 and 1 Corinthians 15), which obedience to the Law cannot overcome and from which membership in the covenant community cannot protect. To be sure, there is also a positive side to Paul's view of the Law, but our focus here is on the negative — the disconnection in Paul of the Law from blessing and of the Law from righteous suffering.

The implication one might draw from the idea that being crucified with Christ and sharing his sufferings is the way to blessing is that this way can be a practice, just as the Law is a practice. And it is true that Paul associates the practice of love with the cross of Christ, which expresses God's supreme love for humanity and Jesus' self-giving love "for us." Nevertheless, Paul never speaks of practicing the cross or suffering. And it might be a mistake to speak of "the way of the cross" in Paul, as if it were a discipline of suffering. Instead, Paul calls for the practice of love, imitating Jesus' other-centered way, obeying God, doing good to all. These practices of the gospel carry the risk of suffering, an inevitable risk for Paul and his coworkers, a likely risk for other believers. In this way, blessing and suffering are linked in the life of believers, both blessing and suffering with Christ being outside their control, both being "granted" to them in God's providence (see Phil. 1:29).

The American "work ethic" and the Confucian idea of self-cultivation through *li* both connect what Paul would call "works" with blessing and prosperity, spiritual or material, and discount death as a power impeding human efforts and draining human achievements of their meaning. In American culture, death is suppressed; in both Native American and Chinese cultures, it is treated as a natural part of the good cosmic order, a piece of the rhythm of life and not an enemy. The Confucian understanding of self-cultivation does have points of similarity with Paul. In particular, the Confucian ethic subordinates *li* (righteousness through propriety) to *ren* (love) in a way that resembles Paul's subordination of the Law to love. The primary difference is that for Confucius, as for most Jewish teachers in Paul's day, subordinating the commandments to love as their purpose and animating principle does not mean that one can do without commandments. On the contrary, the concreteness of *li* for Confucians and of Torah for Jews remains indispensable. By contrast, Paul seems to think that love fulfills the Law apart from the Law through the non-legal "law of Christ." This may be because Paul operates with his own version of Aristotle's idea that the good person needs no law for guidance or as a threatening incentive but does the good naturally and spontaneously. For Paul, it is not the "good person" but the person led by the Spirit who produces the fruit of the Spirit without the Law's guidance or sanctions. But an equally plausible explanation is that the logic of the Law-free gospel for the gentiles leads Paul to the idea that if there is any Christian fulfillment of the Law, it can only be in a way that does not assume the authority of the Law (which shuts gentiles out). Love as the fulfillment of the Law for those who are not under the Law jibes with the Law-free gospel (and also satisfies Paul's conviction that the Law really does aim at righteousness, is "holy, just and good" — Rom. 7:12).

This last way of interpreting Paul points to a distinctive element of his understanding of God's love. God's love for the world is impartial, reaching beyond God's beloved Israel to embrace with equal ardor and mercy the other peoples of the world. Hence, to tie a number of threads together, the Pauline ethic means risking love not only for one's own but also for the "other" — the stranger, alien, or enemy — in a world dominated by the power of death in which there are no guarantees that love will succeed or satisfy the one who loves or will bring a reward in this life. This goes against the natural drives of human biology, which are self-preserving and protective. Except in moments of crisis, the American lives for self and immediate family. The *rioplatense* lives for self and social network. The Confucian as *ren ren* ("loving person") lives for self, family, and community, including, at least in theory, humanity. But humanity is largely an abstraction here, imagined as an extension of one's own self and world, a neighbor who is fundamentally like me and linked to me. The Pauline Christian is supposed to live not for self or only one's own family but for the household of God and humanity (Gal. 6:10), with the consciousness that "doing good to all" means embracing the other. The Pauline mission is marked by the tension of self versus other across ethnic boundaries, and the Pauline ethic of love is attuned to the challenge of love across conflicted boundaries. Welcome one another, Paul says, as Christ welcomed you, and this includes welcoming those we despise (see Rom. 15:7 in the light of 14:1 and ch. 14 as a whole). This ethic of boundary-crossing love is consistent with the way God welcomed us through Christ's death while we were God's enemies (Rom. 5:8, 10). Of course, in reality, Christians who embrace Paul's teachings do not always or even frequently live out the ethic of love for the other. Christians can be as clannish as anyone else, living for self and not for humanity, much less for strangers and enemies. In North America, Latin America, China, and elsewhere, Christians, like most people in the world, are more often than not driven by their natural socio-biological impulses rather than by the highest ideals of their cultures or religious faith. The Pauline ethic turns out to be a formidable challenge.

Cross-Cultural Hermeneutics

Throughout this book we have commented on questions of cross-cultural hermeneutics. Detailed consideration of hermeneutical questions lies outside the manageable scope of this study. But it may be helpful to look briefly at a few such questions in conclusion. We confess in advance that we do not have settled views on these questions. We wish to identify and explore them, not answer them.

First, we have understood our project as engaging the historical Paul, represented by his surviving letters. The distance between the historical Paul and us, in any culture, is a cross-cultural gap. Historical-critical study makes us aware of that gap and helps us distinguish Paul in his culture from us in ours. Connecting Paul with our own cultural settings, we have said, calls for analogical reasoning, finding ways to do fair comparison by noting similarities and differences. But many of the voices we have presented in this book do not operate on the assumption that interpreting Paul requires historical scholarship. More exactly, the historical-critical approach is a modern Western practice of interpretation not found in some of the cultures and sub-cultures that have been our conversation partners. Moreover, even where this style of biblical interpretation is found in a cultural tradition we have engaged, we have listened not only to what scholars have to say about Paul but also to what non-scholars have said. An example is the chapter on African American interpretation of Paul, where we have paid attention to both African American biblical scholarship and many non-scholarly voices preserved in the broad African American tradition stretching back at least two centuries.

Our approach has been to treat all voices, scholarly or not, with respect and to show, where possible, supports in historical scholarship for their perspectives. In this way we have sought to remain true to our own conviction that in engaging Paul across different contemporary cultures we must also do justice to Paul himself in his cultural context. Daniel Patte has recently discussed the partnership this attitude creates between biblical scholars and non-scholars of various cultural backgrounds and social locations. In defining what he calls "scripture criticism," Patte argues that the role of biblical scholars is not "to produce new interpretations."[14] The task of the scholar is to demonstrate the basis in the text for non-scholarly "faith-interpretations" coming from communities of faith and in some cases to suggest how those interpretations might have to be modified in order to have a more secure foundation in the text. According to Patte, the guiding assumption of biblical scholars in partnership with the church is that Christian communities are the proper source of interpretations of the Bible for the church.[15]

A second hermeneutical question is whether some things in Paul are "merely cultural" in the sense that they are unimportant for Christian faith. Are there things that Paul assumes or teaches in his letters that we should not seek to translate into other cultural settings because they are not essential to what we understand to be his basic Christian convictions? The test is whether something can be "removed" from Paul without disturbing the basic pattern of his thought. The difficulty is that one can interpret the basic pattern of Paul's thought in more than one way. J. Chris-

14. Daniel Patte, *The Challenge of Discipleship: A Critical Study of the Sermon on the Mount as Scripture* (Harrisburg: Trinity Press International, 1999), 44.

15. Patte lays out these views in *The Challenge of Discipleship* and in *Discipleship According to the Sermon on the Mount: Four Legitimate Readings, Four Plausible Views of Discipleship, and Their Relative Values* (Valley Forge: Trinity Press International, 1996). For a detailed description of Patte's hermeneutical program, see Charles Cosgrove, *Appealing to Scripture in Moral Debate: Five Hermeneutical Rules* (Grand Rapids: Eerdmans, 2002), 167-70.

tiaan Beker has argued that the apocalyptic cast of Paul's thought is essential to his gospel. Rudolf Bultmann thought it was not. In his autobiographical self-introduction in this volume, Yeo reports how, as a teenager, when he first became fascinated by Paul, he discounted Paul's eschatology as merely cultural and not crucial to appreciating Paul.

The temptation we all face in judging certain things in Paul to be "merely cultural" is to dismiss just those things in Paul that challenge us in our own cultures and to affirm as essential to Paul only those things that suit us culturally. We know that we cannot simply transfer Paul with his culture lock, stock, and barrel into our own cultural contexts. Appropriating Paul involves some selection. But in cases of cross-cultural conflict between Paul and us, how do we know when we should accede to Paul and when we should go against Paul and affirm our own culture? In some cases, making these judgments is easy. A famous example is what Paul has to say about hairstyles in 1 Corinthians 11. He speaks about "what nature teaches." This suggests that he regards his instructions about hair length as universal. We recognize the cultural relativity in what he says, and most thoughtful readers of Paul look for viable cross-cultural principles behind his hairstyle rules. But in so doing, we go against his argument from nature. We usually justify this by saying that matters of hairstyle are not matters of nature but matters of cultural custom and that Paul's teaching about hair length is not essential to his gospel (even if certain principles informing his teaching about hair may be).

But what about Paul's admonitions regarding group conformity and the communitarian assumptions on which they rest? Are Paul's communitarian convictions essential to his gospel? Are some essential and not others? In many ways, Paul's admonitions about group conformity and loyal adherence to him as an apostle appear to reflect basic assumptions of the more communitarian and authoritarian culture in which he lived.[16] This raises an important question. Cosgrove's critique of American individualism relies in part on appeals to Paul's communitarianism. Likewise, Yeo finds in Paul's communitarianism a point of positive connection with Chinese culture, a connection that Yeo highly values. Is Cosgrove unwittingly imposing ancient Mediterranean culture on Americans in the name of Paul? Is Yeo celebrating the value of community in Chinese culture as a

16. See Elizabeth A. Castelli, *Imitating Paul: A Discourse of Power* (Louisville: Westminster/John Knox, 1991).

point of common ground with Paul's gospel when in fact the similarity is more fundamentally between communitarianism in Chinese and ancient Mediterranean cultures?

A third hermeneutical challenge for cross-cultural hermeneutics is that of "modernity." A number of approaches have arisen in Western biblical hermeneutics to deal with conflicts between ancient and modern knowledge, from history to cosmology. The vast majority of ancient Mediterraneans thought that heaven was literally up, and this view is present expressly or implicitly at many points in the Bible. The ancient assumption that heaven is literally up rested on a cosmology or geography of heaven and earth that is no longer tenable in the light of modern knowledge. Moreover, the collapse of this ancient cosmological assumption under the weight of modern science symbolizes a more general supersession of ancient assumptions about the world and history that the Bible reflects but moderns no longer accept.

Western theologians have worked out a number of hermeneutical solutions to this conflict between ancient and modern cultures. Among them are Rudolf Bultmann's demythologizing program, Paul Ricoeur's approach to biblical language as "symbolic" in his sense of the term, and Hans Frei's "realistic" but non-philosophical use of biblical language. This is not the place to discuss these approaches. We wish only to note that *cross-cultural* interpretation complicates the question of how Christians today should appropriate a Paul who is bound to pre-modern knowledge about history and the world. In some respects "pre-modern" is close to "traditional" in the sense in which cultural anthropologists use that term. When members of a non-Western culture are resistant to "modernity" as something "Western" and seek to preserve and rediscover their own cultural identity by reclaiming their traditions, they express a contemporary cultural form that is not "modern" in the typical sense of that word. Often it is "traditional" in a contemporary sense, that is, a contemporary recouping and refashioning of their ancient, evolving traditions to meet present needs. What relevance do Western hermeneutical approaches have for non-Western Christians who see modernity as a Western cultural invention that Europeans and Americans have sought to impose on the rest of the world? It is easy for Westerners to regard resistance by non-Western Christians to modernity as a form of Christian fundamentalism. But not all Christians who resist modernity are fundamentalists. Labels become very confusing here. Is a Native American Christian church that conforms to fundamentalist Western Christianity "modern" or "fundamentalist"? It may be both in different ways, just as Western Christian fundamentalists are both modern and anti-modern. But in the Native context, the question of how far to be modern, anti-modern, or fundamentalist is also the question of how far to be Western. And being non-Western or anti-Western may mean being "traditional" in a self-chosen contemporary way as opposed to being modern.

We three authors have all been shaped by Western educations and embrace Western hermeneutical approaches to Paul. For us the challenge is to find bridges from Western hermeneutics to non-Western hermeneutics, which may or may not be "philosophical" in the Western sense of that word. The challenge is also to learn from non-Western approaches — discovering not only new approaches to the hermeneutical questions that preoccupy us but also new questions that have escaped our attention. But this is a set of questions for another book.

Index of Modern Authors

Index of Subjects

Index of Ancient Texts